DISSENT ON TRIAL:
The Story of a Political Life

DISSENT ON TRIAL:
The Story of a Political Life

by

WILLIAM SCHNEIDERMAN

MEP Publications
Minneapolis

MEP Publications
c/o Anthropology Department
University of Minnesota
215 Ford Hall, 224 Church St. S.E.
Minneapolis, Minnesota 55455

Library of Congress Cataloging in Publication Data

Schneiderman, William.
  Dissent on trial.

  Bibliography: p.
  1. Schneiderman, William. 2. Communist trials—
United States. 3. Communists—United States—Biography.
I. Title.

KF224.S25S36 1983   345.73'0231   82-17940
ISBN 0-930656-25-3   347.305231
ISBN 0-930656-26-1 (pbk.)

Printed in the United States of America

Contents

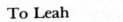

To Leah

Foreword

This book is history—by one of its participants who played a major role in the struggles of the thirties, the war years, and the McCarthy period.

The thirties were stirring times. Elected in 1932, President Franklin D. Roosevelt in his first hundred days launched the New Deal and the National Recovery Act. The period was especially important for the trade-union movement. Before the end of the next few years, the impact and growth of trade unionism had their effect on the entire Pacific Coast and throughout the United States, including the western states of Canada.

July 1934: the San Francisco General Strike took place. It followed the International Longshoremen's Association's coastwide strike starting May 9. The ILA, covering all Pacific Coast ports, was joined by nine other, mostly seafaring, unions and organized into the Joint Marine Strike Committee. The strike lasted ninety-nine days.

With dozens of ships lying at anchor in San Francisco Harbor, the docks choked with cargo which could not be hauled away because the Teamsters had refused to haul, on July 3 the shipowners decided to open the port. When the strikers, joined by many other trade unionists, attempted to march along the waterfront on July 5, they were met by members of the San Francisco Police Department. In the ensuing battles, two strikers were killed and hundreds wounded.

Led by San Francisco's Mayor Angelo Rossi, the San Francisco Industrial Association, which had taken charge of the strike for the shipping companies, prevailed upon California Governor Frank Merriam to call out the National Guard. The Guard took control of the waterfront.

The San Francisco Labor Movement, through its Labor Council, met this attack by voting for a General Strike, which began July 12 and lasted for four days. During those four days, 35,000 San Francisco workers joined unions. The General Strike ended after the dock and shipping companies agreed to arbitrate all issues in dispute between them and the ILA.

Because of the strike, General Hugh Johnson, Director of the National Recovery Act, was sent out from Washington, D.C. His message to the people of San Francisco and to the country at large

7

said that the waterfront and General Strikes were not labor disputes but were, in fact, a Communist takeover plotted and directed from Moscow. He took to the radio and called upon the patriots of San Francisco to run the leaders of the striking longshoremen (of whom I was one) out of town like rats.

Also at this time William Randolph Hearst, head of the Hearst newspaper empire, telephoned from Europe to John Francis Neylan, a well-known San Francisco lawyer. He instructed Neylan to confer with the Mayor, set up a special office in the Palace Hotel, and coordinate the efforts of the main five Bay Area newspapers (three of them Hearst-owned) in a united front to break the strike. But the working people of San Francisco did not waver in their support of the longshoremen.

There was no question about the position of the Communist Party USA and its all-out support of the maritime and General Strikes. The Communist Party marshalled all its forces, including its newspaper, the *Western Worker,* to support the unions. General Johnson and the shipping companies, the Chamber of Commerce, and employer groups seized upon these facts as proof that the strike was not a labor dispute but a "Communist Revolution" ordered and directed from Moscow, a charge which played a major role in the second trial so graphically described here.

By 1935, in the midst of a new crisis on the waterfront, the leadership of the Communist Party in California was headed by William "Bill" Schneiderman, the author of this book. He was a trained, knowledgeable organizer in California, Minnesota, and New England, with a history of leadership and fearless fighting for the working-class and trade-union movement since his teenage years and his school and college days. From the time he took over until his retirement, Bill Schneiderman gave leadership to the Communist Party in San Francisco and in California. His role led to one of the first trials to revoke a person's citizenship for being a Communist, his case finally landing before the United States Supreme Court. He was represented then by Wendell Willkie, 1940 Republican candidate for president against Franklin D. Roosevelt. Willkie represented Bill as a matter of principle and without fee. The Supreme Court of the United States overturned Schneiderman's lower-court conviction, and restored his citizenship.

During the hysteria of the McCarthy period in the early fifties, Schneiderman was charged and tried again under the new anti-Communist law, the obscene Smith Act. Bill, acting as his own counsel, went on trial with fourteen others in the Los Angeles Federal Court before a judge who was not at all backward about exhibiting his prejudice against the defendants (all Communist Party officials). Although the decision was against Schneiderman and his codefendants, it again eventually was overturned by the United States Supreme Court.

The various charges and arguments in the Smith Act trials in the District Court in Southern California form a substantial part of this book. It is a fascinating history of the troubled, turbulent efforts of those times to outlaw the Communist Party of the United States and not only to jail all its leaders but likewise as many of its members as possible.

Thus this book is a valuable document covering the defense of the working class, the unions, and their allies in our country. Between the lines we are made aware of the courage and effectiveness of Bill Schneiderman's leadership.

Harry Bridges, President Emeritus,
International Longshoremen's and
Warehousemen's Union

1   The Spark is Kindled

"Ladies and gentlemen of the jury: My name is William Schneiderman. I am one of the defendants in this trial, and I am here representing myself as my own counsel." It was February, 1952. How vividly the scene comes back to mind: the packed Federal courtroom in Los Angeles, the vigilant marshals, the intent jury, the grim-faced judge flanked on one side by the special prosecutor from Washington, and on the other by the fifteen defendants and their attorneys; as does the recollection of my long, weary journey by train across the continent, shackled with leg-irons, to join my fellow-defendants awaiting trial.

Once before I had endured this ordeal, as target of a prosecution which eventually resulted in the intervention of a president, a would-be president, and the State Department, and a bitter struggle within the Supreme Court before the issues supposedly were resolved. Supposedly: for now it appeared that we were engaged in a repeat performance of that earlier drama over a decade before. It was the era of McCarthy madness.

For me it had all begun hardly a stone's throw away from this courtroom, twenty-five years before. If a starting date can be placed on the commitment which brought me here, it could well be an August day in 1927.

* * *

On the morning of that day of bitter anguish, I sat alone in the dim light on one of the back benches in the old church across from the Plaza, the historic landmark of the birth of the City of the Angels. I had come here not to pray, but to hide. At the time I gave no thought to the anomaly of a Jewish youth of twenty-one seeking sanctuary in a Catholic place of worship, the *Church of Our Lady of the Angels*. As I sat there in the gloom, I brushed aside a momentary feeling of guilt for intruding on the privacy of the few worshippers, mostly the poor of the neighborhood, sitting in the pews or kneeling before the altar. Would they have understood and sympathized with my purpose, I wondered? For my mission was in behalf of two men, described by one of them as "a good shoemaker and a poor fish-peddler," who were destined to live their last days in agony. It was August 23, the day Sacco and Vanzetti were to be executed.

And while the state of Massachusetts in all its majesty was taking the lives of two poor immigrant workers for a crime they did not commit, the City of the Angels had decreed that no protest meetings could be held, no memorial services could be conducted by those who believed in their innocence. An indoor meeting had already been broken up, and even now the police were massing to prevent a demonstration from taking place in the Plaza across from the church.

To protest was forbidden, to mourn publicly was prohibited. As I sat there in the gloom, waiting through the long morning for the hour when the demonstration was to begin, emotions of anger and frustration, and sorrow for the victims, overwhelmed me. Nothing I had read in books or experienced in real life had quite prepared me for this. I had learned since boyhood something about inequality and injustice; I knew there was a benevolent law for the rich and powerful, and another, harsher law for the poor, but up until now this lesson had penetrated the head rather than the heart.

There was something about the fate of these two humble workingmen, who bore their ordeal with such courage and dignity, which touched the heart. It moved vast numbers of people throughout the world, many of them in high places, to speak out in their behalf. Nonetheless, repeated appeals to the higher courts, last desperate pleas by their supporters to the Governor and the President were futile.

The legal system of those in power had fashioned a web from which there was no escape, using prejudice and hysteria to turn truth into lies, and lies into truth, making a mockery of the words "equality" and "justice." Until now, the words in the books I had read were abstract ideas, and the figures dealing with wealth and poverty were just statistics. But this searing experience made vividly alive to me the cost in human life and freedom of inequality and injustice. In looking back, it seems to me that it was this fateful tragedy, more than anything else, which impelled me to become so deeply involved in a struggle which twice in my lifetime brought me before a tribunal of justice.

At the appointed hour I walked from the gloom of the church into the bright sunlight of the Plaza, only to find that my long vigil had been fruitless. The task assigned to me was to evade the police lines and mount the speakers' platform. I was to be the youth speaker; other speakers were to try similar strategems to reach the square without being stopped. But I found no speakers, no crowd; the square was empty. Since I had entered the church, hundreds of policemen had blocked off all streets entering the Plaza and prevented anyone from approaching. As the people gathered on each street, they were shoved back and those who resisted or did not fall back fast enough were arrested.

I managed to evade the police lines and join the crowd as it fell back, and a few hundred of us formed a march down to the First Street police station where the prisoners were held. There the crowd set up a chant, "Free the prisoners," and would not leave. I shall never forget the grim, determined faces of the people standing there—mostly garment workers, carpenters, and painters from the East side. They were the worn, lined faces of men and women who had fled the tyrannies of the Old World to look for Paradise, only to find the ghettos of the New World. They had then fled the sweatshops of the East to the lure of the Golden West, but Paradise still eluded them. They could not escape, for the fate of Sacco and Vanzetti foreshadowed their own fate. So they stood grim and determined there, as if they were saying: this far and no further!

And a remarkable thing happened; the police authorities, who had been so ruthless in preventing the meeting in the Plaza only an hour before, hesitated to move against the crowd. Perhaps the city fathers shied away from the stigma of making hundreds of additional arrests on such an emotion-packed issue; or perhaps it was simply that there was not room enough for all of us in their already crowded jail. Whatever the reason, to our astonishment and joy, they released the prisoners, and we had wrested some solace from this tragic day.

The Friday before, history was made at the Central Labor Council. For years this central body of the Los Angeles trade-union movement had been under a tight dictatorship headed by its secretary J. W. Buzzell. But this particular Friday night an unusually large turnout of delegates packed the hall. I was working at the time in the office of the Upholsterers Union, and was a delegate to the Council from the Office Workers Union. I was a novice then, but I was to learn that night how a group of workers, long cowed into submission, can rally to a great cause.

The news about Sacco and Vanzetti had charged the atmosphere with tension, and the uneasy officers did not show their usual arrogance; they had been warned that a protest resolution on the case would be introduced. On all past occasions they had ridden roughshod over all opposition; it was a rare meeting when they got any opposition at all, since dissenters faced the threat of expulsion (as I was to find out later that year).

But this Friday night was different. The explosion was triggered by the entry into the hall of Lt. Hynes, head of the "Red Squad," and another plainclothesman. "Red" Hynes had always raided meeting-halls, broken-up meetings, confiscated literature, arrested speakers, and beat up prisoners with impunity. (No newspaper would print the story for, after all, only "radicals" were involved.)

His appearance at Labor Council meetings had the tacit consent of the officials and had never been challenged before. Previously it had the effect of intimidating the delegates. But this time pandemonium broke loose. Cries of "Throw him out" went up from all over the hall. A burly delegate from the Electricians Union, Dave Gorman, finally made himself heard above the commotion; he made a motion to order the two policemen to leave or have the sergeant-at-arms throw them out. While the chairman pounded vainly with his gavel, a roar of "aye" went up from the delegates. Although the motion was not recognized, mayhem was probably averted when Hynes and his companion, seeing the seething anger of the overwhelming majority, wisely decided to get up and walk out.

Thus the stage was set for what was to follow. The delegates quieted down and the business of the meeting droned on for a while as usual. But when Dave Gorman rose again to present a resolution from the Electricians local, the hall was recharged with expectation. In calm, measured tones he branded the Sacco-Vanzetti trial a frameup and requested the Council to endorse the protest demonstration, scheduled by a defense committee to take place at the Plaza.

The Council officials were frantic. They denounced the demonstration as "radical" and "anarchist." They threatened the delegates with disciplinary action. But it was to no avail. As the debate raged on, the officials against the rank and file, it was apparent that for once the pall of fear had lifted, and the Buzzell machine could not control the meeting. When the vote on the resolution carried with only a few scattered "no's" against it, a great cheer went up from the delegates. As they streamed from the hall, slapping each other on the back, they were celebrating more than a victory for a resolution adopted; they were jubilant that their self-respect had been restored; they held their heads higher, heartened by their liberation from fear. It was a night to be remembered!

* * *

The spark was kindled in me by the memory of our grueling poverty in the slums of Chicago where I grew up. I was two years old, the first of five children, when my parents brought me to the land of promise from old Russia in 1908. The promise mocked us in the rat-infested tenements where we lived, and in the sweatshops where my father worked. The hardest time was the winter, when we had only enough money to buy coal a pail at a time, and a pail of coal went fast when you were trying to keep warm.

When I was twelve, my father contracted tuberculosis, the dreaded "consumption" which was the occupational disease of the garment workers. He was forced to leave for California's warmer climate, only to find his trade locked out by the employers there. Again the land of promise mocked him, this time by the employers' "open shop" policy which was to keep Los Angeles nonunion for years to come. We were to join him as soon as he could find work, but in the meantime our family was destitute. We lived in a flat so crowded that I had to sleep on chairs in the kitchen. I became the "head of the family" and went to work as a newsboy by day and behind a soda fountain until midnight. The generosity of a kindly uncle finally enabled us to make the long move west.

After Chicago, Los Angeles in the twenties seemed like a fairyland. The air was clean and pure, and you could see the mountains miles to the north. Palm trees were everywhere, and the neat bungalows seemed a far cry from the tenements of Chicago. But we had not really escaped the grim pursuer; poverty continued to stalk us. My parents, usually cheerful even in the face of adversity, looked old and worn before their time. My father's shoulders were stooped from long hours at the sewing machine; my mother no longer sang at her household chores.

I went to work in a warehouse office, finished high school at night after a ten-hour day, and worked my way through two years at the University of California at Los Angeles (then known as U.C. Southern Branch). I finally had to give up school to help support the family, over the protests of my parents who were fiercely determined that I should finish college. (I was not to get my college degree until forty years later, when my teenage daughter quipped "Class of '22 to '62—slow learner.")

There was always an awareness of being "poor" and a stoical inurement to hardship, but also a gradually growing rebellion against acquiescing that this was the way it had to be. In fact, my introduction to working-class consciousness took place at a very early age, although it was neither dignified nor voluntary.

I was eleven years old when a Socialist election campaign parade, led by its candidate, J. Louis Engdahl, took place on the

Chicago West Side in 1917, carrying antiwar placards and protesting the high cost of living. I was with a street gang of juveniles
out for a lark, throwing rocks at the parade and almost breaking it
up.

My father and mother were horrified when they heard of my part
in this episode. My gentle father, who had never raised his voice to
me, took me over his knee and delivered a lecture rather forcefully:
"Do you know who you were throwing rocks at?" Smack! "They
are workers, just like your father!" Smack! "So you were really
throwing rocks at your father!" Smack! I tearfully accepted this
stinging rebuke, promising never to "throw rocks at my father"
again. And whether or not this painful introduction on my back-
side really contributed to my class consciousness, I never did.

(Years later, when I was introduced to Engdahl, who by then
was editor of the *Daily Worker*, he was somewhat startled when I
greeted him: "Yes, we've met before; I threw rocks at you in 1917.)

My high school days were a period of discovery. My reading
began with the agnostic Robert Ingersoll, Henry George's *Progress and Poverty*, and Lewis H. Morgan's *Ancient Society*, before I
discovered Marx and Engels. I took part in a group called the "A to
Z Club." Heated discussions took place on subjects like atheism,
the morality of war, and whether human nature could be changed.
I was impressed by the argument made by Henry George that
human conduct could change when there were changes in the social environment.

The Russian Revolution, of course, was the great catalyst for
minds in ferment. In my early boyhood, the talk at home often
veered to reminiscenses of the early revolutionary days in Czarist
Russia, the pogroms against the Jews, and the desperate
strategems used to evade the police or military service. And I was
intrigued by the coincidence that my birthdate in December, 1905,
was in the midst of the first Russian Revolution.

Then came the 1917 Revolution, which was to fire the imagination of those who had visions of a better world, and to arouse
such bitter hostility that it took sixteen years for the United States
to recognize the Soviet Government. The holocaust of World War
I and its disillusioning aftermath created a revolutionary ferment
throughout Europe.

In the United States the aftermath brought depression, strikes,
and persecution. Woodrow Wilson was to admit that the war for
democracy was really a war "for commerce and markets." The notorious Palmer raids, which were to launch J. Edgar Hoover on his
career, arrested thousands of suspected radicals, and hundreds of

foreign-born workers were deported. The formation of the Communist Party in 1919 resulted in the indictment of some Party leaders, including Anita Whitney in California, under "Criminal Syndicalism" laws. These were passed in many states in the midst of the postwar hysteria and were used as a dragnet against radicals much in the tradition of the early Alien and Sedition laws.

So the "war to end all war and make the world safe for democracy" was a sham after all. The disillusionment of the postwar generation turned to cynicism and escapism. For many in the labor movement and in intellectual circles, however, it marked a turn to the left.

I joined the Young Workers League when I was sixteen, and the Workers Party at eighteen (later named the Young Communist League and the Communist Party). The Party's followers were made up of former left-wing Socialists who had broken with the Socialist Party over its support of the war and its hostility to the Russian Revolution, and trade-union militants inspired by William Z. Foster, organizer of the packinghouse workers and leader of the 1919 steel strike.

The first Communist speaker I heard was, oddly enough, a minister, Reverend Robert Whitaker; it was from him that I first heard the Marxist thesis about the class nature of society and was introduced to the works of Marx and Engels. I was introduced to the workings of imperialism when I heard lectures by Scott Nearing, author of *The American Empire*, an exposé of U.S. exploitation of Latin America. As Lenin's works became available, his analysis of imperialism as the rule of monopoly capital made a deep impression upon me.

My education proceeded rapidly enough so that in my last year of high school I headed a team of young Communists which challenged the debating team which had just won the city high school championship to debate the subject: Socialism vs. Capitalism. The challenge was accepted and Upton Sinclair, the Socialist who had gained fame as the author of *The Jungle*, and *The Brass Check*, agreed to serve as co-chairman with one of the school officials. The publicity for the debate created a great deal of excitement, and on the night the debate was to be held, the hall was packed to overflowing. But to our disappointment, the high school champions did not show up. Sinclair announced that the school authorities had put pressure on them, and they were forced to back out at the last minute. He thereupon delivered a highly enlightening lecture on the ties between the school administration and the business interests of the city, which made quite clear why they did not want to expose the school youth to any discussion of socialism.

My university days were marked by my first participation in political activities. Senator Robert LaFollette, Republican liberal from Wisconsin, was making his bid for the presidency in 1924 on a third-party ticket, but he spurned the support of proponents of a Farmer-Labor Party. When the movement for a Farmer-Labor Party failed to take hold, the Workers Party put up its own presidential candidate, William Z. Foster. I helped form a "Foster for President" club on the campus, and our competition with the larger "LaFollette for President" club created more interest and discussion among students than did the main contest between the Republican incumbent, Calvin Coolidge, and the Democrat John W. Davis, a Wall Street lawyer.

It was on the campus that I first heard an eyewitness report on Soviet Russia by Anna Louise Strong, author of *The First Time in History*. The large assembly hall was filled with a rapt audience of students as she described the colossal effort to build a new social order on the ruins of the old in the face of famine, blockade, and active intervention by Allied military forces, including a United States expeditionary force headed by General Graves which invaded Siberia. I also heard on the campus Charles Steinmetz, the famed electrical wizard and the top scientist of the General Electric Company, who corresponded with Lenin about plans for the electrification of Russia. The subject of the speech was "Science in the Service of Man," with socialist overtones.

I took part in a campaign against compulsory ROTC training and distributed antimilitarist leaflets, a project which was aided by a prominent pacifist, Fanny Bixby Spencer. When I myself refused to take my second year of ROTC, the university administration reclassified me as a noncitizen who was not entitled to the benefit of the nominal fee then charged at a state university. The relatively high fee for aliens and nonresidents of California would have made it prohibitive for me to attend school. Since I had applied for my citizenship papers at the earliest date I was eligible, I challenged the decision and won my appeal.

As a result of my activities on the University of California campus, I later learned, the authorities were discussing how they could bar me from graduation. I was never faced with that test, however; after two years I had to leave school and go to work full time.

* * *

My first arrest was a mistake. I was hitchhiking back from San Diego with my friend Nat. I first saw him when he was a Western Union messenger boy; he was delivering a telegram to us while we were conducting a Young Communist open forum; he liked what he heard and stayed. Unlike as we were, we became fast friends. I was the intense young man with many goals not too clearly defined, and pursued sporadically. I was going to teach history or literature; I was going to write a play; I was going to organize the masses. Nat looked upon my many enthusiasms with cynical amusement. He had bummed around the country in boxcars. He viewed all ambitions with skepticism. He was a drifter who wanted to be left alone. But his tough exterior concealed a gentleness and compassion which he revealed to very few.

On the highway to Los Angeles we were stopped by the Highway Patrol and brought into Santa Ana. We had no idea why we were picked up until we were brought to their brand new jail. We were wanted in San Diego, it seems, for "deserting the Navy." A call had been put out for two AWOL sailors wearing civilian clothes. We were the first ones who seemed to answer their description, so they held us in custody and sent word to Navy headquarters in San Diego to come and get us.

Our protests did no good. One look at us should have told them that they had the wrong fellows. Nat had the pale sickly look of a tubercular patient, and I didn't look particularly robust either; lack of time for physical exercise and burning the midnight oil for night school had not contributed to body-building. A Navy recruiter would have passed us up with a sneer.

We were put into one of their spanking new cells, and I had my first sensation of having a barred cell door clanging shut on me. There is a finality about it that can be frightening, especially if you are alone and nobody on the outside knows or cares. It helps to have indignation, for it feeds the spirit of resistance, which in turn obliterates the fear.

My initial shock was overcome by my indignation. I was so infuriated at the cops' refusal to acknowledge that they had made a ridiculous mistake that I banged on the bars and shouted for the guard (an unforgivable sin for a prisoner). When he came running, I demanded the right to send a telegram to our friend Fanny Bixby Spencer; she had been an official in the state penal system, and although a well-known pacifist, still had some influence in official circles.

The guard refused my request and threatened disciplinary actions if I didn't "pipe down." When he walked away, I started to pace the floor of the cell. Nat had not said a word; he stretched out on the lower bunk, lit a cigarette and watched me restlessly pacing.

Finally he said: "Calm down, Bill. When you've been through this as often as I have, you'll find out it doesn't get you anywhere. They'll find out it's a mistake, but we don't know how long it will take, so just take it easy." Our ordeal didn't last very long this first time, but in later years I had more than one occasion to remember his advice.

Before I had a chance to renew my demand to send a message out, we were suddenly released. San Diego sent word that they had found the two sailors, but the cops did not even deign to say: "Sorry for the mistake." When we got out on the highway outside of Santa Ana, the comedy of errors was repeated. A squad car drove up and picked us up again; they had not received word that the sailors had been found. They paid no attention to our plaintive protests that we had just been released and brought us into police headquarters again. We were freed at the station, but no apologies, of course, and it was nearly dark before we wearily headed for the highway again.

* * *

Stimulating as my school experience had been, my greatest education came from my contact with workers in the Party and the trade unions, where I learned about the labor movement, its strength and its weaknesses. Although I had come to accept the thesis of Marx and Lenin that a revolutionary transformation from capitalism to socialism could only come through the power of the working class, the scene in the twenties was far from promising. The American Federation of Labor of Samuel Gompers and William Green consisted primarily of craft unions, and the basic industries were neglected and unorganized. It played no independent political role; it bartered the support of the officialdom to the highest bidder of either party. In return for their collaboration with the employers the officials received favors and concessions which made them richer and more powerful ("labor banking" was the vogue), but which vitiated the unions as instruments of struggle for the needs of their members.

The big debate in Communist and left-wing circles in the early years revolved around the pros and cons of a Labor party. The experience of the British Labor party was held up both as an example, because of its political power, and as a warning, particularly after the Labor Government came into office in 1924 under Ramsay MacDonald and promptly proceeded to betray its platform. On the other hand, the organization of a Labor party and a break with the two-party system would have been a big step forward for the American workers and given them an independent political role.

During this period, William Z. Foster, who had great prestige as the organizer of the steel industry and the packinghouse workers, formed the Trade Union Educational League. Its program was a popular one: amalgamate the craft unions into industrial unions; form a Labor Party; support recognition of Soviet Russia. The left wing gained a considerable following in the unions for this program, notably in the Chicago Federation of Labor, the railroad brotherhoods, and among the miners and the garment trades. But attempts to form a Farmer-Labor Party were abortive when the LaFollette campaign for President was launched in 1924.

The small Communist Party during this period was rent with factionalism, beset by sectarian rhetoric and a heritage of dogmatism which left its mark for a long time to come. Nevertheless, the issues raised by the Party and the left created stirrings in the labor movement, and its program remained valid through the years; it was the forerunner of the CIO program of organizing the basic industries into industrial unions, in which Communists took a prominent part; and its advocacy of a third party based on labor is still a challenge to which the labor movement will sooner or later have to face up.

* * *

The year 1927 was an eventful one for me. That year I got my U.S. citizenship, little dreaming at the time that it would be challenged in the courts twelve years later, or of the fateful circumstances in which this case would make history in the United States Supreme Court. It was the year in which the Sacco-Vanzetti case propelled me into a deeper commitment to my chosen cause. And it was the year in which I had an unusual confrontation with the national leadership of the American Federation of Labor.

As a delegate to the Central Labor Council, I was a marked man ever since that tumultuous meeting of the Council on the Sacco-Vanzetti case. Shortly thereafter, the national convention of the A.F. of L. was being held in Los Angeles, and I was elected a delegate from my local union, which at that time was a federal local directly affiliated with the national A.F. of L.

I nervously awaited the opening of the convention, knowing that I was on the spot. No Communist had appeared at an A.F. of L. convention since 1923, when Bill Dunne, representing the Butte miners as a delegate from the Butte Federation of Labor, was unseated at Portland, where he had delivered a scathing denunciation of the conservative leadership and its reactionary policies. I was a nobody, and certainly not able to match his experience and colorful eloquence. I was naive enough to believe that I would be given a chance to speak, but I did not reckon with the well-oiled machinery that kept the A.F. of L. conventions running smoothly without a ripple of opposition year after year.

At the door of the convention hall I was stopped and brusquely told to report to what I thought would be a credentials committee at a conference room in the Alexandria Hotel. (The A.F. of L. officials would sneer at this seedy hotel today, but in those days it was one of the swankiest in town.) When I was ushered into the presence of the "credentials committee," I found three men in the room. One was Frank Morrison, Secretary-Treasurer of the A.F. of L., white-haired and dignified. The second was Vice President Matthew Woll, with his wing-collar looking every inch a banker; in fact, he was quite at home at bankers' and businessmen's conventions in his dual role as head of the National Civic Federation, where he often spoke on his favorite theme, the "Menace of Communism."

To be greeted by a reception committee consisting of two of the three top officers of the A.F. of L. (William Green was then president) was surprising enough. But the third man, to my even greater astonishment and dismay, was none other than Lieutenant "Red" Hynes of the Police Department. Only the year before he had been responsible for having me fired from my job, a malevolent pursuer who was to dog me for twelve more years until our confrontation on the witness stand of my first trial. (By that time his power had been broken by the political upheavals and the democratic upsurge of the Roosevelt era.)

I blurted out indignantly: "What is he doing here?" Morrison looked me over, seemingly surprised at my youth, and said: "I understand you have a Communist record." I replied: "What difference does my politics make? I am a duly accredited delegate and here are my credentials from my union." Morrison turned and nodded to Hynes, who said: "Yes, I know him to be a Communist." He then rattled off a list of meetings I had attended (some of them broken up by his "Red Squad"), and speeches I had made right up to the August events around the Sacco-Vanzetti case.

Morrison then said to me: "You are barred from the convention," and before I had a chance to reply, the three of them arose and left the room. This was the extent of the "hearing" I got from the "credentials committee," with an assist from the same police agent who had been ordered out of that memorable meeting of the Central Labor Council. I was subsequently barred from the Council as well, in absentia. It was a first-hand lesson in how democracy was practiced by the high command of the A.F. of L. leadership in the twenties.

However, in the lower echelons the officialdom did not always have its way. At the local and district level across the country there were frequent examples of strikes, and of rank-and-file left-wing slates being elected to office, in defiance of the international leadership of their unions. I had a small but satisfying part in one such election while I was working in the local office of the Upholsterers Union in Los Angeles.

I discovered there had been a misuse of funds by some of the officials running for reelection in the local union. After my expulsion from the A.F. of L. convention and the ensuing publicity, these officials decided to use my case to smear a rank-and-file slate that was running against them. The slate was making some headway because "section work" was being introduced and the skilled upholsterers were being replaced by unskilled people who only had to perform one operation; wage scales and working conditions were going down and the union was doing nothing about it.

The incumbent officials waited until election night, and before the voting took place announced that I would be fired because I was a Communist; the opposing candidates who defended me were also attacked as Communists.

Fortunately, I was able to get the floor by demanding that I be allowed to report my findings on the misuse of funds. As I read off the names of scores of members whose dues had not been receipted, the audience, initially hostile to me, began to turn against the officers. When the members heard what was happening to their funds, cries of rage went up from the crowd. They saw the attack on me as a red herring to cover up the officers' misdeeds. A wild scene ensued, in which the officers tried to shout me down, but they were themselves drowned out by the incensed members. When the voting finally took place, the rank-and-file slate was elected.

The swift turnabout of the upholsterers was a dramatic but not uncommon example of what happens when a group of workers can penetrate the smokescreen of the "Red" scare to see the real issues involved. It was a lesson in the anatomy of "anti-Communism," which when dissected consists largely of blind prejudices based on conditioned reflexes to labels which have been predetermined to be evil. To paraphrase Samuel Johnson, the "Red" scare (like patriotism) has often been used as "the last refuge of a scoundrel."

My exclusion from the Central Labor Council had an amusing aftermath, when early in the following year I was invited to come to San Francisco to head the newly formed California District of the Young Workers League. When I arrived in San Francisco, I visited the Central Labor Council meeting on a Friday night from long-standing habit. I was sitting in the visitors' section when

John O'Connell, the venerable secretary of the Council, read a communication from his Los Angeles counterpart, J. W. Buzzell. The gist of the letter was that a notorious Communist named William Schneiderman, who had been ousted from the Los Angeles Council, had arrived in San Francisco, and to watch out for him. (So "Red" Hynes had supplied him with my itinerary, too!) O'Connell looked around the hall and asked : "Is there a delegate of that name here ?" All the delegates looked around at each other; amid the craning of necks, I was glad I was not a delegate and that I was a stranger to them, and I looked around innocently, too. There being no answer, the chairman said, "Let's get on with the next order of business." That was my inauspicious introduction to the San Francisco labor movement, which was to change so dramatically in the next few years.

2 The Thirties: Bread Lines and Picket Lines

Unlike Los Angeles, San Francisco was reputed to be liberal and strongly prolabor. I was soon to find out differently. In 1928 there was a long and bitterly fought strike at the textile mills in Gastonia, North Carolina. The union there was getting little or no help from the official labor movement. There were mass arrests and indictments had been issued for some of the leaders. One of my first experiences in San Francisco was when we undertook to organize a protest movement and to raise money for the strikers.

One of these meetings was an open-air demonstration behind the old *Examiner* building near Third and Market Street. As the crowd gathered, the police tried to desperse them; and as speakers mounted the platform, they were immediately hauled down and roughly shoved into paddy wagons, some of them badly manhandled. When it was my turn to speak, I mounted the platform and imprudently shouted: "There aren't enough jails in San Francisco to hold all of us!" A cop growled: "There's still enough room for you," and pulled me down and jabbed me in the stomach with his club. Doubled over in pain, I was shoved into the packed wagon. I was still in a daze when we were brought to the Southern police station, which was already overflowing with the others arrested.

As we were being led past the cage holding the women prisoners, one of the militant women leaders yelled through the bars: "They're beating up our boys in the other cells." At this all the prisoners set up an uproar, beating on the bars, stamping their feet, shouting and cursing. The bedlam was so great that the police officers on duty, their faces red with rage, could not be heard above the din, although they were shouting at the tops of their voices.

The protest was effective, however. I was still too sick at the time to see exactly how it happened, but the women were released and the Labor Defense Council went to work and got the men out by nightfall.

I had occasion to test San Francisco's liberalism again before the end of the year when we tried to organize an outdoor election rally. There seemed to be an unwritten law that when Republicans and Democrats held outdoor rallies, they miraculously avoided interfering with traffic, but when Communists held a rally, somehow we were always "blocking the street."

Furthermore we had the temerity to hold the meeting on the Market Street traffic island in front of the old Bank of Italy of A. P. Giannini, the godfather of the Bank of America. I barely had time to mount the box and give the names of our candidates when I was arrested for "obstructing traffic," although we had not had time to gather a crowd yet. My trial was not a particularly heroic demonstration. For some unexplained reason our campaign committee chose a lawyer who was more experienced in "fixing" cases than in trying them. He maneuvered the trial to come up the day before Christmas. When I appeared in court, the Irish judge had obviously begun celebrating Christmas early and was in an expansive mood. Amid an exchange of "Merry Christmas" with the attorney, the case was dismissed.

*   *   *

It was a cloudy day when I was riding down El Camino Real from San Francisco with a gentle, elderly woman by my side at the wheel of the car. We turned off to the coast, and as we approached the Watsonville area, we were stopped by a roadblock of sheriff's deputies. One of the deputies peered into the car and asked for identifications. My companion smiled sweetly at him and said: "I am Anita Whitney, and this is my nephew. We are on our way to visit some friends in Watsonville." The deputy seemed satisfied and waved us on.

The cause of this blockade was a strike of Mexican-American pea-pickers, an unusual event in 1929 in the California agricultural fields, which had not seen a strike since the days of the IWW. If one can imagine the brutal exploitation of the farm workers before the days of the present United Farm Workers Union, ten times over, it would give some inkling of the conditions in the twenties, which caused the pea-pickers to strike even though many were defying the threat of deportation. The growers reacted with fury. They were convinced that the strike was caused by "outside agitators," and mobilized all the police forces of the area.

The strikers were not organized, had no union experience, and had the additional difficulty of language. Some of our sympathizers in the area contacted them, notified us that they were eager to have help, and urged us to send a speaker to a strikers' meeting being called in Castroville. The problem was how to get through the blockade. I volunteered to go, arguing that because of my youth I would least likely be suspected of being a union organizer, and to cinch it, proposed that Anita Whitney go along with me.

Anita Whitney was the niece of a Supreme Court Justice, daughter of a California State Senator, and one of the founders of the Communist Party in the state. Her trial and pardon by the Governor had made headlines, but that was years ago. She had the appearance of an elegant lady, but she was a courageous fighter in all people's causes, and was fearless in the face of danger. And so it was that we made quite an innocent-looking pair and successfully ran the blockade.

The Castroville hall was packed when we arrived. Curiously enough, the deputies were not in the immediate vicinity of the hall, or we might have been prevented from entering. The meeting was chaired by a Mexican-American who was younger than the rest, could speak English and acted as interpreter for us. We were introduced as "friends who have come to help us." The audience must have wondered that we made a strange-looking pair of union organizers; nevertheless they greeted us warmly.

In my speech, which had to be translated sentence by sentence, I explained that we were Communists, and that we were trying to organize an Agricultural Workers Union. The American Federation of Labor had no interest in organizing the unorganized, especially the unskilled, and it was necessary to form independent unions or be left completely helpless at the mercy of the growers. We would furnish organizers, and also organize solidarity actions among the unemployed to try and prevent strike-breaking.

When I concluded, a worker arose to ask a question in Spanish. The chairman turned to me and said: "He wants to know what is the difference between the Communist Party and the union." I answered as best I could, in the course of which I explained that socialism meant taking over the means of production, which the Party stood for, but that under capitalism a union would have to fight unceasingly for the most immediate elementary needs of the worker.

Something in my phrasing must have caught the questioner's attention with great favor, because he arose and spoke rapidly again, and when he sat down there was laughter and scattered applause in the hall. The chairman translated: "He says he doesn't want scraps from the table of the bosses; he wants the whole works; he wants to join the Party."

When we left, the chairman promised us that they would discuss our proposal to form a union, and would notify us through our local contacts in the area. But the growers never gave them a chance to make that decision. The reign of terror was stepped up, strikers were picked up for deportation, and the rest were either driven back to work or replaced by scabs. The odds were simply too great against them. It was not until the thirties that the Party actively began organizing efforts among the field workers. The growers invoked the Criminal Syndicalism law to jail a number of Party members during the Imperial Valley strikes. But the seeds had been sown.

* * *

The lines that formed at the Party headquarters on Turk Street wound all the way from the second floor down to the street. A demonstration of thousands of unemployed had just taken place in the Civic Center, and following an appeal by the Communist Party speaker to join the Party, hundreds of workers streamed down to the Party offices and waited patiently in line. As the Party's Organizational Secretary, it was my task to interview each one briefly and pass them on to a membership committee for final approval for membership.

The country's desperate economic plight was reflected in the occupations listed on some of their applications: "Engineer"; "Teacher"; "Construction Superintendent"; "Small Businessman, Bankrupt"; these designations appeared almost as frequently as those of industrial workers. All were unemployed and this was still in the first few months that followed the Wall Street crash.

I was startled by one application that read "Ex-policeman." The man was powerfully built, with broad shoulders, and huge hands; he looked like a wrestler, and I could visualize him in a policeman's uniform under very unpleasant circumstances. Was he being sent into the Party as a spy, I wondered? Why, then, would he admit his former occupation?

He must have seen the question on my face and smiled,"I was in the Boston policemen's strike, and when the strike was broken, I could never get back. I've been in the building trades ever since." I still hesitated. I remembered that "Red" Hynes, before he became head of the Red Squad in Los Angeles, had been doing his spy work freely at radical meetings, and he had been discovered just by accident.

Being unwilling to make a snap decision on the expoliceman, I recommended to the membership committee that his union record for the past years be thoroughly checked if possible, although he indignantly protested against the delay. But as we did not have the facilities to get this information from the various cities he had worked in, nothing ever came of it. I have often wondered whether we had driven away an honest worker who had received his first baptism in a policemen's strike, or whether we had saved ourselves from one more spy or provocateur.

*   *   *

There is no dearth of chronicles about the devastation which struck the land in the early thirties. The government bureaucrat hands out statistics, the economist talks learnedly about cycles, and the historian depicts movements and trends to describe the times. But most of the chronicles do not delve too deeply into the tragic consequences on the lives of individuals, of families, of a whole class; and they miss the feel of the struggles which profoundly changed the face of the nation. To have taken part in any part of that conflict is to have participated in a small way in the making of that history. I was plunged into the midst of the struggle when the Party assigned me in 1930 to be district organizer in Connecticut, a district which included surrounding border towns in Massachusetts, Rhode Island, and New York state.

New England was one of the areas struck hardest by the unemployment crisis. The arms and munitions plants of Bridgeport, the brass foundries of New Britain, and the textile mills of various towns were shut down almost completely. I was sent there from California at a time when the Party headquarters in every state were swamped with requests to organize the unemployed. The cities had no provisions for unemployment relief, the state and federal government agencies turned a deaf ear to pleas for aid, and the American Federation of Labor made no move to organize the people out of work. We stepped into the vacuum.

I hitchhiked to seventeen towns in which we had set up Party branches, where we held demonstrations in the public squares or parks attended by hundreds, sometimes thousands. In many cities and towns the authorities did not interfere with these demonstrations, but where they did, they came up against some tough militancy. In New Britain the brass workers, largely Polish-American, fought a bloody battle with the police when they were told they could not hold a public meeting, and some of the speakers were beaten and jailed. The same happened in Stamford. In New London a group of sailors from the nearby naval base arrived at a meeting where I was speaking, threatening to break it up and yelling epithets like "get that Bolshevik bastard," but the workers formed a solid phalanx around me, and the Navy men, seeing themselves outnumbered by men a little huskier and more determined than they were, finally left amid the jeering and the catcalls of the crowd.

My means of transportation improved to the point of luxury when I acquired an ancient Ford of 1919 vintage, and in my speeches I would joke about the car, saying that it reminded me of capitalism because it was on its last legs (which we firmly believed at the time). I don't know whether Marx would have approved this method of presenting his ideas, but the audience appreciated it.

The corps of Party organizers around the country was a young and dedicated lot, who made up in enthusiasm what they lacked in experience. Mostly jobless youth or just out of school, they did not hesitate to go into the coal fields of Pennsylvania to organize the miners, into the South to organize textile workers or sharecroppers, or into the agricultural fields of California to organize the migratory workers. When sent into danger, they were fearless or learned to suppress their fears. One of them was Harry Sims, a quiet, idealistic youth in his late teens when I met him in Connecticut. He was an organizer for the Young Communist League when he volunteered to go into the Kentucky coal fields where striking miners were appealing for help. He was there only a short while when he was shot to death by company thugs who were terrorizing the strikers. He was only one of many victims among the miners and their families.

Wages for party organizers were more theoretical than actual, but then we were no worse off than most of the unemployed. After breakfasting on coffee and a roll, I would travel from town to town and not eat again until arriving at a friendly house in the evening. In fact, I was once accused of favoring certain towns because I got better meals there. The most unusual place that fed me was the mansion of a wealthy suburbanite in swank Portchester, New York. In that town, a most unlikely place for Communists, we had a party club made up of the servants of the rich. It was they who took me into their kitchens when the coast was clear.

* * *

In the fall of 1930, downtown New Haven witnessed an unusual sight. A large group of teenage Italian girls were marching down the street from a nearby garment shop. They looked more like kids playing hookey from school than workers from a factory, except that there was nothing light-hearted about their manner. Their march ended at a storefront with a sign in the window "Communist Election Headquarters," and they crowded into the room.

Their leader, who looked no older than sixteen or seventeen, explained to me that they had walked out of the shop when their boss had announced a wage cut. "Someone said the Reds would help us, so we came here," she said. They were unorganized, and the A.F.of L. showed no interest in organizing the garment shops. They were on piece-work, working a fifty-four-hour week under an intensive speedup system. The breaking point came when their piece-work rate was cut by the equivalent of five cents an hour.

It was a time of hunger. Factories were shut down, masses of un-employed roamed the streets, and those plants which remained open, many of them on a part-time basis, felt free to cut wages. The fear of losing his or her job, when hundreds of replacements were waiting in line, hung like a sword over the head of every worker still fortunate enough to be employed. Only the most extreme provocation could cause an unorganized group to leave their jobs at such a time, with the odds so heavily against them.

We set about organizing the girls into a union and setting up picket lines, but we ran into an unexpected obstacle. Their parents, the girls' leader explained, would not let them attend meetings with strange men, and Reds at that. I began to spend my evenings visiting their homes to meet their parents and to show them that Communists did not wear horns and had no designs on their daughters. Since the parents were mostly poor workers or unemployed, I usually found a cordial welcome after an initial wariness. Almost too cordial, in fact, because in each household the father would produce a bottle of potent homemade wine. It was still in the days of Prohibition, and I was not accustomed to drinking anything stronger than a concoction called "near-beer;" but I did not dare refuse the hospitality of my hosts, so I often ended the evening with my head spinning and my stomach churning.

I soon found that their reluctance to let their daughters attend meetings was not so much due to the strict mores of a Catholic family, but had an economic reason. Their cupboards were almost bare, most of the parents were without jobs or worked one or two days a week, and the family income often depended on the few dollars the girls brought home from the shop. But their feelings were mixed between fear for the loss of this income and pride in the girls' militancy against the wage-cut. In our discussions they usually conceded that the strikers had no choice but to fight back.

In the meantime, the Trade Union Unity League, the left-wing center for organizing independent unions, answered our appeal for help. From the New York headquarters came June Kroll, an ex-perienced organizer of the needle trades. Accomplished as a speaker and in handling people, she showed a remarkable skill during her stay in teaching her young pupils the elementary things about conducting a meeting, organizing a picket line and other strike activities. Soon they were mimeographing their own leaflets and passing them out in the downtown streets.

But strikebreakers began to infiltrate into the plant, and it became neccessary to appeal for support in the form of mass picket lines. The Unemployed Council, spokesman for hundreds of jobless workers, mobilized its members to support the girls at the factory gates. Up to that time the police had stayed in the background, but when mass picket lines were formed, they moved in, although no violence had occurred.

I was there on a late afternoon when a contingent of cops charged the picket lines with drawn clubs, ordering the crowd to disperse. They were careful to single out the unemployed workers for attack, not the strikers. Rough tactics against the teenagers might have had political repercussions in a community with a large Italian population. What the police did not count on, though, was that the girls refused to accept this gentlemanly amnesty. They cursed and swung their signs at the cops who were using their clubs on the men.

I was caught up in a swirl of clubs and fists as the pickets fought back. Some went down with bloodied heads and faces, but the cops kept flailing away. I remember being struck a glancing blow on the side of the head as I was futilely pounding my fists on the back of a cop who was bent over a fallen picket and using his club. Someone dragged me away, and I sat down on a curb in a daze. The fight ended as suddenly as it began; the pickets retreated, but not before a number of them had been arrested.

The police had made one mistake, however. Among the arrested were two of the most militant girls who had fought back. When the case came to court, it was difficult to create a separation among the defendants between the unemployed and the strikers, and since the authorities were reluctant to send the girls to jail, all the defendants were freed with suspended sentences.

A short time afterwards, the garment factory owner offered a compromise settlement, and the girls went back to work, the germ of unionism implanted.

* * *

In the spring of 1931 food riots swept Minneapolis, and in order to divert attention from the widespread hunger among the jobless, the authorities started a "Red scare" and were seeking to indict a number of Party leaders of the unemployed. In this emergency I was rushed to Minneapolis and stayed as district organizer. The Party and the Unemployed Councils decided to organize a protest demonstration. In view of the fact that the police had repeatedly broken up peaceful demonstrations there, the plan was to organize marches from the neighborhoods, timed to arrive at a central square at different times. If the police cleared the square of the first contingent and made arrests, the next contingent would wait until the square was clear, then march in and put up speakers again. I was assigned to be one of the speakers with the second contingent. When we arrived at the square, the police had not yet cleared the area. The demonstrators fought back. They broke off the handles holding their placards and used them as clubs to defend themselves against the police wielding their lethal weapons.

In the midst of the melee, I jumped up on a box with a megaphone, and yelled: "We are here to ask for bread, and they answer us with clubs. . . ." That was as far as I got. One cop kicked the box out from under me, and another one grabbed me and hustled me off to a waiting police car. When I arrived at the station, it was already crowded with prisoners and more kept arriving. In the meantime, the crowd driven out of the square reformed its ranks and marched to the police station. We heard the police officials in the station talking nervously, trying to decide what to do. Finally, one of them went outside and announced to the crowd: "We are asking you to disperse. We will release the prisoners if you disperse." And so we were finally freed.

* * *

The mayor of Bemidji concluded his remarks by saying: "We have come a long way in the last twenty-five years. Child labor and the twelve-hour day are gone. We can look forward to the next twenty-five years to make even greater progress. That is why I believe in gradual reform and not the revolutionary way."

The occasion was a debate between the mayor and myself on the subject "Capitalism or Socialism; Reform or Revolution."

I rose in rebuttal.

"It is all very well for the mayor to say he is willing to wait for twenty-five years, while he sits in his comfortable house and draws his comfortable salary. But what about you farmers who face foreclosures? What about you unemployed, with no relief in sight? What about the Indians who out of desperation and hunger stormed the warehouse where surplus food is kept under lock and key? Perhaps the mayor can afford to wait, but can you afford to wait twenty-five years?"

I was in the midst of my campaign for governor of Minnesota. Bemidji was way off the beaten path in the northwestern part of the state. I went there because the mayor was reputed to have been a socialist, but had not lifted a finger to deal with the plight of its citizens. So desperate was the situation that the starving Indians broke into a warehouse to search for food. Only then did the authorities bestir themselves and supply some all-too-meager aid.

Bemidji was only one disaster area in the midst of widespread distressed areas thoughout the state and the nation. The Farmer-Labor Governor Floyd B. Olson was by Republican standards a far-out radical and socialist, but in this crisis he did not go far beyond the politicians of the two major parties in trying to meet it except when subjected to great pressure by his constituents.

It was the summer of 1932, and I was hitchhiking from town to town thoughout the state of Minnesota. Anyone seeing the young man of twenty-six with an unruly mop of red hair, an open collar, and a carefully wrapped package under his arm, thumbing a ride on the highway would scarcely suspect that he was seeing a candidate for governor making his campaign tour. And a unique tour it was!

The package was a bundle of leaflets announcing the candidate's campaign rally in the next town. It read: "Work or Wages! Jobs or Relief for the Unemployed! Come hear the Communist candidate for Governor speak on the issues of this election! Vote Communist!" The meeting place was announced as "Courthouse Square" or "Park," and left a blank space for an address and the time of the meeting to be filled in with a pen.

I would arrive in a town, go to the city hall to find out if a permit was needed, then pass out the leaflets in the park and in working-class neighborhoods. By the time of the meeting a crowd of several hundred was usually gathered with at least one watchful policeman, and I would mount the speaker's platform consisting of an empty wooden box or crate from a nearby grocery store. Usually I knew no one in the town, in which case I would act as my own chairman, explain the purpose of the meeting and introduce myself as candidate.

I would speak for half an hour or longer, depending on how long my voice would hold out. As the campaign progressed I found I could speak longer, up to an hour. The main theme of my talk was the economic crisis which left fifteen million unemployed, as an example of the failure of capitalism as an economic system to meet the needs of the people. While appealing to the crowd to vote Communist, I also urged the formation of Unemployed Councils to fight for the demands of the unemployed and frequently stayed to help set up a council before moving on. I also carried some pamphlets to sell, which helped finance my tour. (The most popular pamphlet was called "Will Beer Bring Back Prosperity?" It dealt with the promise of the Democrats that repeal of Prohibition would bring jobs.)

We organized demonstrations in every town where I spoke. The Unemployed Councils and farmers' groups organized a state-wide hunger march which converged on the State Capitol while the legislature was in session. While other speakers and I addressed the huge throng outside, a delegation of workers and farmers called on the governor and addressed the legislature with a series of demands for unemployment relief and for a moratorium on foreclosures and evictions.

Governor Olson confined himself to indoor meetings for select audiences in his campaign. He was a polished orator and a shrewd politician who knew how to speak in Yiddish in a synagogue, and Swedish, Finnish, or German to other ethnic audiences. He made one attempt at an outdoor night rally, but some angry unemployed workers ripped out the electrical connections for the lights and he did not try again.

But as the campaign wore on, the hopes aroused by the promises of a New Deal had their effect, and Olson rode in on the Roosevelt landslide. I received 5,000 votes and William Z. Foster received about 100,000 votes nationally for President. Nevertheless, we had presented our platform to vast numbers of people. Our immediate demands had received a favorable response and left their impact on future legislation, and our advocacy of socialism had reached an attentive audience.

All this time I was living on five dollars a week and rented a room which had an extra cot in it. Minimal as my living standard was, it was luxury compared to that of other activists. One of them, Jack Bartley, was an ex-lumberjack who had come down from the north woods to the city and became a leader of the Unemployed Council. A big, handsome man, his good looks marred by a missing front tooth when he smiled, he was clothed in a threadbare overcoat he had found somewhere, too small to fit his burly frame. But beneath his shabby appearance was a man of culture and wit, who could quote poetry and reel off long passages from Shakespeare, or tell amusing stories and anecdotes. He often had no place to sleep, so I invited him to use my extra cot. In order to keep this from the landlady, he would slip in late at night and leave early in the morning. But somehow the landlady found us out, and one day when I came home I found the extra cot gone, although she made no fuss about it. That night Jack slept on a park bench.

The backbone of the Party in the district was the left-wing Finnish community, organized in a string of cooperatives and workers' clubs with their own halls throughout Minnesota, northern Wisconsin, and upper Michigan, and with their own newspaper, *Tyomies*, one of three Finnish-language dailies in the country. Scores of these Finns were elected to school boards and other local bodies, even though their left-wing political opinions were well known in their communities. There was hardly a town or farm where the Finns resided where I was not welcomed with a cup of coffee, a meal, or a place to sleep. Many of the party functionaries and Young Communist League organizers were Finnish workers or farmers, or their sons and daughters, and some of them went on to become trade union organizers during the upsurge of the labor movement. One of them was Gus Hall, later to become a CIO steel organizer in Ohio and eventually the General Secretary of the Party.

* * *

It was a warm, sunny day in 1933 in the shabby little mining town of Hancock, and when I arrived the crowd was gathering early at the old Finnish Workers Hall. The copper mines, an ugly blot on the beauty of the upper Michigan peninsula, were shut down. Miners, farmers, their wives, and a large number of youth were streaming into town for the demonstration. They came on horseback, or with horses and buggies, and in old jalopies from the small surrounding towns for miles around.

There was tension in the air, for no public demonstration had been allowed in Hancock since 1912, the year of the bitterly fought miners' strike. The walls of the Finnish Hall still showed the bullet marks dating back to that bloody battle. Hancock had been ruled with an iron hand ever since; so great had been the terror and intimidation that although a great wave of demonstrations and hunger marches was sweeping the country, it had not as yet been reflected in "Copper town." But hunger had overcome fear, and the miners and their allies had decided to march.

The plans were to march through the town and back to the hall where I was to speak. But for this relatively mild exercise in freedom of speech, the police chief and sheriff had mobilized a large number of deputies and announced that they would not allow the march to take place. A permit for the parade had been refused, and the word was spread that the police had threatened to shoot.

We held a council of war. Anderson, the chairman of the meeting, informed the committee in charge that armed deputies had been placed along the parade route since early morning. Faced with the danger of an armed confrontation, what to do? The demonstrators were militant and enthusiastic, but did they know all the possible consequences? It was unthinkable to call off the march, but we also had a responsibility to weigh the consequences and avoid giving the deputies an excuse for bloodshed.

We decided to go ahead with the march, but prepared alternate routes for the march in case we were stopped. Anderson addressed the crowd: "We are not looking for trouble, but we are not going to be cowed by thugs who are doing the dirty work for the mine owners and the banks. We are marching to demand jobs and relief, and no one is going to stop us." The crowd roared its approval, but listened more quietly as the chairman outlined the plan to avoid clashes; some of the younger men grumbled openly.

The march began, several blocks long with waving banners, placards, and clenched fists. Groups of spectators looked on in amazement, for nothing like it had been seen in Hancock within their memory. We had proceeded several blocks when suddenly, as we turned a corner, we found facing us a line of policemen and sheriff's deputies, and behind them straddling the street was a fire truck with the hoses uncoiled held by firemen who were pointing the nozzles at the marchers.

As we came to a halt, the police chief pulled a gun from his holster and waved it at the crowd, yelling: "Get back! Get back!" He seemed terribly excited, his face red, his eyes bulging, just the trigger-happy type that would start shooting without provocation. Behind us, some of the younger marchers were pushing and shoving, with cries of: "Let's go! Cut the firehose!" It was a dangerous moment, and Jack and I turned to the crowd and exhorted them to turn down a side street and follow our alternate route.

It was a chilling experience to see that gun pointed at us, to know that we were teetering on the edge of bloodshed. But we succeeded in turning the angry crowd into a cross street away from the deputies and fire engine. As we swung back into the main street, however, we discovered that we were not to escape so easily. Cheated of their excuse to shoot, the police and deputies called on their reserves, the fire department. Gertrude Betts, a preacher's wife, was an eyewitness and described the scene in her diary:

> They turned the fire hose full force on the line of marchers. It was like being hit by a stone wall. The force of it almost knocked me down. The teacher with me and I had Loretta (her 5-year-old daughter) between us, holding her hands, or she

would have been washed away. The hose had to be played back and forth to give one a chance to catch his breath. A continuous stream would strangle and smother one. It doesn't seem too bad just reading about it, but when it strikes, the breath is knocked right out of one, or perhaps one is knocked down flat—it has to be experienced to be understood. We managed to get into a doorway of a business building and so avoided any further the full force of the water. We were so out of breath and exhausted, we could hardly stand. My corset and shoes were wet for two days. In spite of all this, our lines reformed and we went marching, wet and all, back to the hall. This was our baptism, not by fire, but by water. We were slammed full force by the fire hose into the progressive movement. A fire hose or a police club have far greater and more lasting meaning than the brutal forces back of them ever realize.

The marchers triumphantly returned to the hall by the alternate route, their clothes drenched but not their spirits. In my speech I spoke of the ravages of the unemployment inherent in the capitalist system, of the need to organize politically outside the two-party system, especially the unemployed and the farmers. And I spoke of fascism, since Hitler had just come to power, and emphasized that it could happen here. The demonstration concluded with adoption of a series of demands upon the town and county authorities.

After the release of tension, the mood of the crowd was jovial, as though we had won a great victory by simply exercising the rights which had been denied the people for so long. That there were no casualties was due to the discipline shown by the demonstrators in the face of provocation. Hancock would never be the same again.

* * *

The incident at Hancock was just a tiny eddy in the tidal wave which struck the country such a devastating blow that it took many years for it to recover. The term "depression," invented by politicians and economists, gives no real inkling of the full-blown economic crisis which engulfed the country and much of the capitalist world. The term suggests merely a drop of so many percentage points in the economic index, giving no intimation of the vast amount of human suffering and turmoil brought about when there are fifteen million unemployed, and wage cuts for millions more who are lucky enough to be still working. It gives no hint of the dark shadow of hunger and despair hanging over the land when there is no unemployment relief, no unemployment insur-

ance or social security; families evicted from their homes and farmers foreclosed from their land; banks closing their doors; shanty-
towns named "Hoovervilles" springing up on the edge of the
cities; and the poor standing in bread lines or rummaging in gar-
bage cans for food or standing on street corners selling apples.

It was in this situation that the Communist Party in 1930 began
to organize the jobless into Unemployed Councils. Hundreds of
thousands marched under the slogan "Work or Wages." Their
demands were for unemployment relief, unemployment insurance, and no evictions. The farmers were organized into Farmers
Committees to demand relief and a moratorium on foreclosures.
Some of the unemployed groups were formed spontaneously, and
some were organized by Socialists and other groups, but the initi-
ative for a national movement came from the Communists. There
were hunger marches to city halls, county court houses, state cap-
itols, and to the Capitol in Washington, D.C.

The established organizations of labor, representing the better
paid crafts, did nothing. The A.F. of L. leaders, business-oriented
as they were, talked and wrung their hands, but did nothing. They
were more at home with labor banking than with hunger marches,
and they fumed more at the Communists than at government policies, not to speak of the system which created unemployment.

It has become a standard accusation by those in power, echoed
by the top leaders of organized labor and by middle-class liberals,
that the Communists "used" the unemployment issue to foment
unrest for their own purposes. One might ask: Does not a trade
union which goes out to organize workers "use" the fact that they
are discontented with low wages or poor working conditions to
win members and build the union? One might ask: Do not the
Republican and Democratic parties "use" whatever issue they can
seize upon—whether it is taxes, the economy, civil rights, racism,
or war—to win votes for their party, with a demagoguery so cynical that a politician's pre-election promise has become notorious
for its unreliability?

As for fomenting unrest, the Communists did not invent the
unemployment issue; it was capitalism which created it. The
Communists did not create the discontent; it was brought about by
the economic crisis, and the failure of the ruling class responsible
for it to alleviate its effects. What the Communists did do was to
organize the discontented, and there's the rub! For the true
measure of their role should be: what did it accomplish for the
unemployed?

It wrested temporary relief from local and state governments,
even while Hoover was still in office, and it created such a powerful national movement that the Roosevelt administration was

compelled to put into effect sweeping reforms. The mass pressure of the unemployed movement was undoubtedly a major factor. Historians who have not let their anti-Communist views interfere with their objectivity (and they are very rare indeed), are compelled to acknowledge the Communists' historic role in bringing about these advances.

* * *

The mining town of Crosby, Minnesota, lying south of the Mesabi iron ore range, had the distinction of being one of the few places in the country which mined that rare metal, manganese, used in the process of hardening steel. But the mines were closed and times were hard. There was no work and on the nearby farms, the farmers were nearly as hard up as the miners, and many had to depend on what little relief or public work projects were available.

Local elections were usually perfunctory. The businessmen, the mine owners, and the bankers decided who was to run, so there wasn't much to choose from on election day. But this time there was a difference. The Unemployed Council had been conducting a campaign for unemployment relief and more public works jobs. One of the leaders of this fight was Emil Nygard, the strapping young son of a farmer who had worked in the mines.

When the municipal election campaign opened, the two businessmen's candidates for mayor found to their surprise that they would have a third candidate in the field against them. In a three-way race almost anything could happen. What was even more unprecedented was that the candidate, Emil Nygard, was known as a Communist. Furthermore, he campaigned on a platform demanding more relief for the unemployed and the neighboring farmers and promised that if elected, he would appoint a Workers' Advisory Committee to be observers at the city council and keep reminding them of the workers' needs.

This unexpected challenge created a great deal of excitement in Crosby. The response of the unemployed miners was so disturbing to the established order of things that the mine owners struck back with a campaign of redbaiting. But their most effective argument was that the mines were closed due to the importation of Russian manganese. Roosevelt was blamed for opening up relations with Soviet Russia, but somehow the closing of the mines was placed on the shoulders of the Communists. Thus did foreign policy become a major election issue in an obscure little Midwestern mining town.

When Nygard apprised our district headquarters of the situation, I immediately contacted Walter Frank, head of the AFL

Building Trades Council in Minneapolis, who had just recently returned from a trip to the Soviet Union as part of an independent American labor delegation. Frank was a progressive trade union official, but was far from being a Communist. He agreed to speak in Crosby on his impressions of Soviet Russia and also to deal with the question of Russian manganese.

Frank's meeting was advertised as a reply to the mine owners' charges, and he spoke to a packed hall, including many supporters of the incumbent as well as voters who were just curious. The audience was intent, even the hostile ones, as Frank described a strange land where there was no unemployment, although it was still recovering from the ravages of war, counter-revolution, and foreign intervention. Far from causing the loss of jobs for American workers, Russian orders were supplying Americans with work. The Caterpillar Tractor plant in Minneapolis was at that time working on a big Russian order for tractors, without which it would not have been working full-blast, if at all. As for Russian manganese, Frank pointed out that the low-grade ore mined in Crosby was never in competition with the higher grade manganese which the steel industry had to import from abroad. The mines were closed, he said, not because of Russian manganese, but because the steel mills were simply shut down; and he charged that the mine owners were using a smokescreen to cover the failure of the economic system to provide jobs or adequate relief.

The Frank meeting marked a turning point in the campaign, and as a result Nygard was elected by a plurality over the other two candidates. One of his first acts was to plant trees on the main streets and to hire jobless miners for other public works. In the face of a hostile City Council majority, he made a valiant effort to implement his program, but the resources of the town to supply jobs or relief were limited, and the businessmen clamped down an effective boycott to prevent more from being done. When the Workers Advisory Committee reported how Nygard's efforts were being blocked, the unemployed knew whom to blame. And when there was a walkout on a public works project over a grievance and the mayor warned any potential strikebreakers that they might face charges of disturbing the peace, the workers knew for once they had a sympathetic ally in the mayor's office.

The word got around beyond Crosby. When Nygard led a "Workers and Farmers Hunger March" to the State Capitol, to place their demands before the governor and the state legislature, the story of the small-town Communist mayor, the first elected in the United States, made national news. There was a great curiosity about him which we naturally made the most of. He spoke in New

York in Madison Square Garden, and in Milwaukee, which had a Socialist mayor, Daniel Hoan, whose record was no different from that of other old-line politicians.

But we found that this national speaking tour was a mistake and cut it short. Some of the townspeople grumbled that the mayor should stay at home and attend to business, and his political opponents capitalized on this sentiment. But none of the opposition's arguments made much headway until the next annual election approached, when the mine owners came out with the flat statement that the mines would not reopen as long as Nygard was in office.

Then, to secure the outcome of the election, they arranged that only one candidate would oppose him. In the previous election Nygard had received a plurality in a three-way contest. This time he would have to win by an outright majority. This proved to be impossible in the face of the mine owners' threat. There had begun a slight revival stirring in some industrial areas, and the whole town, as well as the surrounding farmers, had been looking hopefully for signs that the mines might be working again soon. Those hopes were dashed by the ultimatum and many voters reluctantly concluded that the only way they could get work was to switch their vote. Thus was Nygard defeated in a "free" election. And still the mines remained closed.

* * *

The truck rolled to a stop at the barricades which blocked the front gate of the Armour meat-packing plant. The driver leaned out and called: "What's going on here?" A husky figure, bundled up in a heavy lumber-jacket against the cold, came forward from the group of pickets standing at the gate and spoke briefly to the driver, who shrugged his shoulders, backed up and drove away.

The man in the lumber jacket was Joe, the head of the strike committee. As the key man on the killing floor, he had been instrumental in organizing his department and in shutting down the plant when they were confronted with a wage cut. A man of natural leadership, he had been the first to respond to our urging the workers to form a union.

It was the winter of 1933 in South St. Paul, Minnesota, a company town dependent on the Armour and Swift plants, which had been unorganized since a strike was broken in the early twenties. In the absence of any effort by the A.F. of L. union to do any organizing, the Trade Union Unity League was attempting to form an independent union of packinghouse workers. In the wake of

Roosevelt's National Recovery Act, workers had been led to believe that they now had the legal right to organize, a right which was not actually put into law until the Wagner Act of 1936.

The organizing of the Armour plant began in the fall with the patient step-by-step recruiting of individual workers whom a few of us visited systematically in their homes over a period of weeks until we had won over some of the key people in the plant. From then on, the recruiting proceeded rapidly and we were soon passing out leaflets openly at the gates.

When winter weather came, the company struck back by laying off a number of workers and announcing a wage cut; with economic recovery still feeble, and mass unemployment persisting, the company could afford to be arrogant, but the response of the workers to this intimidation was immediate. Before the end of the day shift, they streamed from the plant and set up picket lines in time to stop the night shift from entering. The union was weakest among the night-shift workers, but the majority of them respected the picket lines, although only a few of them participated actively in the strike.

From the moment the strike began, for the next eight days, I dropped all my other duties, although I was the district organizer of the Party, to devote full time to help the fledgling union. Three of us manned the strike headquarters, a storefront near the Armour gates. Joe, the head of the strike committee; Norman, the organizer of the Trade Union Unity League, who had started the organizing drive; and I myself, who had become somewhat known to the workers when I passed out *Daily Workers* at the plant gates, and when I spoke at open-air rallies the previous year as the Communist candidate for governor. Such was the temper of the times that no one questioned my presence. I picketed with the strikers. I ate with them, and I slept on the floor of the headquarters with the others when the strike committee asked for volunteers for night-guard duty.

The barricades at the gates created a furor in the press. We had not anticipated them. This unexpected development was a result of the militancy of the strikers and the improvisation of Joe, who argued it was easier to keep out truckloads of supplies and scabs by piling up lumber with a few pickets at the entrances than by trying to man mass picket lines around the clock and run the danger of having the trucks run right through them.

The St. Paul *Pioneer Press* and the Minneapolis *Tribune*, Republican newspapers, demanded in editorials that the National Guard be called out to give safe conduct to the trucks. Fearing that the Farmer-Labor Governor Floyd B.Olson would give in to this demand, the strike committee organized a delegation to see the governor, who received them and assured them that he had no intention of intervening. At one point there was an amusing interchange when the suave governor turned to Norman, who spoke with a strong New York accent, and asked: "Do I understand that yours is a vertical union?" (meaning an industrial union which cut across craft lines, unlike the A.F. of L.). Norman replied: "Vertical, horizontal—all I can say is it's an industrial union."

The refusal of the governor to call out the National Guard caused the company to turn to other means to break the strike. Freight cars loaded with supplies and scabs rolled into the yards at the rear of the plant at night, and it proved impossible to stop all of them. Meanwhile the company began to work on some of the weaker union members, who were on strike but did not participate in picketing or other strike activity, simultaneously with a redbaiting campaign launched in the newspapers by Harold Stassen, the young and ambitious district attorney.

With the strike beginning to lose ground, the strike committee decided it was essential to shut down the nearby Swift plant, and made an appeal to the workers there to support the strike. From the beginning there had been a great deal of sympathy at Swift's for the strike, but there was no union there, the workers were more intimidated, and the redbaiting had been more effective.

When a mass meeting of the Swift workers was called, the other side worked feverishly to influence them against a strike, but we did not know to what extent the city authorities, the police, and the district attorney's office had involved themselves until the meeting took place, and we found cops surrounding the hall. The speakers for the strike committee were Joe, Norman, and I. Joe was well known and respected in the community, but was somewhat inarticulate on the platform. Norman also was not a very good speaker. I was the only experienced speaker, but unfortunately, I had contracted laryngitis, which reduced my voice to a hoarse whisper, so all in all we made a very poor presentation. But it is problematical whether a better presentation would have turned the tide, for the company stooges had done their work well, together with the outside pressure and the accompanying redbaiting. The vote showed a substantial majority against striking.

As we left the platform, we were met by the police and placed under arrest, and a court order conveniently timed for the occasion forbade the blocking of the plant entrances by pickets or barricades. By morning, sheriff's deputies and police had removed the barricades, and this together with the negative vote of the Swift workers effectively broke the strike.

Harold Stassen became the "hero" of the Republican Party for his strikebreaking strategy, and was to exploit this to the full when he successfully ran for governor of Minnesota as the man who knew how to deal with the Communists.

But his victory over the strikers was not quite complete. As the prosecuting attorney in our trial, he was confident that a small-town, property-owning jury would convict us. To make sure, the home-town boy was released. He was nearly right. It was a typical small-town jury, and our hopes that their sympathy for the strikers, some of whom were their neighbors, would overcome their prejudices, inflamed by Stassen's redbaiting, proved false. One man on the jury, a retired businessman, was the last person we would have expected to hold out for acquittal. Yet when the hung jury was dismissed, and they filed past us, he gave us a broad smile and wink. What we did not know was that he had been a packinghouse worker who had been blacklisted after a strike in the early twenties, and turned his hand to business because he could not get a job. And although he had become successful enough to retire, a spark of his working-class background still remained alive and was rekindled by the strike and the prosecution of its leaders. It was he who stubbornly refused to go along with a "guilty" verdict and hung the jury. The charges against us were later dismissed.

Nevertheless, Stassen had accomplished his main purpose of breaking the strike. He was to exploit this to build a political career, rising from an obscure district attorney to governor of Minnesota, governor-general of the Philippines, president of the University of Pennsylvania, and perennial candidate for the Republican presidential nomination.

My three years in Minnesota were memorable in another way. While running for governor, I was invited to speak on the campus of the University of Minnesota. I was greeted at the door by a vivacious young woman with sparkling eyes and a radiant smile, who introduced me to the audience. A spark ignited between us. On our first date, she got an inkling of what life with me would be like. I was stopped for a minor traffic violation while driving an out-of-state car, and instead of giving me a ticket, the policeman arrested me and took me down to the police station. Leah had to spend the evening raising bail for me. When we were married, the shadow of my first trial was hanging over me. But nothing daunted her, and we have shared our joys and sorrows ever since.

Her own talents as an organizer confronted us with a dilemma when I was to return to California. She was chosen by the International Ladies Garment Workers Union to organize the sixth largest dress shop in the country. No one had ever succeeded in organizing the Boulevard factory in Minneapolis and David Dubinsky, the international president of the union, had made a wager with the regional director that it couldn't be done. Leah not only organized the shop, but led a union fight to defeat the employers' attempt to open a runaway, nonunion shop in St. Cloud, a small town near Minneapolis. The Social Democrat Dubinsky never knew that he had to depend on a Communist to get the job done, but the workers knew there was a difference, for she won their trust as none of the old-line officials had been able to do. After that, she could have written her own ticket, but as so often happens in a male-oriented society, she chose to join me in California.

3 Moscow Interlude: Dimitrov and the People's Front

They came from every corner of the earth. Many had to slip illegally across borders where fascist or military dictatorships were in power. It was whispered that some never made it, and suffered the extreme penalty. It was 1935, and the drama of the Seventh World Congress of the Communist International was unfolding in Moscow. I was fortunate enough to be at this history-making event which had such far-reaching consequences. Hitler had come to power in Germany, jailing Communists, Socialists, and all other opponents. The purge of the Jews was well under way. The fall of Spain, Czechoslovakia, and Poland were still to come. In the meantime, the Western powers debated whether they could do business with Hitler.

It was in this atmosphere that the Congress met and sounded a theme that was to echo throughout the world as the rallying cry for the resistance to fascism: the United People's Front. The year before, the Communist Party of France had joined in a united front with the Socialists in the municipal elections with brilliant success. But generally the bitter polemics between the Communists and the Socialists, after the latter's support of the imperialist war, their betrayal of the postwar revolutionary upsurge in Germany, and their rejection of a united front with the Communists, had divided the working class and its trade unions in the major European countries.

The somber news from Germany gave us all a feeling of urgency. I had caught a glimpse of what had befallen Germany when as my ship passed through the Kiel Canal on the way to Leningrad in 1934, I saw the children lined up on the bridge above us, waving and shouting "Heil Hitler." At a stop of a few hours in Hamburg, I saw the Nazi Storm Troopers marching through the avenues. As I walked the streets, I stopped a worker near the docks and saw the fear on his face when he refused to acknowledge a friendly greeting, or answer my question when I asked how many were unemployed in Hamburg. This was the city which had elected Ernst Thaelman, the leader of the Communist Party of Germany, to the Reichstag; now he was in jail, soon to be murdered. And the question haunted me: How could we stop this awful disease and stamp it out before it spread and infected the entire world?

All the famous names of world Communism were there: Stalin, still at the height of his power, and the other Soviet leaders; Thorez of France; Togliatti of Italy, Wilhelm Pieck of Germany, Dolores Ibarruri of Spain, Bela Kun of Hungary; Tito of Yugoslavia; Pollitt and Gallagher of Great Britain; Katayama of Japan; Wan Ming of China; and William Z. Foster and Earl Browder of the United States. Many were members of parliaments in countries where Communist Parties were powerful. Others were in exile or risking their lives as leaders of Parties that were outlawed. Some were destined to become premiers or cabinet ministers of their countries after leading the underground resistance against the Nazi occupation during the war that was to come. One of them, Bela Kun, had headed a revolutionary government in Hungary which had come to power peacefully in 1919, only to be overthrown by a reactionary counter-revolution which set up a fascist regime under Horthy.

But the dominant figure of them all was Georgi Dimitrov, the hero of the Reichstag fire trial, and it was eminently fitting that he should deliver the main report to the Seventh World Congress on what became known as the "People's Front Against Fascism."

An exile from his native Bulgaria (where he became prime minister ten years later), Dimitrov was in Germany when Hitler came to power. He saw firsthand how the Nazi Party, misnamed the National Socialist German Workers Party, financed by the biggest industrialists and bankers, used terror, cunning, divisiveness, and demagogy to fasten its hold on the country. He saw that the only organized force that could have stopped it, the working class, was too divided to present an effective opposition. The main division was between the Communists and Social Democrats and their respective trade unions; the Social Democratic leaders had refused to consider any unity of action with the Communists. The main burden of the struggle against the fascists fell on the Communists.

Those historians who see Hitler's rise to power as a struggle between fascists and Communists simply echo or give comfort, perhaps unwittingly, to the Nazis' theme that they were saving Germany from the "Communist danger." They have missed one of the great lessons of history. As the Protestant pastor Martin Niemöller said sadly about the Holocaust: "When Hitler attacked the Communists, we were silent because we were not Communists; when he attacked the Jews, we said nothing because we were not Jews; when he attacked the Catholics, we did not speak out because we were not Catholics; by the time he got around to the rest of us, it was too late.''

In order to seize power completely and destroy the Weimar Republic and its constitution, Hitler had to appear as the savior of Germany against Communism. To convince the unconvinced masses, he organized a monstrous frameup. Nazis set fire to the Reichstag building (where the German parliament sat). He announced that it was a Communist plot against the government and ordered the wiping out of the Communist Party. Most of its leadership were seized, tortured, and eventually executed. Tens of thousands of Communist members were arrested and sent to concentration camps which very few survived. The powerful Communist Party was decimated, and the members who escaped had to resort to underground resistance at great risk to their lives.

The frameup required a "show trial." For this purpose the Nazis arrested Dimitrov and two young Bulgarian colleagues: Ernst Torgler, a Communist parliamentary leader in the German Reichstag, and a young half-witted Dutchman named Van der Lubbe, who was known to be a Nazi stooge. The arrest of the three Bulgarians was needed to give the appearance of a sinister international conspiracy. Van der Lubbe was needed to supply the "confession" that he set the fire at the behest of the Communists.

The Reichstag fire trial is now history. The heroic stature of Dimitrov became evident to the entire world. He dominated the scene in the courtroom. Time and again he defied the fascist judges and presented a magnificent defense of his principles. At the same time, within the limits imposed by the court, he carried out a skillful exposure of the frameup. Of Van der Lubbe, he said scornfully to the court: "This miserable Faust is here in the dock, while Mephistopheles has disappeared."

It was an unforgettable scene when Hermann Goering, the number two Nazi, was brought in as the chief witness for the government. When Dimitrov challenged him with withering questions, Goering lost control of himself. He raged and screamed at Dimitrov: "You will be hanged, but the Third Reich will be here for a thousand years." When a member of the court spoke of Bulgarians as a "barbaric people," Dimitrov retorted: "The people of Bulgaria are not barbarians. . . . Only their fascist rulers are barbarians, but I ask you, in which country does not fascism have these qualities?"[1] The enraged court ordered him expelled from the courtroom.

So glaring, so blatant was the frameup that even a Nazi court could not withstand world reaction to this dramatic confrontation, where the accused became the accuser. Dimitrov and his companions were acquitted. But Hitler's main aim had already been accomplished—the destruction of the Communist Party, the excuse for a reign of terror against all opponents, the destruction of Germany's parliamentary democracy, and the establishment of a fascist dictatorship. (The Third Reich, which Goering boasted would last a thousand years, lay in ashes ten years later.)

When Dimitrov arrived in the Soviet Union, the Communist International was already in the process of discussing the events in Germany and their meaning. But his firsthand assessment of the situation added depth to the discussions. While Hitler's rise to power could be traced directly to the support of the ruling class of Germany and the pro-fascist sympathizers in the highest circles of Great Britain and France, had there been a united working class this rise would not have been inevitable. Effective resistance was weakened by the refusal of the Social Democratic leaders to consider any form of united action with the Communists. The masses represented in the powerful Social Democratic and Communist parties could have presented a more formidable bloc against the Nazis had there been unity. But the deep and bitter rift that persisted, since the Social Democratic leaders had taken sides against a socialist revolution in Germany after World War I, frustrated the desire of Socialist workers and Communists alike to join together against the Nazis. There were frequent examples of the workers of both parties doing common battle in the streets against the storm troopers, but in elections their votes were split on divided tickets. Our labeling of the Social Democrats as "social fascists" only deepened the rift.

The discussion took a sharply self-critical turn when it came to assess the role of the Communists themselves. They were led by Dimitrov and Wilhelm Pieck, the chairman of the German Communist Party. (Ernst Thaelman, the General Secretary of the Party, had been arrested and never heard from again. Pieck had escaped the same fate only because he was out of the country at the time of the Reichstag fire; he had returned secretly to organize resistance and knew firsthand about the heavy casualties suffered.)

Their conclusions were that the Party leadership had committed many errors, chief of which was that it had made insufficient efforts to achieve unity with the Socialists. The most strenuous efforts should have been made to reach some pact or understanding with the Social Democratic party leaders, without which any direct appeal to the Socialist rank and file was ineffective. This applied also to the separate trade unions led by Socialists and

Communists, which together could have been a powerful center of resistance.

This opinion was reinforced by the experience in the French municipal elections a year earlier, in which Communists and Socialists united with a single slate and won a major electoral victory. I had heard Maurice Thorez right after the elections give an account of this landmark victory, and defend the policy of his party against the doubters in other Communist parties who still looked with suspicion on any form of unity with the Socialists.

I had my own experience on a smaller scale with these doubters, when shortly after my arrival I recounted at a meeting of the Comintern, to which I had been invited, our policy in Minnesota to enter Workers and Farmers tickets in local elections in rural areas. One of the Russian leaders present was skeptical of this tactic, citing the corruption in American politics for his doubts. Such an attitude held by a few was not conducive to a united-front policy, as the later discussion led by Dimitrov made clear.

Dimitrov defined fascism as something qualitatively different from bourgeois democracy. It was the "open terrorist dictatorship of the most reactionary, most chauvinist, most imperialist sections" of the ruling class. Despite the limitations which Communists see in capitalist democracy, he said, it should be defended from the threat of overthrow by fascism, and its democratic rights must be fought for at every step against the encroachments of fascist ideology and methods. He called for a United Front of the working class, but beyond that a People's Front to embrace people of all classes who opposed fascism. This historic call became the rallying cry of antifascists everywhere.

In the following year it became the basis for the electoral victory in Spain which brought into power a People's Front government (whose later overthrow by Franco was due to the open intervention of Hitler and Mussolini and the help they received from the "neutrality" of Britain, France, and the United States). Through the rest of the decade it was the central focus of Communist policy, and under other names and forms has continued to be so ever since.

The United Front policy has been much maligned by liberals as well as by reactionary historians. We see the "Front" as a battle line, but it has become fashionable to twist its meaning to a "front" as a facade, a screen to disguise or conceal some sinister purpose. Of course, if one takes the attitude that everything the Communists say or do is sinister per se, then this useful semantic distortion becomes possible. McCarthyism made good use of the "Communist front" scare.

But the fact is that the Communists were rallying people to the antifascist fight when hardly anybody else was, whether in defense of the Spanish Republic or in the underground resistance in fascist countries. We were the "premature antifascists." Who is to say that if the People's Front had won out in Britain, France, and the United States, history might not have avoided the catastrophes of the concentration camps, the ovens, and the holocaust of World War II?

* * *

My stay in the Soviet Union was not long enough to make me an expert, so I cannot speak as learnedly as those "experts" who were never closer to Russia than New York or Washington, or the Hoover Institution at Palo Alto, California, from which were issued periodic prophecies of the doom of the Soviet regime. But I had always been intrigued by a saying of the famous journalist Lincoln Steffens (who was not a Communist) on his return from visiting that land: "I have seen the future, and it works."

One must remember that in the first decade after the revolution the main subject of debate in the rest of the world was not whether socialism would bring more freedom or less freedom, or whether it would produce a superior economy; the chief question raised by the pundits of the bourgeois world was whether it would work at all, and how soon it would fall. Steffens, who had gone there as a skeptic, found out in his own way what Marxists have been saying—that socialism works for the people.

I found no utopia. We should not be blind to the shortcomings of a socialist society which still has a long way to go to reach the goals it has set for itself. We have often made the mistake of holding that the Soviet Union could do no wrong; but even when we were wrong and criticism was justified, it was because we refused to go along with the anti-Sovieteers in their relentless efforts to undermine and destroy what the Soviet people have achieved with so much sacrifice.

From its starting point, in spite of all obstacles, Soviet society came further in a shorter time than had ever been achieved in history before. The year before the Seventh World Congress was the year that the Soviet Union emerged for the first time from a period of hardships brought on by famine, counter-revolution, and foreign intervention. For the first time life was a little easier; bread was plentiful as a result of the collectivization of agriculture, and although shortages existed in many commodities, no one went hungry. The abolition of illiteracy, unemployment, and hunger was a monumental achievement which the capitalist world, even the wealthiest nations, have not yet accomplished. On our visit to Saratov, on the Volga River, a guide took us to a huge empty field and said: "Come back in five years, and you will see the largest ball-bearing plant in the world here." History proved him correct.

The excesses of Stalin had not yet begun, or at least were not known, and the atmosphere was one of buoyant optimism. Foreign correspondents and diplomats have invariably referred to life in Moscow as "drab" and "dreary," and to the people's "unsmiling faces." By Western bourgeois standards, of course, "drabness" consists of a lack of neon lights, night clubs, luxury goods in stores, and Broadway musicals.

I saw no drabness. I saw cheerful people on the streets, on the beaches, in the amusement parks, at the circus, and at the cinema. I saw ordinary working people thronging to the always packed ballet, opera, and theater.

Leah learned to speak a little Russian, so we were able to chat with anyone at random, to verify our impressions. There was a feeling of pride among the Russians at their achievements in overcoming stupendous obstacles, a feeling that things were getting better. But the curtain of hostility and misrepresentation kept this from most Americans.

An amusing incident comes to mind. It involves Kathleen Norris, the noted American novelist, whose politics, if any, were conservative. I met her at a San Francisco rally for Loyalist Spain, of which her brother, Frederick Thompson, was the chairman. When he introduced us, she told me about a visit to the Soviet Union she had made some years before and described what she considered to be "quaint sights." One of them, she said, was to see people walking down the street nibbling on pieces of bread. "They were obviously hungry," she said. I thereupon pinpointed the year she was there. She was obviously surprised at my accurate guess, and I explained that I was there the same year. When I arrived the newspapers had been publicizing complaints by shoppers that they were being short-weighted when buying bread, which was sold by the kilogram. As a result of the newspaper campaign, the store clerks would cut a sizable hunk of bread, put it on the scale, and then keep adding small pieces to make up the exact weight. Due to a shortage of paper, the bread was handed to the customer with a skimpy piece of paper, and the little pieces were picked up in the other hand. I was not long in Moscow before I was doing what the Russians were doing, walking down the street carrying the cut loaf in one hand and nibbling on the small pieces in the other. Kathleen Norris had quite a laugh at my explanation and admitted that appearances can be deceiving. (At least in her case her erroneous impression was not due to malice or bias.)

Hitler's rise to power had thrown the shadow of fascism over the continent of Europe, and had renewed the fear of another war and its dreadful toll. Much of Soviet production had to be diverted to defense, holding back even greater advances. It took sixteen years for the United States to recognize the Soviet state, but even then the economic blockade was never completely lifted, and nearly all of the economic progress made since then has been from its own resources.

I came away from my sojourn there echoing Lincoln Steffens's words. I confess that I did not have a clear idea as yet of how this "future" would be achieved in the United States, but I believed that we would find our own way to achieve it, and perhaps learn from the achievements and mistakes of those who had gone before. It would not be long after my return to the United States that I would be forced to explain and defend these views before a Federal District Court and the Supreme Court, and fight for the right to express them.

4   The Great Upsurge:
The General Strike
and Its Aftermath

In October, 1935, I came back to California to serve as District Organizer, and later as State Secretary and State Chairman, posts which I was to hold for twenty-one years. On my return I was immediately plunged into a maelstrom of events which tested the Party's ability to give leadership to the unfolding struggles— struggles on a different level from those of the previous years when the unemployed movement dominated the scene.

In the aftermath of the General Strike and despite the longshoremen's victory, the struggle on the waterfront was by no means over. The seamen's unions were trying to enforce union conditions by "job action" against ships containing "hot cargo," which the longshoremen were refusing to unload. The shipowners had not given up their fight against the maritime unions; their main weapon was redbaiting. Their particular target was the key Longshoremen's Union and its Australian-born leader Harry Bridges, who had to fight a series of attempts to deport him because of alleged Communist Party membership.

Using the excuse that the unions were "Communist dominated," the employers conducted a bitter struggle against them, which resulted in one crisis after another on the waterfront. They tried to create division among the workers by cultivating those members who were anti-Communist, and by the use of informers. (A senate committee investigating violations of civil liberties, headed by the liberal Senator Robert LaFollete, uncovered the large-scale, well-financed efforts of the shipowners to penetrate and disrupt the maritime unions and the Communist Party.) But these efforts had only a limited effect, because a new day had dawned in labor's ranks.

The General Strike of 1934 in San Francisco, in the midst of the great strike wave which swept the country that year, had left an indelible mark on the labor movement and politics of California and the West Coast for some time to come. It was a period, with the country just coming out of the depths of the economic crisis, when the strike wave and the unemployed struggles preceding it proclaimed that the American working class was beginning to act consciously as a class.

The General Strike, and the longshoremen's strike which precipitated it after two pickets (one of them a Communist), were shot and killed by the police, demonstrated two lessons of enormous importance to the labor movement which most historians have ignored. First of all, the General Strike Committee of the San Francisco Labor Council was able virtually to run the city for several days by a permit system in a responsible and orderly manner, so that essential services were maintained where necessary for food, health, and safety. (Any citizen, group, or business could apply to the strike committee and their requests were heard and acted upon.)

Secondly, unity and solidarity were shown by all sections of the San Francisco Bay Area labor movement in support of the longshoremen, in spite of the redbaiting attacks on their "radical" or "Communist" leadership; this support radiated out to include not only the working-class population, but to many small business people and professionals as well.

Panic swept the ruling class, to whom the strike was outright "revolution." Vigilantism was rampant; printing presses were smashed, meeting-halls and offices raided and wrecked, and in Sonoma county two left-wing sympathizers were tarred and feathered. The press charged a Communist plot to incite revolution. The terror and the redbaiting were deliberately calculated to break the strike.

Reading about it from afar, thousand of miles away, I never dreamed that eighteen years later the government would claim that I "ordered" the general strike as a "dress rehearsal" for revolution. (In 1934 I had been away from California for four years, yet the incredible charge was made that the working class of San Francisco was pulled like a puppet on a string from Moscow, and that I was pulling the strings. Thus the history of the general strike was to become a central feature of the trial to come, in which the prosecution would seek to weave a sinister web of conspiracy around the events which led to the historic confrontation in San Francisco).

But it was not the Communists who shot down two workers, the incident which triggered the general strike. The Communists did not create the "shape-up" on the docks, and long hours and low pay, which caused the bitter longshoremen's strike. The Communists did not manufacture the overwhelming sympathy of the other trades for their struggle, nor the support for them shown in the community as a whole.

What was the Communists' role? After a period of unsuccessfully trying to organize workers into independent unions (because of the failure of the A.F. of L. leadership to organize the unorganized), the Communist Party turned its attention to helping organize workers into A.F. of L. unions. A change in the situation favored this turn in policy. As part of Roosevelt's "recovery" program, which was mainly aimed at putting Big Business back on its feet, the National Recovery Act of 1933 contained the deceptive term "free choice," actually to restrict A.F. of L. unions from organizing and to encourage company unions. The Wagner Act had not yet been enacted, and a worker still ran the risk of being fired for joining a union.

What they didn't count on was that Section 7a created the illusion of legitimacy; up to that time the right to organize into trade unions had never been legally recognized by the Federal Government, and the long and bloody history of labor struggles attested to the fact that the only rights the workers had were those they fought for and won on the class battlefield. The expectations created by Section 7a and by Roosevelt's promises let loose a wave of strikes and organizing activity, most of it initiated outside of the A.F. of L. bureaucracy, by the unorganized themselves. There was a wave of unrest among the rank and file of A.F. of L. unions, whose leadership was sitting on its hands, a situation which eventually led to the formation of the CIO.

It was in these circumstances that members of the left-led Marine Workers Industrial Union, affiliated with the Trade Union Unity League, began meeting with other militants among the longshoremen and seamen, set up rank-and-file caucuses and a popular mimeographed newspaper, *The Waterfront Worker*, which won such wide support that eventually a new, militant leadership emerged, and the company union was replaced by locals of the A.F. of L. International Longshoremen's Association and the International Seamen's Union. After an eighty-three-day strike the longshoremen won the hiring hall and the six-hour day, but the seamen's unions had a long, difficult, and more complicated struggle. The sailors were under anarcho-syndicalist control; the officers unions were under conservative leaders, most of them anti-Communist. The cooks and stewards were under left leadership, as were the marine firemen for a time. Nevertheless the struggles on the waterfront made solidarity essential, when a series of strikes and "hot cargo" disputes required each union to respect the picket lines of the others. It was this need for mutual support which led to the next logical step, the federating of the West Coast longshoremen and seamen's unions, despite their differences in political outlook, into the Maritime Federation of the Pacific. When the CIO was formed, all these unions later broke with the A.F. of L. and nearly all affiliated with the CIO.

An exception was the Sailors Union of the Pacific headed by Harry Lundeberg, which remained affiliated with the A.F. of L. Seamen's International Union. Lundeberg was strongly influenced by anarcho-syndicalism. Highly ambitious to be the top dog on the waterfront and bitterly jealous of Bridges' prominence, he allied himself with the Trotskyists and drove suspected Communists out. He led his union out of the Maritime Federation and into constant clashes with the other seamen's unions and the longshoremen.

An illustration of his methods was brought home to me personally when I paid him a courtesy visit while he was ill, some time before he had broken with the Communists and other left forces on the waterfront. I found him in bed in a room at the Southern Hotel, at Seventh and Mission Streets. At the time he was worried about the union's legal difficulties arising out of some "job actions" which succeeded in tying up ships over legitimate grievances of the sailors. I suggested a lawyer I had heard of, Aaron Sapiro, who had successfully represented steel workers in Pennsylvania with similar legal problems, and urged Lundeberg to bring him out to the Coast. (I knew Lundeberg wouldn't use local attorneys associated with Bridges.)

This was a big mistake on my part. Sapiro was bitterly hostile to Bridges and his allies, and helped influence Lundeberg in his union policies to isolate the sailors from the other unions on the waterfront. At one point, when Lundeberg went on his anti-Communist rampage, he stood before his membership meeting in San Francisco and brazenly told them that while he was bedridden, Schneiderman had come to his hotel room and tried to intimidate him to carry out Communist policies. (It was no wonder that he became the darling of the Hearst press, and as he moved further to the right, began to support Republican candidates for public office.)

With the beginning of economic recovery from the depth of the Depression, the struggles of the maritime unions and the victories won had a galvanizing effect on the rest of the labor movement in California and on the West Coast. Even before the CIO launched its battle for industrial unions in the basic industries, successful organizing drives began in California in the warehouses, the canneries, the lettuce fields, and other industries in the rest of the state. The passage of the Wagner National Labor Relations Act, the national organizing drive and the sitdown strikes of the emerging CIO gave an added impetus to the upsurge in California, which merged with the nationwide struggles. As a result, the left-led maritime unions took a leading role in the formation of the CIO West Coast organization, a fact which John L. Lewis acknowledged when he appointed Harry Bridges as the CIO's Pacific Coast Regional Director.

Bridges was a dynamic figure, slight and wiry of build, and cocky of manner. He was no orator, but when he addressed a meeting of his peers, speaking in an informal, conversational tone with a slight Australian accent, he made telling points by the substance of his speech rather than its rhetoric. The strong support he received from the rank and file, in spite of the redbaiting attacks on him, was due primarily to the program he advocated, but was also due to the faith of the membership in his incorruptibility, in a world full of corrupt officialdom.

The left which launched the revolt on the waterfront included Communists and non-Communists, and some with a syndicalist background from the days of the IWW. Many believed in socialism but were not attached to any party. There were differing ideologies among them, but all were bound together by a common denominator—the economic demands which they hammered into a program of action. The Communists on the waterfront were not "outside agitators," as the press charged, but maritime workers who had become disillusioned with the breakdown of the capitalist system during the Depression and saw in the Communist Party the only force that appeared to be leading the fight for jobs and to organize the unorganized.

Bridges took a firm stand against redbaiting. During one confrontation with the waterfront employers, when they refused to negotiate with the "Communist leadership" of the longshoremen, Bridges told the San Francisco Labor Council, to a roar of approval from the delegates, "When the Waterfront Employers Association will let us select their leadership, we'll let them choose ours."

When the charge was made during his deportation hearings that he met with Communists and accepted their support, he readily acknowledged it. Did he meet with Schneiderman? "Yes," was his reply. Where? "He would come to my office, but so did Republican and Democratic party people."

He had a shrewd sense of tactics in the war with the shipowners, and an instinctive understanding of how far the rank and file was willing to go on economic and political issues. He had, also, a contempt for what he considered "theory," and sometimes would go for an immediate tactical advantage at the expense of longer range goals. We would often argue with him, not always successfully, on such points of disagreement. But overall he was one of the most effective of the new crop of leaders that emerged in that period when militant unions with rank-and-file democracy were showing the way to the rest of the labor movement. (In later years he had many disagreements with Communists in the union, who became increasingly critical of some of the policies he advocated, but he remained a staunch supporter of American-Soviet friendship when many former left leaders were running for cover.)

The longshoremen's influence spread far beyond the waterfront. Organizing activities mushroomed, from the warehouses of the city to the lettuce fields of Salinas, and the growers began to raise the alarm about the ILWU's "march inland," as though they were mobilizing against a foreign invasion. When the Salinas lettuce workers went on strike, the growers used vigilante gangs as well as the legal law-enforcement machinery against the strikers; There were no Communists involved in that strike, but that did not stop the growers from using the "Red scare" and the same ruthless tactics as they did in the Imperial Valley a few years before, when Communists were organizing farmworkers and leading strikes there, which resulted in seven organizers (five men and two women) being arrested and given harsh prison sentences under the then-operative Criminal Syndicalism Law.

The entrance of new young forces into the leadership of various unions revitalized the labor movement, and the influence of the left was strongly felt in central labor bodies and the State Federation of Labor. I witnessed an incident which took place at the State Federation of Labor convention in Sacramento in 1936 which illustrated the unhappiness of some of the old-line leadership with the new trends. Each day the delegates were given a different colored pass to get into the convention. On the day that Bridges was scheduled to speak, the cards happened to be red, and as I stood in line for a visitor's pass, I heard a paunchy business agent, who had just been handed his red card, snap, "It's a fine state of affairs when you need a red card to get into an A.F. of L. convention."

It was no wonder that the government, prompted by the waterfront employers, carried on a relentless effort to deport Bridges with an unprecedented series of deportation hearings, in which it sought unsuccessfully to prove he was a Communist through an assortment of stool pigeons and "guilt-by-association" techniques.

The political climate in California, for decades under Republican rule, underwent an equally great change. The greatest challenge the Republicans had faced till then was in 1934, when Upton Sinclair and his EPIC (End Poverty in California) movement captured the Democratic gubernatorial primaries, but was defeated by Republican Governor Merriam in a frenzied redbaiting campaign. Sinclair, with his Socialist background and his proposal that the unemployed operate the idle factories, represented to many a challenge to a system in which the confidence of the people had been shaken very badly by the economic crisis. His campaign, therefore, had a crusading zeal uncharacteristic of the Democratic party, and his supporters had built a chain of EPIC clubs throughout the state that operated sometimes independently of the Democratic Party, many of whose regulars either sat on their hands or openly supported the Republicans.

The Communist Party in 1934 had not shown the same flexibility on the political arena that it had demonstrated so well in the trade-union field. It had opposed the Sinclair movement as a diversion to keep the militant upsurge in the country within the two-party system. It was the period when "Social Fascism" was the label we put to Social Democracy. It was Social Democracy in western Europe which had opposed the revolutionary upsurge after World War I and the Russian Revolution, and it was Social Democracy in the United States on a smaller scale in certain unions, which had allied itself with the employers and the government against the workers. But while all this was undeniably true, there was a grievous error in the promulgation of the theory of "Social Fascism," and applying it indiscriminately to all Socialists.

It was Hitler's rise to power and the suppression in Germany of the Communist and Socialist parties and the bourgeois democratic opposition, which caused the various Communist Parties to reevaluate their position. The ground was laid for a historic change when the Seventh Congress of the Communist International promulgated the new United Front policy.

The People's Front policy had an enormous influence in developing a democratic upsurge in Western Europe, especially in France and Spain, where People's Front governments were formed in 1936. In the United States a loose coalition of democratic forces had formed about the same time around the Roosevelt New Deal. (The coalitions fell apart, in France and in the United States with the outbreak of the war in 1939, and in Spain with destruction of the Spanish Republic by the fascist onslaught of Franco, Hitler, and Mussolini, aided by the embargo imposed by the United States under the guise of "nonintervention.")

On the political field, a struggle was going on in the California Democratic Party between the regulars and the progressives who had supported Sinclair. In addition to the EPIC clubs, pension clubs were springing up all over the state, some in the Townsend movement and others in the so called "Ham and Eggs" organization, all seeking some form of social security.

By the time I came back to California, we saw the need to shake off the past sectarian attitudes toward these emerging forces and began to develop united-front relations with them. In the absence of any realistic perspective of a breakaway movement from the two-party system at that time, the main objective of the left was directed to the bringing together of the progressive forces in the Democratic Party and the pension movement with the new upsurge in the labor movement into a cohesive, independent political force.

As a result, the coalition that emerged in California was a movement that was somewhat to the left of the Roosevelt New Deal, but supporting it. Although part of the national coalition around Roosevelt, it was a peculiarly California phenomenon with a special characteristic. It was more of a grass-roots movement, with a populist tinge, and the labor unions, especially the left leaders among them, had more of a say in it.

The CIO became a powerful political force in the state, even though the American Federation of Labor continued to have a larger membership. The AFL benefited, too, from the vigor and militancy of the CIO and the maritime unions, and while there was competition, there was also a considerable amount of labor unity between the two bodies, especially in the San Francisco Bay area, where the memory of the General Strike remained in the minds of the workers.

Following the big victory for Roosevelt in the 1936 reelection campaign, the left forces in the Democratic Party and the labor movement set their aim on the 1938 gubernatorial elections. The Republicans had reigned for forty years, and except for their near miss in the Sinclair campaign, they were well entrenched. A "Committee for Political Unity" was formed which represented a coalition of progressive Democrats, trade unions, pension clubs, and independents which waged a successful campaign to elect progressives to the state legislature and State Senator Culbert Olson to the governorship.

The Communist Party, although it ran its own ticket for some state office and received as high as 150,000 votes, allied itself with the progressive forces and was looked upon as an unofficial part of the coalition. The newly launched daily *People's World*, successor to the *Western Worker*, was recognized and accepted as a valuable ally, and in its first edition carried greetings from members of the state legislature and trade-union locals. Indicative of the recognition of the Party's role is the fact that U.S. Senator Sheridan Downey, Governor Olson, and various state legislators showed no hesitancy in meeting with me and other Party leaders to discuss the election campaign or legislation we were supporting.

It was inevitable that a certain euphoria was prevalent in Party ranks, and illusions as to how much could be achieved through the Democratic party. When one of our workers exulted after the election: "We won! We won!" I had to caution him, "The Democratic party won." It was not too long afterwards that we were to find how limited the victory was.

* * *

If one would judge by our history books, the civil-rights struggles began in the 1960s. But long before them, the consciousness of the nation was first aroused to the national oppression of the Negro people by the Communists. The Communist Party recognized that Black people were doubly oppressed, as workers and as a racial minority. Consequently we were almost alone when we conducted a persistent fight for equal rights for Blacks, for political, economic, and social equality at all levels.

Lynchings in the South were still prevalent, with little or no public outcry. But the legal lynchings to which Blacks were subjected were even more numerous, and it was in fighting against some of these that we brought nationwide attention to the evil. Angelo Herndon was saved from a death penalty in Atlanta, and a young Black lawyer in the Herndon case, named Ben Davis, later became a national leader of the Communist Party and a New York City Councilman. The frameup of the Scottsboro boys in Alabama resulted in a campaign which resulted in mass protests in the entire country and throughout the world, and eventually ended in a notable victory. It was the first time that the system of all-white juries was challenged in the courts, and a breakthrough achieved (although to this day the practice has not been completely wiped out in the South.). Numerous other such campaigns come to mind, notably the Willie McGee case in Mississippi, and the case of Wesley Wells in California; Wells was saved from a death penalty by a commutation of sentence from a Republican Governor after we had initiated a statewide campaign in his behalf.

Blacks were generally barred from political office, and we joined in a fight for Negro representation in public life. When Gus Hawkins first ran for Congress, where he is now one of the senior members, from a predominantly Black district in Los Angeles, there were many white progressives who argued that it made no difference whether a white liberal or a Black candidate ran in such a district, and very often they leaned toward the white liberal. They did not understand the necessity of Black representation as a right, and at times we did not have many allies when we were fighting for that right. At that time the fight for recognition of Blacks had to be made at every level, and poll taxes and other discriminatory legislation even barred them from voting in the South.

Even more important was the struggle we conducted in every locality against discrimination in jobs, housing, and schools. Many craft unions and industries barred Blacks and other minorities, or relegated them to Jim Crow locals or auxiliaries. I can still remember when Walter Stack, a Communist, then a business agent of the Marine Firemen's Union, stirred up a storm when he admitted the first Black member into the union and a job. The union had been lily white. It was not until the war that Blacks could work as streetcar men and in other trades, and we undertook the battle against the hostility which threatened their jobs.

With white workers monopolizing most jobs, we began to raise the question in the unions of giving some preference to Black workers, so that they could be admitted to unions and job opportunities that had been denied them in the past. But this proposal, dubbed "super-seniority," met opposition even in the progressive unions as a threat to the seniority system, and made little progress at that time. Yet it was the forerunner of the "affirmative action" program that is now widely accepted, at least formally, by unions and government agencies.

As the war made a small dent in segregated housing, Communists frequently had to mobilize neighbors and friends to protect Blacks from racist violence for daring to move into white neighborhoods.

Basic to our understanding of the importance of the fight for equal rights for Blacks was our recognition of the special character of the struggle of a nationally oppressed people. We had reached the conclusion that in the so-called Black Belt, cutting across state lines and running through most of the South, where the Negro people were a majority, they constituted a nation and were entitled to the right of self-determination, up to and including the right of secession. They had a common territory, economic life, culture, and psychological makeup, and by this definition appeared to have all the attributes of a nation. We, therefore, raised the slogan of the right of self-determination. (The slogan was later dropped, and the question has become moot with mass migration from the

Black Belt to the North, and industrialization of the postwar South.)

The demand for self-determination was never taken up by the Black liberation movement, probably because it was not considered a practical demand. The Black people were directing their struggle, not to separation but to integration into American life with full economic, political, and social equality. In this sense our slogan was not a realistic one and did not take into full account all the historical and psychological factors which gave their struggle a unique character in the United States. Nevertheless, our demand for self-determination helped to raise the national consciousness of Blacks, and was a prelude to the rise of Black pride and awareness which accompanied the civil rights movement of the sixties.

Our pioneering role brought us recognition from a strange source. It was the FBI that paid us an inadvertent compliment; anyone fighting for Negro rights was a "Communist" and put on their "subversive" list. Those giants of Black culture and struggle, Dr. W. E. B. Dubois and Paul Robeson, had their passports revoked, denying them the right to travel; William L. Patterson, head of the Civil Rights Congress, was harassed. The government jailed the Communist leaders Ben Davis and Henry Winston, thus conferring a badge of honor on the party of Black and white unity.

* * *

Although the economic and social issues of the lingering depression were still paramount, the fight to free the frameup victims Mooney and Billings played a prominent part in the 1938 election campaign, so much so that Olson repeated the promise of Sinclair to labor that if he were elected governor, one of his first acts would be free Tom Mooney.

Mooney, the San Francisco labor leader who with Billings was framed in 1916 for a bomb explosion that took place during a "Preparedness Day" parade, was a remarkable character. For over twenty years he tenaciously conducted his defense campaign from his jail cell in San Quentin, and his case became famous throughout the world. He was saved from the death penalty by a protest demonstration of Russian workers at the American embassy in St. Petersburg (now Leningrad), which brought the case to the attention of President Woodrow Wilson, who commuted his sentence to life imprisonment.

The most spectacular event in the worldwide campaign for his release took place at the 1932 Olympic Games in Los Angeles. Six young people (four of them Young Communist League members) were sitting close to the track, and as the Parade of Nations was about to start, took off their outer clothes revealing track suits which bore the slogan "Free Tom Mooney" on the front and back, jumped over the railing and ran around the oval track at the huge Coliseum before 100,000 astonished spectators. Since the police and other security forces were standing at attention while the national anthem was being played, no one molested them until they had finished circling the track, when they were finally arrested and given fifty to one hundred days in jail.[1]

Mooney was an ardent believer in socialism, and a warm friend of Robert Minor, the Communist leader, writer, and cartoonist, who organized the first defense committee in his behalf. The labor movement took up the cry for his pardon, and his case was constantly in the courts over the years. I got to know him when a labor-oriented district attorney in San Francisco allowed Mooney out of jail to live in an apartment while his appeal was being heard—that's the way things were in San Francisco in those days.

Mooney was a dynamic personality, strong-willed, and persistent. Although imprisoned since 1916, his spirit was never broken, and he kept up to date with the latest developments in the labor movement and in politics. While at his temporary living quarters in San Francisco, he held court in his apartment for a constant stream of prominent personalities who came to see him. And although this strange arrangement was widely known, no reporter picked it up, no newspaper printed anything about it, because there was an almost universal belief in his innocence.

His instinctive distrust of politicians, even progressives, served him well. The Democrats had won a decisive victory in the elections, capturing both the governorship and the state assembly. It was expected that on Inauguration Day Governor Olson would announce a pardon for Tom Mooney. But word began to spread that the Governor was having second thoughts. He wanted to delay the pardon to a later date. When Mooney heard this, he summoned his attorneys and said to them: "If I'm not pardoned on Inauguration Day, I'll never get out of here; he will find some excuse to back out of his promise." He then dispatched a scathing letter to the governor, repeating this, and in his characteristic style told him: "The only thing you'll ever be remembered for is that you pardoned Tom Mooney." Egotistical as it sounded, subsequent events proved him to be a prophet.

Whether it was this letter, or the intense pressure of many labor leaders, the wavering governor was finally persuaded to carry out his promise. It was an impressive and moving sight, that January day in 1939, when the newly inaugurated governor announced, in the chambers of the State Assembly before an audience that included politicians, labor leaders, and rank-and-file workers, that he was righting an injustice of over twenty-years standing in pardoning Tom Mooney.

But the drama of the scene was surpassed by the reception Mooney received on his arrival from San Quentin in San Francisco. I had visited him in San Quentin some time earlier, with one of his attorneys, to discuss the welcoming meeting being planned by the Mooney Defense Committee. They were going to have it in the huge Civic Auditorium. But Mooney objected and wanted it out of doors in the Civic Center. We argued with him, pointing out that in January there was a likelihood of rain. The matter was left unresolved when we left, and the committee continued to plan for the Civic Auditorium. But we hadn't reckoned with Tom Mooney's persistence. When we visited him again, he triumphantly announced that he had studied the weather charts and found that it had rained only once in twenty-five years on that day in January. So we capitulated—Civic Center it was!

It was a bright, sunny day when the cavalcade accompanied Tom Mooney and his escorts over the bridge into San Francisco. There was a tradition that when a President arrived in the city, the whistle of the Ferry Building at the foot of Market Street was blown three times to announce his arrival. The old ex-teamster who manned the tower, peering out over the bridge, saw the procession of cars approaching and true to the tradition sounded the whistle three times to tell the city that Tom Mooney had come home. And what a homecoming! Cheering thousands jammed the streets as a parade formed down Market Street, with trade-union guards wearing armbands policing the demonstration.

My most lasting memory of the occasion was when Mooney, with an instinctive sense of drama, pointed as he marched by to the roof top where he had stood watching the "Preparedness Day" parade on that fateful day twenty-two years before, when the bomb went off. It was a crucial point in his proof of innocence, because a newspaper photographer had taken a picture of him there, which was several blocks away from where the bomb exploded and where the prosecution witnesses had placed him.

At the Civic Center 100,000 people were gathered. The list of speakers included Lieutenant-Governor Ellis Patterson, Robert Minor for the Communist Party, and a host of labor leaders. I stood at the top of the stairs in front of City Hall, looking out from that vantage point over the vast throng, and thought to myself: Sacco and Vanzetti were not so fortunate. But it was one of the most satisfying experiences of my life.

Speaking at demonstration of the unemployed in Minneapolis,
1931. (p. 33)

Schneiderman speaking at demonstration of the unemployed in
Minneapolis when running for governor of Minnesota in 1932. (p.
34)

Longshore pickets surrounding produce trucks during the 1934 strike. (p. 212)

Tom Mooney leading victory parade down Market Street in San Francisco after his pardon by Governor. Harry Bridges is in the first row of marchers (between the tracks, to the left of woman). (p. 67)

William
Schneiderman,
1941

Newspaper cartoon prompted by a witness's testimony before the Committee on Un-American Activities that Schneiderman came to California from Russia "to overthrow the government." The caption on the buggy with the two-year-old Schneiderman reads, "California, here we come." (p. 84)

5 Munich: The Road to War

The honeymoon period ended abruptly. Storm clouds were already gathering on the horizon as Hitler moved into Czechoslovakia, and Japan into China. Pickets were protesting the shipment of scrap iron to Japan, and San Francisco longshoremen were refusing to cross the picket lines. The American League Against War and Fascism campaigned for collective security against Hitler and won wide support, especially among people in the arts, sciences, and professions. The heroic battle of the Spanish people against Franco stirred deep emotions in the democratic camp and great pride for the Americans who fought there in the Abraham Lincoln Brigade.

But those who favored appeasement of fascism were busy, too. Lindbergh and the America First Committee were preaching: You can do business with Hitler. The "non-intervention" policy of Roosevelt toward Spain, while Hitler and Mussolini were openly supplying Franco, led to the fall of the Spanish Republic, the battle for which was aptly described as "the opening guns of World War II." The Munich Pact signed by England's Chamberlain and Hitler was an ominous go-ahead signal to Nazi Germany that the Western powers would not prevent its swallowing up the smaller nations and carrying out its avowed purpose of moving against the Soviet Union. The fascist axis of Germany, Italy, and Japan, in a pact aimed at "fighting Communism," got ready to strike.

The Soviet Union had vainly appealed for collective security pacts with Britain and France, first to defend Czechoslovakia and then Poland, but to no avail. Chamberlain's appeasement policy was aimed at deflecting Hitler from the West, and turning him to the East. It was on this background that the Soviet Union, finding its efforts to form an anti-Hitler alliance fruitless, signed a Non-Aggression Pact with Germany.

It is one of the great ironies of history that those who denounced the pact as "perfidy" conveniently ignored the perfidy of the Western capitalist powers in tacitly approving at Munich Hitler's takeover of central Europe and encouraging him to attack the Soviet Union. Who was the Soviet Union disloyal to, the "allies" who were plotting its destruction? Only later, when the Soviet Union was saving them from annihilation by its stand against the Nazi invasion, did the military commentators admit that by this pact it was buying valuable time to prepare for the inevitable confrontation that was sure to come. Whether Stalin had illusions that the pact would avoid such an attack I do not know, but in fact it did buy time so that the Soviet Union was better prepared. When one bears in mind how nearly destroyed the Soviet Union was in 1941, it becomes clear how much closer to catastrophe it might have come had the Nazis attacked two years earlier.

But while all this was acknowledged later by military commentators when the Red Army was holding back Hitler's onslaught, at the time of the pact the media managed to mold public opinion in line with the official State Department line that the Russians were partners of the Nazis. I had occasion to challenge this official line in a debate with the editor of the San Francisco *Chronicle*, Paul Smith, before a membership meeting of the San Francisco Longshoremen's Union, Local 10. I had the advantage of being well acquainted with the struggles on the waterfront, and in my argument I pointed out that when the longshoremen were forced to go on strike, their strategy was to try to sign separate agreements with the individual shipowners in order to break the united front of the Waterfront Employers Association, which was intent on breaking the union. "Well, that's what the Soviet Union did in signing the Non-Aggression Pact with Germany—to break the united front of those powers who were plotting war against it," I said. I made the same point in a debate with the foreign editor of the *Chronicle*, Albion Ross, before a membership meeting of the Marine Cooks and Stewards Union. The majority of the maritime workers understood this very well, in spite of the editorial thunderings of the *Chronicle*. But they were the exception.

Hitler's invasion of Poland, which opened World War II, was triggered, not by the German-Soviet Pact, but by the Munich pact and the refusal of Britain and France to negotiate a collective security agreement with the Soviet Union to defend Czechoslovakia and Poland. Even after the occupation of France and its neighbors, the prolonged period of the "phony war," when resistance had collapsed and no fighting was going on, indicated that the policy of appeasing Hitler was still in effect. With no serious opposition in the West, Hitler was marshalling his forces to move on his Eastern front. The policy of Munich was being carried out.

With these factors in mind, the Party defended the German-Soviet pact and denounced the war as an imperialist war between rival capitalist powers. For this we took a lot of abuse for a "flip-flop," but I think that the reasons for the pact were valid. In retrospect, however, I believe that we were in error in not differentiating between the Nazis and their adversaries, in spite of the temporary identity of their aims.

Ever since the Dimitrov thesis at the Seventh World Congress of the Comintern, we had stressed that we would defend bourgeois democracy against fascism. Had the United States been under threat of invasion by Hitler, we would have taken such a stand. But the complex factors in the war were such that in its early stages it was not a war against fascism but a jockeying for position, for a deal at the expense of the Soviet Union. It could well have ended in a negotiated peace with Hitler that would have left him the master of Europe, if not the world. We should have made this clear and stressed that if the Munich concept were abandoned, and the war aims of the Allies genuinely directed to the destruction of Naziism, it would have changed the character of the war, and we would support such a struggle.

When Hitler invaded the Soviet Union in June, 1941, precisely such a change took place in the character of the war, and because we said so, we were ridiculed. Churchill had to change his tune and recognize what should have been clear all along—that the destruction of the Soviet Union would leave Hitler free to subdue Britain as well and whatever other country, including the United States, he chose to attack or intimidate by his new position of power. If there was a "flip-flop," it was the abandonment of the dream that if Hitler would turn East, the West could be saved. Munich was replaced by the antifascist alliance with the Soviet Union, which the United States supported and then joined as a full-fledged partner after Pearl Harbor. If there were any objectivity in the ranks of those who write about history, they would rewrite their self-righteous estimates of those sorry days of the Munich period and recognize that the capitalist world could not save itself from its own follies; and they would be a little more humble in reviewing their own lack of wisdom and foresight rather than dwelling on the mistakes that the Communists may have made.

Even then the Munich spirit did not completely die. It was an almost unanimous opinion of the pundits that the Soviet Union would last only a few weeks, and there were not a few who hoped for such an outcome. When the Nazis crossed the Soviet border, the reaction of a United States senator from Missouri was, "Let the

Germans kill Russians, and the Russians kill Germans and kill each other off."[1] His name was Harry S. Truman. The same sentiments were held, but not voiced so frankly, by powerful appeasement forces in the country. After Pearl Harbor they discreetly held their silence but exerted their influence on war strategy.

The political situation in the country changed rapidly after the outbreak of the war in Europe. The social objectives of the New Deal were replaced by military priorities and marked a turn to the right by the Roosevelt Administration. The left, which had supported the New Deal coalition and been in the mainstream of American politics throughout the thirties, now found itself under attack by the Administration and by liberals who had joined with us when we were leading the way in fighting for a united front against fascism.

The Party had made great strides toward becoming a mass party. Although it never got a large vote, in its heyday it reached a membership of about 100,000 nationally, and in California close to 10,000. In the period when we were leading the unemployed movement, organizing the unorganized into unions, and calling for a united antifascist struggle, Fred Kirchwey, editor of the *Nation*, the liberal magazine, was once quoted as saying: "A Communist is one who does things that we liberals could do so much better, but never get around to doing."

We were not quite prepared for the new role of bucking the stream. Our election successes had created illusions among some members about the nature of the Democratic Party, especially in California where it had a certain grass-roots character and organization unlike anywhere else (except possibly Minnesota with its Farmer-Labor base). Browder, the leader of the Communist Party, was already sowing the seeds of a theory which, when it came to full bloom in the forties, denied the class struggle. It is no wonder, then, that we lost some ground, which was not regained until the entry of the Soviet Union and the United States into the war vindicated our position.

In the meantime, however, persecution of Communists began. The House of Representatives' Committee on Un-American Activities, which had been at odds with the Roosevelt Administration for its notorious redbaiting witch hunts, now intensified its activities with at least the silent consent of the White House. I was subpoenaed, but never called, probably because at about the same time the Justice Department filed a denaturalization suit to deprive me of my citizenship. In the ensuing period I was twice called before the State Assembly Un-American Committee, headed by renegade liberals. Browder went to jail for a technical violation of passport regulations. Hundreds of foreign-born were arrested for deportation.

In California, Governor Olson and most Democrats went along with the political winds. The Democratic Party, which in the heyday of the New Deal fooled so many people into believing it was a people's party, reverted to type and revealed that the big-business interests still had the last word. Under intense pressure, such as was exerted in the depths of economic crisis, these interests would yield concessions to head off mounting movements of struggle, but basically the two-party system did not change. The design of alternating power but retaining it in the hands of the ruling class was still in effect. The influential Democratic clubs, which gave a progressive coloration to the party in California and an appearance of rank-and-file participation during the period of the democratic upsurge, were paralyzed and intimidated to the point of silence or acquiescence to the redbaiting offensive. The progressive wing of the Democratic Party collapsed.

Olson, once a stalwart liberal, had from the beginning of his administration shown himself to be weak-kneed and vacillating when under attack, as the Mooney incident should have forewarned us. When his appointees and program had come under attack from the redbaiters, he retreated and soon found himself on the defensive on many issues. Disappointing as his record was even when the climate was favorable, his actions changed for the worse when the political situation changed, and began to resemble those of his Republican opponents. To absolve himself of the stigma of accepting the support of the left, the Governor joined the wolf pack and turned on the Communist Party.

* * *

"Mr. Speaker and Members of the Assembly: First of all, I wish to protest against the indecent haste with which this bill, to rule the Communist Party off the California ballot, is being rushed through this Assembly. It makes a hollow mockery of the democratic process and an empty gesture of this hearing."

The scene was the State Capitol in Sacramento on September 21, 1940. I was at the rostrum addressing the State Assembly, with many of the state senators crowding into the hall to take in these extraordinary proceedings.

Only a few hours before, on a Saturday afternoon, the Party's attorney George Andersen, had informed me that Governor Olson had suddenly sent a bill to outlaw the Party to a special session of the State Legislature. In unseemly haste and without advance notice, the State Assembly was preparing to consider the bill without hearings and rush it through for passage. I jumped into Andersen's car with him, and we started racing to Sacramento at such speed that my fear for our safety temporarily overshadowed my concern over whether we would get there too late.

It seemed like a hopeless mission. Our unpopular position on the war had turned the liberal Democrats against us. In the midst of the prevalent anti-Communist campaign and with an election coming on, they were determined to cleanse themselves of any association with the left forces who had helped elect them, and so they outdid the reactionaries in throwing overboard con-stitutional liberties which had been won in the great democratic upsurge of the previous decade.

When we reached the Capitol building, we found that the bill had been introduced in the State Assembly by Jack Tenney and Sam Yorty of Los Angeles, two opportunists who had ridden the liberal wave to win public office, but who were now trying to live down their past by their leadership of the State Assembly Com-mittee on Un-American Activities, which was doing a hatchet job on liberal and left forces. I knew them well. In former days I had frequently met with them when they were part of the liberal bloc, to discuss Fair Employment Practices Legislation for which I was lobbying, as well as other bills. They had at one time posed as so "left" that they introduced a resolution in 1936 to support the Spanish Republican government during the Spanish Civil War, much to the dismay of many of their liberal colleagues, who felt that the defeat of this resolution (which never had a chance) would hurt the cause it ostensibly supported. Now the fury of their attack against the left exceeded that of any of the Republicans. Tenney had an additional motive. A rank-and-file slate in the Musicians Union defeated him for re-election as president of the union, and he attributed his loss to the Communists. Thus it was quite appro-priate that the renegade liberal should sponser the bill to outlaw Communists.

At the Capitol we were greeted by a grinning Tenney. I furiously protested against the unprecedented railroading procedure of voting on a bill without even the formality of a hearing. "Even a condemned man is allowed some last words before sentencing," I stormed. Members of the press, who were standing nearby, heard the loud altercation and crowded around us. Tenney, somewhat embarrassed by the presence of the press, lost some of his arrogance and said, "I'll tell you what we'll do. We'll have the full Assembly meet as a Committee of the Whole, and you can address them before we vote."

George Andersen argued that a vote should be put off until full public hearings could be held, but to no avail. We were not at all happy with this meaningless, condescending gesture which showed such "magnanimity," but which put up a facade of democratic process to cover fascist-like acts. "The condemned man is to be allowed his last words," I said bitterly, "but the verdict has already been decided, hasn't it?"

And so it was that I faced this sea of hostile faces. Some looked bored, some just curious, and a few must have felt guilty, but many showed outright hatred. If a motion had been made to hang me, I am sure some them would have voted for it. Such was the thin dividing line, I thought, between liberal democracy and the rule of the iron fist. Tenney and Yorty sat smirking at the show they were putting on. The State Assembly, at Tenney's request, had reconvened to meet as a Committe of the Whole, and I stood at the rostrum in this empty gesture of "democratic" procedure to address them. There were only three friendly faces in that audience who had the courage to defy that mob: Assemblymen Pelletier of Los Angeles and Richie of San Diego, and Senator Robert Kenny, who had come over from the State Senate to attend the proceedings.

I had not seen the bill until it was handed to me just before they gave me the floor. I had no time to read and study its provisions, nor to prepare testimony in defense of my Party. No other organization had been given enough time to send a representative to express opposition to this bill. But to keep up the pretense of a hearing, they gave me twenty minutes to address the Legislature.

"This is not a routine matter on which you are voting so casually. This bill strikes at the heart of the Constitution of the state and the nation. You are not voting for or against Communism when you vote on this measure. That is not the issue here. You are voting whether a legally constituted political party, complying with the Constitution and the laws of the land, a party with a few thousand members but which has polled as high as 150,000 votes in this state, shall be denied its constitutional rights. You are striking at all political minorities' right to freedom of opinion and expression . . . .

"Our party's constitution pledges its members to oppose with all its power any effort to overthrow or destroy the institutions of American democracy, whether such efforts come from within the country or from abroad . . . . Thus none of the provisions of the bill you have before you can possibly apply to the Communist Party, and we deny that we come in any way under the provision affecting organizations advocating force and violence or controlled by a foreign power.

"It is very strange that the Governor and certain members of this

Assembly should be so anxious to throw the Constitution out of the window, by speaking about 'subversive' and 'un-American' influences. There are members sitting in this Assembly tonight, and the Governor of California himself, who met with leaders of the Communist Party and accepted our support and assistance in the 1938 elections. They did not think we were 'subversive' or 'un-American' then. Somebody has changed their colors, and it is not we. We are still fighting for the same progressive American ideals that we did in 1938. It is the Governor and his colleagues in this Assembly who have gone over to the camp of reaction, war hysteria, and to trampling democracy underfoot . . . .

"The bill pleads the need for 'national defense.' Do you really think you can defend the country by suppression and measures that smack of fascism? Some of you talk a great deal about the danger of fascism. We Communists were fighting fascism and Hitlerism long before most of you had found it 'fashionable' to do so, and when some members of this Assembly were openly admiring the methods of Hitler and fascism, and trying to copy them here . . . .

"You may pass this bill, but we will fight it because it is unconstitutional, undemocratic, and un-American. You cannot outlaw an idea, and you cannot outlaw an American working-class political party, because you cannot solve the problems of peace and security for the American people that way. It is the people you are voting against, and the time will come when you will have to reckon with the people for your action on this bill."

When I had finished my speech, the Assembly voted for the bill, with only Pelletier and Richie voting against. Kenny was the lone dissenting vote in the Senate when it reached there, and the bill was sent to the Governor for his signature. It was a foregone conclusion; nevertheless it was a bitter pill to swallow. But, as often happens in the people's struggle against repression, the victors of the moment did not have the last word. Their victory was only temporary, for we took the fight to the State Supreme Court, and the bill of the turncoat liberals was declared unconstitutional. The law was nullified, and we appeared on the ballot again in the next election, when Governor Olson went down to defeat against Earl Warren.

*　*　*

The war years tested the mettle of the Party at a different level. The entry of the Soviet Union into the war gave the prospect for the first time that the seemingly invincible Nazis could be beaten, and aid to the Soviet Union became of crucial importance to the

United States. The political atmosphere abruptly changed again, for how could anti-Communism remain a rallying slogan for Americans when the Russian communists were fighting our battles for us? (An Englishman quipped to me, "The reason the Russians are able to hold off the Germans, when the Allies failed, is because the Red Army is the only army in the world that is not afraid of Bolshevism." And he laughed heartily at his own joke.)

When Pearl Harbor plunged the United States into the war, Communists threw themselves into the war effort wholeheartedly. Many volunteered for the armed services and distinguished themselves in battle. Others entered the war industries and worked for maximum production. The Communists' role in the war effort was so well recognized that when I applied for extra gasoline ration coupons so I could travel around the state on my official duties, they were granted as a matter of course "in the interest of the war effort."

The Party itself conducted an educational campaign on the character of the war as an antifascist war, on the outcome of which would depend whether we and the rest of the world would live under fascist rule. We supported a no-strike pledge by labor, a controversial position for which we have been criticized. But with Hitler and Japan ruling over most of Europe and Asia, and America, Britain, and the Soviet Union with their backs against the wall, we believed we had no other choice in those critical days.

The big issue of the war years was the opening of a second front in Europe. With the Soviet Union in the East bearing the brunt of the fighting and suffering enormous casualties, while the Western front was quiet, it became clear that victory depended on forcing Hitler to fight on two fronts. Churchill and some of the American appeasers who were only half-heartedly supporting the war (to them it was the wrong war and the wrong enemy) favored delays and peripheral actions. Some American military men favored concentrating on the Pacific, relegating the war against Hitler to a secondary role. With Stalingrad and Leningrad under siege, it seemed Truman had blurted out what was on many minds—"Let them kill each other off." The campaign for a second front, therefore, became a fight to convince the American people who was the main enemy and what was the nature of the war. Had the Soviet Union failed, the prospect was at best for a negotiated peace in which Hitlerism would live to threaten the world again, and at worst a fascist victory. The Party's rallying cry for a second front won wide support and helped to bolster the Roosevelt Administration and defeat the appeasers.

A serious blemish on the Party's war record, however, was its reaction to the internment of the Japanese-Americans on the West Coast. We remained silent with the excuse that it was a necessary war measure. But there was no mass internment of German and Italian aliens. It was a concession to racism, therefore, when we did not protest the internment, and the expropriation of the property of Japanese-American residents. Although Earl Warren and others responsible for the internment later formally recognized its injustice, to this day the Japanese-American victims of racism are still seeking to get adequate compensation for the loss of their civil rights and virtual theft of their properties.

At the outbreak of the war, when the roundup began, one of the people arrested was Karl Yoneda, a longshoreman on the San Francisco waterfront. But by an ironic twist, when the FBI discovered that he was a Communist, he was released. He joined the Army and served overseas against the Japanese. Nevertheless, the authorities sent his Jewish wife Elaine and their American-born child to the concentration camp where the Japanese-American internees were held throughout the war.

While this tragedy was unfolding, my own situation was growing more precarious as a decision in the denaturalization suit against me hung in the balance, and the prospect of deportation hovered like a cloud over my head.

6 Wendell Willkie

I am not likely to forget that chilling Monday morning after December 7, 1941. The shock waves of the stunning disaster seemed to be still reverberating through the air. Storefront radios were blaring the grim details of the first casualties at Pearl Harbor, as the president was making his "day of infamy" speech and Congress was getting ready to declare war.

At this precise moment in history, of all the unlikely places in the world for me to be, I was finding my way through lower Manhattan's canyons in the Wall Street area to keep an appointment with Wendell Willkie. Turning in at 15 Broad Street, I could not shake off the air of unreality about it all. A more incongruous meeting would be hard to imagine: A Communst faced with the loss of his citizenship and deportation, and a Wall Street lawyer who only the year before had been the Republican candidate for president.

The irony of it was all the greater because only yesterday, before the war news had been broadcast on the radio, I had attended a meeting of the Communist Party's National Committee which condemned the Republican appeasers who were not unwilling to make a deal with Nazi Germany and Japan before Pearl Harbor made it impossible. I felt relieved that Willkie was not one of them.

As we faced each other across his desk, I studied the familiar craggy face with the famous smile, the rumpled suit and the gravelly voice which had become so well known to millions during the 1940 presidential campaign, and wondered again about his motive in offering to take my appeal, without fee, to the United States Supreme Court. We were poles apart; yet this man, who as head of Commonwealth and Southern Corporation had served as spokesman for the big Southern public utility interests in their battle against the New Deal and especially against the publicly owned Tennessee Valley Authority, undertook to defend an unpopular cause like mine, risking the wrath of his colleagues and clients.

Willkie was a product of his time and his class, but other factors in his background contributed to the makeup of his character and the realities of the war against fascism had a bearing on his conduct. I was puzzled by the ready explanation given by some that political expediency was the sole reason for his entry into the case. It did not advance his popularity in his own circles, and his biographer and friend Joseph Barnes noted later that he was put under the pressure of unfavorable and even hostile reaction: "His enemies were sure that it marked his final capture by the sinister forces of internationalism, liberalism, Jewry, and the Kremlin," Barnes related. "SAYS WILLKIE FAVORS REDS OVER G.O.P." ran a Hearst headline over a speech by Representative Paul Shafer, Michigan Republican."[1]

A friend of Willkie's later told me this anecdote: When Willkie was running for president in 1940, and was being depicted as Wall Street's candidate, he was pelted with eggs by workers in one Ohio industrial town. He turned to his friend who was traveling with him, and asked: "Why are they doing this to me?" Later during the war years, when he supported Roosevelt's war policies and had committed himself to my defense, he was walking to his office one day with the same friend, and one of his former colleagues from a Wall Street office walked up to him and said: "Wendell, I could spit at you." Willkie turned to his friend of the 1940 campaign and said, smiling ruefully: "I've come a long way, haven't I?"

They never forgave him; whether supporting Roosevelt or defending a Communist was the worst sin, it was hard to tell. So when he ran again in the Republican presidential primaries in 1944, he was pretty much a loner, a maverick who could not be trusted.

* * *

It was some time in 1940 that the idea which culminated in our meeting first jelled in my mind. My citizenship had been revoked. The Appellate Court had upheld the decision and my case was on its way to the United States Supreme Court. It was the year in which the so-called interventionist wing of the Republican party "blitzed" the Republican convention, and Wendell Willkie, with his attractive, dynamic personality, snatched the nomination away from the isolationist Senator Robert Taft. But in the campaign against President Roosevelt, Willkie was having a hard time living down the image of "the barefoot boy from Wall Street," the derisive term coined by that wily phrasemaker, Secretary of the Interior Harold Ickes.

Willkie surprised the liberals by writing an article on civil liberties called "Fair Trial" for the liberal weekly, the New Republic.[2]

He criticized the House Committee on Un-American Activities, then having a witch-hunting field day, and concluded that Earl Browder (then head of the Communist Party) was jailed, not for a technical violation of the passport law, but for his politics.

When I read the article, I brought it to Carol King, one of my trial lawyers who lived in New York, and asked: "Are you thinking what I'm thinking?" She replied: "I'm way ahead of you. I've already sent Willkie a copy of the brief and the Supreme Court's writ agreeing to review the case." She remembered Willkie's telling her later, after he had read the brief, "After that I could not, with my beliefs, have remained satisfied with myself if I refused to accept the case, if two conditions were true: (1) that Schneiderman was a decent fellow personally, and (2) that the record sustained the brief. That was the reason for my making inquiries about Schneiderman and asking you to send me the record."[3]

And thus began a strange friendship between this radical lawyer, an expert on naturalization and immigration law who defended left-wing clients (Harry Bridges was one of them), and the corporate lawyer who made two tries for the presidency before death ended his ambition during the 1944 primaries. Carol King's idealism and remarkable personality impressed Willkie, and she in turn was firmly convinced that his interest in the case was not merely political expediency, but a genuine concern to right an injustice. To the doubters who scoffed at such a possibility she would say with a mischievous twinkle: "Perhaps he has a conscience which bothers him now and then, and this is his way of appeasing it."

* * *

Willkie studied me with a curious interest. I was probably the first Communist he had ever met. He saw before him a short, slightly paunchy, balding young man of thirty-five, pale from countless meetings in smoke-filled rooms, nearsighted but too vain to wear glasses, and a raspy voice from speaking at too many outdoor meetings without a microphone. I did not learn until later that he had asked Bartley Crum, a liberal Republican lawyer in San Francisco, to investigate me to make sure that there was nothing in my personal background which might embarrass him or detract from the issues in the case. He must have been relieved that I did not resemble the public image of a Communist which the Un-American Activities Committee propagated.

In any case, only a week before our meeting, he wrote to his friend Bartley Crum: "I am sure I am right in representing Schneiderman. Of all times when civil liberties should be defended, it is now."[4] This was December 3, the week before the United States entered the war, while the Nazis were at the gates of Moscow.

Before getting down to discuss my case, we talked for a few minutes about the subject uppermost in our minds. He had just talked on the phone, he said, with Arthur Krock of the New York Times, dean of the White House correspondents. We were caught napping, he related grimly; the Japanese had crippled us in the Pacific. If only the Russians could hold out! The country must be mobilized for an all-out war effort. What effect, I inquired, would appeasers like Lindbergh and the America First Committee have? He waved the question aside with a grin: "We won't hear from them for a while." As we talked it suddenly dawned on me that he was addressing me, not as a client to be held at arm's length, but as an ally; "we" were now allied in this war against the common enemy, fascism. It was "we" and "they."

Before Pearl Harbor, this was far from clear. When Hitler invaded the Soviet Union, the *New York Times* reported that Congressional reaction to "the newest turn of the European war was reserved except among isolationists."[5] The reporter, Turner Catlege, went on to quote Senator Harry Truman that our policy should be to let the Germans and the Russians kill each other off. It reflected a hope in some ruling circles that the Soviet Union would be destroyed, a hope which unfortunately lingered on for years to come, and which for some has never died. It was a prophecy of Truman's role in the cold war to come.

Charles Lindbergh and the right-wing America First Committee had for some time been spreading the gospel that "you *can* do business with Hitler." On the other hand, Willkie was among those in the Republican Party who recognized more farsightedly, with Roosevelt, that fascist Germany also threatened the United States, and was prepared to accept the Soviet Union as a valuable wartime ally. (After visiting beleaguered Moscow in 1942, Willkie added his voice to the call for a second front in Europe.)

So "we" talked. He told me that his interest in my case had preceded Russia's entry into the war, and wryly acknowledged that, even now, to defend an acknowledged Communist was no quick road to political popularity. I observed, much to his amusement, that I found some people on my side who looked suspiciously at me for accepting his help, but that for my part I was glad to find someone on the other side who was not looking for ways to put me in jail.

He then related how his grandfather had fled Germany after the defeat of the 1848 revolution to escape tyranny, and how this had influenced him to want to protect the freedom which immigrants came here to seek. He said that this would be the theme of his argument to the Supreme Court and added: "And I'm going to remind Felix (Justice Felix Frankfurter, then sitting on the Supreme Court) that in our college days we discussed socialism and debated it. It wasn't taboo. It wasn't a crime to advocate it."

He was to follow this theme when he appeared before the Supreme Court to argue my appeal. The civil libertarian arguments of the Republican corporate lawyer did not persuade Justice Frankfurter, the Roosevelt liberal whom some businessmen attacked as the "arch radical of the New Deal." (I was not to learn until many years later of the behind-the-scenes role of President Roosevelt in the prosecution of the case, and of Frankfurter in trying to win a majority in the Supreme Court against my appeal.)

* * *

My citizenship case started as a farce, and almost ended as a tragedy. When the House Un-American Activities Committee opened its hearings in 1939, I had no inkling that I would be one of its prime victims. (By an odd quirk of history, Willkie had publicly attacked these same 1939 hearings, not suspecting that one of its victims would soon be his client.) The Dies Committee, named for its notorious chairman, Representative Martin Dies of Texas, had already established a reputation for a reckless disregard for the truth which over the years grew into a national disgrace. Congress never had the guts to abolish it for its "abuses" as long as it served a useful purpose, for reactionaries and scared liberals alike, in the anti-Communist crusade and later in the cold war.

The height of absurdity in its wild charges was reached when the Committee, while investigating Hollywood actors and writers, solemnly reported that the child actress Shirley Temple was a part of a Communist conspiracy in Hollywood. But I will always believe that none of its charges were quite so bizarre as the one leveled against me.

An obscure informant, one of the many who were encouraged by the Dies Committee to broadcast unsubstantiated charges, testified under oath that after supposedly serving a term in Sing Sing penitentiary in 1913, I was ineligible for citizenship. The Committee was pained to find that I had not been stripped of my civil rights by the Justice Department. This was faithfully broadcast by the news media, and the Justice Department proceeded to conduct an investigation.

They undoubtedly discovered very quickly what the Dies Committee and the media had never bothered to find out, that in 1913 I was seven years old, at which tender age I could not possibly have been precocious enough to be in a New York state prison (especially since I lived in Chicago at the time); and much as the Dies Committee might have looked upon me as a notorious desperado, I had never been in any penitentiary. Nobody, of course, took the trouble to correct this "error" which was broadcast to the nation (once the Dies Committee smeared you, you didn't expect retractions).

However, the Justice Department did discover something of great interest: born in Russia, brought over here when I was two years old, I applied for citizenship at the age of eighteen when I was an active Young Communist, and received my final naturalization papers at the age of twenty-one when I was already a Party member.

In late 1939, after the signing of the German-Soviet Non-Aggression Pact and the outbreak of war in Europe, the hunt for Communists was in full swing. Hundreds of foreign-born Americans, many of them non-Communists, were arrested for deportation. Most of them were never deported, but their cases dragged on for two or three decades with all the attendant hardships which accompanied this type of persecution.

The Justice Department, in the interests of American foreign policy, saw in my case a convenient way to whip up prejudice against American Communists. It filed a suit in Federal Court to cancel my citizenship. The suit charged that I had obtained my citizenship fraudulently in that I had signed a pledge that I was not a "disbeliever in organized government" (as the law then read); and that as a member of the Communist Party I was not attached to the principles of the United States Constitution. If the suit succeeded, I would be subject to deportation. Worse yet, it would set a precedent ranging far beyond my individual legal problem; it would involve the legal status of the Communist Party and the constitutional rights of all naturalized citizens, whose status would be vulnerable to retroactive review if their political opinions did not please the authorities.

7 Trial by Headlines

I was not in an optimistic mood when my first trial began on December 5, 1939. As I sat in the courtroom, the headlines screamed about Poland and Finland; I felt as though I were being tried in those headlines. The spectators' section was half empty. There was fear in the political atmosphere, and we had not had time to organize a defense campaign. The trial was called in such unusual haste that I had very little time to prepare my political defense, or my lawyers a legal defense.

I had to defend myself against the charge that I was a "disbeliever in organized government," and that by virtue of my membership in the Communist Party I advocated "the overthrow of the United States Government by force and violence." But the issue was far broader than a legal one: could the government, having once granted citizenship, retroactively revoke it twelve years later? Could the government claim unlawful intent on the part of a member because of his membership in a party which was legal and on the ballot in many states, with candidates in four presidential elections? Thus the issue concerned far more than Communist Party members. Once the principle was established, it could be broadened to include those who might be called "Communists," or who belonged to a political or trade union organization in which Communists also participated. It could threaten any naturalized citizen of whatever persuasion, or any applicant for citizenship, depending on the political climate.

My attorneys were George Andersen, Carol King, and State Senator Robert W. Kenny. Andersen, a self-taught lawyer who was propelled from a respectable law pactice into defending radicals and unions by the San Francisco General Strike, had successfully fought in the courts to place the Party on the California ballot and to defeat efforts to rule us off the ballot. Carol King, counsel for the American Committee for Protection of the Foreign Born, came from New York to join the case as an expert on immigration and naturalization law. She had earlier served as an associate defense counsel in one of the Harry Bridges deportation trials. Senator Kenny of Los Angeles volunteered to enter the case, also without fee, because he saw a vital principle of civil liberties at stake. He was especially anxious to confront the principal prosecution witness, my old nemesis "Red" Hynes. As a former judge in Los Angeles, Kenny was fully familiar with the policeman's notorious activities. (Kenny later became state attorney- general, ran unsuccessfully against Earl Warren for governor, and was subsequently appointed a Superior Court judge.)

The prosecutors were headed by United States Attorney Frank Hennessey. The judge was Michael J. Roche, a stern conservative whose record gave us little cause for optimism. The only comfort we could draw was from the reputation he had among lawyers: according to Andersen, Roche had more of his decisions reversed on appeal than any other judge in the circuit.

It was a strange trial. Aside from "Red" Hynes and a minor prosecution witness, and my own testimony for the defense, the only other witnesses were books, books, and more books—most of them the classics of Marx and Lenin. It was a trial of books.

For some reason, the government did not bring in a parade of stool pigeons to testify. Not that we had any illusions that they were not planted in the Party. When I came back to San Francisco in 1935 to head the California district of the Party, I soon found that I had inherited two stool pigeons who headed the local Party organizations of San Francisco and Los Angeles—Lawrence Ross and John Leach. When we ousted them, they later appeared as government witnesses in the unsuccessful deportation trial against Harry Bridges, where they were thoroughly discredited, and at Un-American Committee hearings. Then in 1936 we were presented with additional evidence. The United States Senate committee investigating abrogations of civil liberties against labor unions (widely known as the LaFollette Committee) sent some staff members to look into the waterfront situation. One of the staff members called me into their headquarters in the old Federal Mint building to warn me that there was an extensive espionage effort on the part of the waterfront employers to infiltrate the Party, as part of their campaign against the maritime unions and their militant leaders. We already knew of the close collaboration of the employer groups with the FBI and the Immigration Department, and we were constantly uncovering evidence of the espionage efforts against the unions and the Party. Because we adopted security measures against stool pigeons to protect our members' jobs and civil rights, we were labeled with the reputation of "secrecy," although all of our political activities were public.

But in this trial the prosecution relied solely on the testimony of a policeman as to my "state of mind" twelve years earlier when I took the oath to support the United States Constitution. This man who had violated the Constitution every time he broke up a meeting, entered offices and seized books and papers without a warrant, was going to be the government's expert on loyalty to the Constitution!

Aside from this travesty, the prosecution had collected mounds of books on Marxist-Leninist theory, together with some obscure, outdated pamphlets, and underlined extensive quotations which discussed the conditions under which force and violence would occur. Wherever the words "force" or "violence" appeared, it was sufficient for the prosecuting attorney to quote it out of context, as though this constituted an advocacy of force and violence against the United States Government. The government's case paid no heed to the time period or countries which the quotations dealt with, or the different historical circumstances and social conditions from which they sprang. Furthermore, there was nothing to show my connection with his "evidence," my interpretation of Marxist-Leninist theory applied to American conditions, or my individual intent.

When the government's star witness took the stand, it was a far cry from his days of glory. William F. Hynes had been a captain then, heading a "Red Squad" of eighteen or twenty men, and boasting that at times he had three to four hundred men under him, as at the Sacco-Vanzetti demonstration. But alas, he was only a patrolman now, with puffy cheeks and bloodshot eyes. Gone was the bully voice; the court had to admonish him to speak up. The arrogance of power was gone, swept out by a reform administration when Mayor Fletcher Bowron was elected in Los Angeles in 1937; one of its first acts was to disband the "Red Squad" and demote its head to patrol a beat. During his heyday, his appetite for using force was not completely satisfied by his career in the police department. At one time he had taken a leave of absence for eight months to take private employment with the streetcar company in charge of strikebreakers during a streetcar strike.

The most damning indictment of his sadism came from his associate's son. Years later, when a number of us were in jail awaiting bail under a Smith Act indictment, the son was brought in on a drug charge, and we heard his grim story: how when he was a boy his father would come home and boast about how many people he and Hynes had arrested and beaten up; how he grew to hate his father and left home; how this son of a law-enforcement officer learned to despise the law and ended up in jail, where he attempted suicide.

And so this paragon of law and order mounted the stand as a government expert on what constitutes attachment to the Constitution.

The United States Attorney:

Q. When did you join the Police Department?

A. In 1922.

Q. Were you ever a member of the Communist Party?

A. I was a member of the Workers Party in 1922.

Q. How long were you a member?

A. A period of approximately eight months.[1]

Hynes was not asked, but he might have been reluctant to tell, why he stayed only eight months in the Party. His career as a "radical" came to an abrupt end one day when he walked into a barber shop and took off his coat before sitting down in the barber's chair. The barber noticed that he carried a gun in a holster under his arm and spread the word around that he must be a cop. His expulsion from the Party launched him on a seventeen-year career as an "expert" on communism.

Q. Have you had occasion to discuss communist matters with many Communists?

A. Yes, I have talked to a great many Communists and Communist leaders in my time.

The nature of his "talks" with Communists was made clear by the following questions put by Senator Kenny:

Q. As a matter of fact, whenever you attended a meeting, you never let anybody speak, did you?

A. Yes, I did, except when they would call me to the platform and make a statement, and the meeting would break up in a riot.

Q. It would break up in a riot?

A. Yes, sir.

Q. Did your men ever use force and violence in these riots?

A. Yes, sir.

The government then proceeded to establish the witness's expertise on Communist teachings.

Q. Have you made a collection of Communist literature?

A. Yes; I have quite an extensive library in Los Angeles.

Q. Approximately how many volumes of documents have you collected, over a period of years, as a result of your activities in the Police Department?

A. Well, we have approximately thirty or forty cabinets full of official documents issued and published from time to time by the

Communist Party. I would be unable to estimate the number. On some occasions, on raids, we seized as may as six or seven thousand pieces of literature; and I recall other times we received as high as three or four thousand pieces of correspondence.

Q. During the period of time that you were a member of the Communist organization, did you then study the program, practices, and policies of the Communist Party?

A. I did.

Q. And, subsequent to that time, have you continued your studies?

A. I have, over a period of years, up until the present time.

Q. Mr. Hynes, might I ask by what means does the Communist Party teach and advise that the workers take control of the government of the United States?

After a series of strenuous objections by the defense, the court allowed the witness to answer.

A. From what knowledge I have gained as a member in 1922 and from what further knowledge I have gained from reading various official publications, published and circulated by the Communist Party, and from observation and actual contact with the activities of the Communist Party in the form of holding demonstrations, actions by the defense section of the Communist Party, their method of bringing about a change of the form of government is one of force and violence.

(So holding demonstrations and defending ourselves against illegal raids on our offices and against the breaking up of peaceful meetings were the damning bits of evidence against us!)

The United States Attorney repeatedly claimed that the witness was an "expert." How did he obtain his profound knowledge of Marxism, the defense wondered, and Senator Kenny queried him on this matter on cross-examination.

Q. When did your interest in political philosophy begin?

A. I have no particular interest in political philosphy.

Q. Haven't you testified that you were familiar with the doctrine of the philosophy of Marxism, Leninism and Stalinism?

A. I testified that I was familiar with what I termed the unlawful advocacy of force and violence on the part of the Communist Party.

Q. You were not trying to make an impartial analysis of what was contained in the books?

A. As to philosophy, I never attempted to make any analysis of them.

Q. You read these books and you are familiar with the various phrases used, I assume?

A. I read portions and underscored those portions which, in my opinion, I felt had to do with force and violence.

Q. But you do not profess to be an expert on the philosophy or on the matters contained in those books?

A. I have never professed to be an expert on any philosophy of Marxism or any other ism. I do profess to know, to be able to read and determine, when a book says that they use force and violence.

Q. You did not read the other portions of the book to find out what relation that might have to the context?

A. In some cases.

Q. Have you read it from cover to cover?

A. I have not read any books from cover to cover that you have mentioned.

Q. You have not read any of the books that you have testified to from cover to cover, have you?

A. Yes; I particularly read Communist literature—those portions that advocated force and violence.

Q. You read for that limited purpose?

A. That was the main purpose.

Q. You were not attempting an academic study of the problem?

A. No.

Q. You were reading in order to obtain evidence for a particular purpose; is that right?

A. Yes, sir.

Q. You testified that you knew Mr. Schneiderman, didn't you?

A. Yes, sir.

Q. Did you ever see him employ force and violence in any way?

A. I did not.

Q. Did you ever see any behavior on his part that brought him into conflict with the laws that you were enforcing, or any law down there?

A. Not to my knowledge.

I spent the better part of four days on the witness stand, most of the time with the United States Attorney hammering away at my understanding of socialism, capitalism, the abolition of private property, and the advocacy of force and violence.

Q. What did you understand by the "socialist system of society?"

A. A system of society in which the basic means of production and exchange would be socially owned by the people, through their representative form of government.

Q. Your objective was to establish a new communistic society?

A. Yes, ultimately.

Q. And the first step would be the control by the workers of the means of production and distribution?

A. The first step would be the establishment of social ownership of the means of production, but control by the workers could not be established except through some form of government which would take the means of production into its own hands.

Q. Do you believe that it will be possible to bring about this socialization by democratic processes in this country?

A. Yes, and I certainly hope so.

Q. You disagree with John Strachey in this regard, do you? He did not believe that it could be brought about by democratic process?

A. No; he said that he did not believe that the dominant group would permit peaceable means to bring about the change in the system of society; and he said, if revolution occurs, it will be because the dominant group will itself use forms of repression which will bring about revolution.

Q. You believe, in the event of the Communist Party becoming a majority party in the United States, they would be justified in using force and violence to bring about change in our form of government?

A. If it were possible for the Communist Party to attain a majority in this country, it would be able by peaceable, democratic, and constitutional means to achieve its program unless some illegal force was used against that majority.

Q. What are your views in regard to the abolition of private property?

A. I believe that essentially private property is not enjoyed by all, because capitalism brings private property, that is, the means of production, to a small group of monopoly capitalists; and our contention is that private property should belong to all the people.

Q. That there should be no private property?

A. No, we believe in the retention of all personal property for personal use; but we do not believe that the means of production should be in the hands of a few, because (they) are used as an instrument of "the exploitation of the many by the few."

Citing an article by Engels in 1894 on "the Peasant Question in France and Germany," I quoted him: "Neither now nor at any future time can we promise the small peasants that individual property and individual working will be preserved in the face of the supremacy of capitalist production. All we can promise them is that we will not forcibly intervene in the conditions of their ownership against their will; we will do anything in any way admissible to make his lot more bearable, to facilitate his transition to the co-operative, if he decides to take this step."

The prosecutor introduced voluminous exhibits of Marxist-Leninist writings to support his contention that I could not be attached to the United States Constitution or be a defender of democracy. My reply: "The Communist Party and its members are obligated to defend our country's democratic institutions against any enemy from within or without, from at home or abroad. (But) we say that bourgeois democracy is limited because under capitalism and especially in its present stage, imperialism, full political freedom cannot exist because it is shackled by the lack of economic freedom for the majority of the people. There exists a formal equality and freedom, but this formal equality merely hides the actual inequality that exists for the working people. The present stage of capitalist society, with its concentration of the nation's wealth and resources in the hands of a few, has built up the control of monopoly capital over the economic and political life of the country. Even the mildest efforts at reforming some of the most evil practices of Big Capital, such as the efforts undertaken in recent years by President Roosevelt, have met with the bitterest opposition of these economic groups (which) have issued more or less veiled threats that if they cannot have their way under the present political forms, they will work for the establishment of fascism in the country."

I gave as examples of inequality: the disfranchisement of Black people in the South, and discrimination; laws which curtail free speech and assemblage; the violation of laws by big corporations with impunity, while the wage earner and unemployed worker do not receive the same latitude. "All these factors lead us to the conclusion that even the most well-meaning and liberal administrations are but instruments of the dominant economic class, that the state is the instrument of the ruling class," I stated.

Referring to the numerous quotations from Marx and Lenin, which the United States Attorney used to imply that the Communist Party advocated the forceful overthrow of the United States government, I answered in my testimony: "The accusations misinterpret and distort (our) position by taking a quotation out of its context without regard to the rest of the context, the historical conditions and forces in existence at the time and the countries about which it was written. The transformation of society from one stage to another has taken place in different ways in different countries. Its reorganization on a socialist basis will likewise have different characteristics, forms, and methods in each country in accordance with its own special characteristics."

Declaring my belief in socialism, I said: "This can only be achieved when the majority of the people choose to follow the socialist path by democratic processes. It would be reducing Marxism to a vulgar absurdity to say that a social revolution could be brought about by any single group or party by a conspiracy." (I could not foresee that twelve years later I would be facing this very charge of "conspiracy.")

To round out our defense, we introduced into evidence the testimony given at the Harry Bridges trial by Professor Brown, Dean of Stanford University's Philosophy Department, and Professor Thompson of its Political Science Department. Both had been used at the Bridges deportation hearing as defense witnesses who were experts on Marxism, and while their interpretations of Marxist theory did not always coincide with that of the Party, it was close enough to serve as an effective answer to those for whom the mere utterance of the word "revolution" was enough to consign the culprit to jail.

The verdict was nevertheless a foregone conclusion. Judge Roche stripped me of my citizenship, and the case started on the long road up through the appellate courts, in a seemingly hopeless cause. But after Hilter's invasion of the Soviet Union and the Japanese attack on Pearl Harbor, the political atmosphere changed. Willkie's startling announcement that he would represent me before the United States Supreme Court, without fee, because of the vital issue of civil liberties involved, strikingly reflected the changes that had taken place, as did the colloquy among the Justices of the high court.

8   Felix Frankfurter:
The Supreme Court, First Round

The United States Supreme Court meets in an impressive setting. When the nine black-robed Justices file in to take their seats in the marble-walled chamber, the courtroom falls into a hushed silence. Spectators barely whisper in their august presence. Attorneys confine themselves to a low murmur until the clerk intones the formal opening of the session.

Here, I thought, was where the fabric of the ruling law, with its built-in class inequality, was woven. From these benches came the proslavery Dred Scott decision and the segregationist "separate but equal" doctrine for the public schools. And here was where Holmes and Brandeis and Cardoza sat, where Black and Douglas wrote their famous dissents, and where Roosevelt sought to purge the "nine old men" who stood in the way of his program. And now, here were the nine Justices who would decide my fate and that of many foreign-born, and perhaps the fate of my Party.

It was not a reassuring sight; Harlan Stone was still Chief Justice, and there were other holdovers whose record on civil liberties was just as bad. Furthermore, the latest liberal addition to the court was Frank Murphy, who had been Attorney General when the Justice Department filed the suit to cancel my citizenship. (Should we have challenged his right to sit on my case, I wondered?) There was Justice Reed, who had been Solicitor-General for the Justice Department before his appointment to the Court. And then there was Felix Frankfurter. Which way would he jump? The only ones who had consistently stood up for civil liberties were the two great dissenters—Justices Douglas and Black. Where were the five votes we needed to win this case? That was the question my lawyers were asking themselves when Wendell Willkie rose to argue the appeal.

I, of course, did not believe that the issue would be decided solely on the merits of the legal arguments presented. The old adage that "the Supreme Court follows the election returns" reflects the fact that issues are usually decided in the political arena, especially when the Court feels the pressure of mass movements. I had no illusion that the campaign conducted by my Defense Committee had created sufficient pressure for a favorable decision, although the committee, headed by Professor Walter Rautenstrauch of Columbia University, had attracted considerable support among liberals, trade-union leaders, and the foreign-born, and had received widespread publicity after Willkie entered the case. But I looked upon the Court as the legal arm of the ruling system, and thus not likely to give a favorable decision on its legal merits to a member of a Party that challenged that system.

However, the political atmosphere in the country had changed since my trial. Hitler's invasion of the Soviet Union, followed by the Japanese attack on Pearl Harbor, brought an about-face in the attitude of the Administration toward the Soviet Union and toward American Communists (the President had released Earl Browder from jail "in the interests of national unity"). When the Circuit Court of Appeals refused to change the trial verdict, it deftly passed the buck to the Supreme Court in the following words: "It may be that prospect of larger policy or changes in the look of international affairs should be viewed to fix the acts proven here in perspective. But as we understand it, as a lower Federal Court, that is not our function." Just as the decision at my trial in 1939 was influenced by the headlines about Poland and Finland, so the verdict on my appeal before the high court was being weighed on the background of the Battle of Stalingrad which was raging all through that bitter winter of 1942, and the growing cries throughout the country for opening a second front in Europe.

Willkie must have come to similar conclusions, although traveling by a different road. He had come almost full circle from the time he had fought Roosevelt's New Deal; with the outbreak of war, he had swung around to supporting the President's war policies, had visited Moscow, and come out for a second front. Now, while presenting an able legal and civil-libertarian argument, he could not refrain from referring to me as "this boy from Stalingrad," much to my embarrassment.

This phrase had an amusing background. Carol King was attending a hearing of one of her clients at the Lewiston Federal Penitentiary in Pennsylvania when she was interrupted by an excited clerk who said she had a long-distance phone call from Wendell Willkie. "Carol, how close is Schneiderman's birthplace to Stalingrad?" he inquired. "I don't know for sure," she replied. "Is it in the same general area?" he persisted. "Well, it's in the Ukraine, a considerable distance south of Moscow." "Would that be in the general direction of Stalingrad?" Willkie asked again. "I think so." "That's all I wanted to know, thanks," and Willkie hung up. The next time Carol saw me she told me of the conversation, and asked: "How far is it from your birthplace?" I replied, "Oh, it must be at least a thousand miles or more." "Oh, my God!" she gasped. "He's going to put it in his argument to the Court. Let's hope the government lawyers and the Justices are as ignorant of the map of Russia as I am."

Willkie was stretching a point, but he was not too subtly reminding the Court that our country had a stake in that desperate battle, that we were engaged in a struggle for survival, and that in this struggle the Communists were our allies.

Now the tide had turned. General Douglas MacArthur proclaimed: "The fate of civilization rests on the worthy banners of the Red Army." Churchill was to write later about the Battle of Stalingrad: "The hinge of fate had turned." In February, 1943, the encircled Nazi army surrendered. In June, 1943, the Supreme Court handed down its decision.

And so it was that the Court may have been listening to a distant thunder when the Justices heard Willkie's arguments and fired questions at Solicitor-General Fahy, who presented the government's case.

When Willkie rose to address the court, he reminded them that this country had prided itself on being a refuge from tyranny. His grandfather had left Germany in 1848 (the year of the Communist Manifesto), after the defeat of the democratic revolution, in protest against the German autocracy.

"One of the dominant ideas upon which the American people were insistent in the formulation of their Constitution was that the citizens should have the right to speak freely and to publish freely any and all views that they might have respecting the form of government and the nature of their political and economic rights," he said.

"The great vice of the opinion of the Circuit Court of Appeals with respect to the entire catalogue of views pronounced to be obnoxious is that it constitutes a wholly unwarranted and unnecessary restriction upon freedom of political belief and thought, freedom of speech and freedom of the press. The main objective which the people of the United States had in mind in adopting the First Amendment was to insure freedom of opinion as to the form of government and political principles and measures," he told the Court. "There is no validity to the government's contention that one cannot be attached to the principles of the Constitution unless he believes in the continuance of the existing framework of the government and the so-called basic principles of the Constitution and its 'general political philosophy.'"[1]

The Court directed its questions mainly to the Solicitor-General:[2]

HARLAN STONE (Chief Justice): You say that Schneiderman's behavior was un-American. The word "un-American" does not appear in the statute. How much of the Constitution must he dislike in order not to be qualified for citizenship?

Fahy referred to the defendant's "unremitting opposition" to the Constitution.

JUSTICE BLACK: Can you point out conduct which shows that he was not attached to the Constitution, that he did not behave as a person attached to the principles of the Constitution? Forgetting the organization of which he is a member, then what is left in the record?

Fahy said that Schneiderman was opposed to organized government. (The citizenship statute barred "disbelievers in organized government.")

JUSTICE FRANKFURTER: Organized government—do you mean he was theoretically opposed to all organized government, or merely that he was opposed to the way our government is organized?

JUSTICE BLACK: You mean that he was opposed to the Constitution from the beginning to the end? Is he required to prove attachment to the Constitution, or must the government prove that he was not attached? . . . . Does not what you say of Schneiderman merely amount to saying: "he believed in socialism"?

JUSTICE FRANKFURTER: Put force and violence to one side, is there a difference between an avowal of faith and conduct? . . . In a naturalization proceeding would disclosure of a state of mind be enough to show lack of attachment? . . . There was in this case no disavowel of attachment except his activities in the Communist Party.

JUSTICE DOUGLAS: Is the Communist Party handing out ammunition? Is the program for the morrow or for years hence? Has it set up a plan for the overthrow of the government?

JUSTICE BLACK: You speak of Schneiderman's violation of law. Violation of what law? . . . Is there a deportation proceeding now pending against Schneiderman? (There was none.) In a cancellation (of citizenship) proceeding how far back can you go?

Fahy said the government only went back to the five-year period prior to naturalization.

JUSTICE BLACK: Oh, no! It went back to 1848 and the Communist Manifesto.

JUSTICE FRANKFURTER: Would it disqualify a man for naturalization if he believed in any other international organization such as the Second (Socialist) International, or the International Chamber of Commerce?

JUSTICE MURPHY: Would membership in a church organization (international) disqualify him?

JUSTICE STONE: What is true faith and allegiance? . . . Is it your contention that a member of the Communist Party cannot be attached to the Constitution of the United States?

JUSTICE MURPHY: Schneiderman believed in economic improvement. Does that show that he was not attached to the principles of the Constitution?

JUSTICE FRANKFURTER: The Communist Party is a legal party, is it not? Didn't it appear on the ballot in a number of states in the recent election including my state? . . . You mean we tolerate native Communists but not alien Communists?

Of course, the questions asked did not always indicate the way the Justices leaned. Chief Justice Harlan Stone, in spite of the tenor of his questions, voted against me. But it was left to Justice Frankfurter (he was still considered a liberal then) to engage in the greatest sophistry to explain his vote to revoke my citizenship. When it was clear he was in the minority on the Court, he wrote to his fellow-dissenter Harlan Stone: "Unfortunately, in the history of nations there is a too frequent change of political partners. What is plain as a pikestaff is that the present war considerations . . . political considerations . . . are the driving force behind the result of this case. . . . This case has nothing to do with the conduct of the war, with our relations with Russia, with one's past or present view regarding the Russian political or social system . . . it has to do, on the other hand, with the conception of American nationhood and the relations of the principles of the Constitution to that nationhood."[3]

What he failed to say was that it was precisely political considerations, in the prejudicial context of the prewar situation of 1939 and 1940, that brought about the prosecution against me, or that, in the absence of the anti-Communist hysteria which provoked the charges and made the trial verdict a foregone conclusion, the Court could now act with less bias and more objectivity on an issue involving the Bill of Rights.

How much these political considerations were uppermost in the government's handling of the case is made clear by Felix Frankfurter's biographer, Liva Baker: "Politically, the case was a hot potato. . . . Roosevelt was willing that the case be tried; the Secretary of State and the Justice Department were reluctant. There was a movement to postpone it. This failed, however, and the case was argued in November 1942, and reargued in March 1943."[2]

Frankfurter did not content himself with registering a dissenting opinion, he tried actively to swing the majority vote his way. In a long statement to a conference of the Justices, which Liva Baker said "provides a significant clue to his later decisions in the cold-war cases," Frankfurter made "as eloquent a statement of his Americanism as he ever made" and likened his feelings about his own American citizenship to a religion. "'I have known the Schneidermans and a good many of them well since my college days,' Frankfurter soliloquized, 'and I have admired, and still do admire, their devotion to their ideals. They are the salt of the earth as far as character and selflessness goes. But they are devoted to a wholly different scheme of things from that to which this country, through its Constitution, is committed.'

"Frankfurter did not mean to suggest," continued Baker, "that mere membership in the Communist Party indicated a lack of attachment to the principles of the Constitution. Perhaps recalling the . . . victims of A. Mitchell Palmer's Red Raids in 1919 and 1920, he told the conference: 'Many a person is a member of the Communist Party merely as an expression of his deep feeling of injustice about the inequities and hardships of our present society . . . however, in Schneiderman, the Court had before it a passionate, dedicated Communist who had belonged to the Party since the age of sixteen, who at that time dedicated himself as an active organizer and important official of the orthodox creed of the Communist Party.'"[3]

Here membership in the Party, he was saying, was not in question presumably, if the member did nothing but pay his dues; it was only if the member actively worked for the political and economic demands the Party put forward, and particularly if he actively advocated socialism, that the Court could decide that he was not a person to be trusted with citizenship. (This was the germ of the concept built upon by future prosecutors to construct the dangerous theory of "conspiracy"; that is, in the area of advocacy what one person could say or do legally, became a "conspiracy" if two or more persons got together and agreed to say or do the same thing.)

Oh, where was the Harvard crusader who had taken up the cause of Sacco and Vanzetti (the beginning of my "dedication"), who had denounced the Palmer raids, who was himself denounced as the "arch-radical" of the New Deal, and who was still living on that reputation as a liberal? So furious was he at the obvious trend of the Court's discussions, that when the majority opinion written by Justice Murphy had been circulated among the Justices, Frankfurter in frustration wrote sneeringly to Murphy: "Thorough and comprehensive as your opinion is on Schneiderman you omitted one thing that, on reflection, you might want to add. I think it is only fair to state, in view of your general argument, that Uncle Joe Stalin was at least a spiritual co-author with Jefferson of the Virginia Statute for Religious Freedom."[4] And he hinted that Black was the real author of the opinion.[5]

Fifteen years later, I was to learn again, in another confrontation in the Supreme Court, that Frankfurter's disarming questions to the attorneys arguing my case in a different trial did not give any real clue to the twists and turns of his mind.

Frankfurter's tirade against Justice Murphy became understandable when the majority opinion, written by Murphy, was handed down: "The constitutional fathers, fresh from a revolution, did not forge a political straitjacket for the generations to come," he wrote. This ringing declaration of faith in democratic principles followed a rebuke to Frankfurter's main line of argument. Murphy said: "We agree with our brethren of the minority that our relations with Russia, *as well as our views regarding its government and the merits of Communism* (emphasis mine—W.S.) are immaterial to a decision of this case."

Replying to the charge that the radical changes advocated by Communists reflected lack of attachment to the Constitution, the Justice declared: "If any provisions of the Constitution can be singled out as requiring unqualified attachment, they are the guarantee of the Bill of Rights and especially that of freedom of thought contained in the First Amendment."

Reviewing the evidence on the key issue before the Court, the opinion stated: "With commendable candor the government admits the presence of sharply conflicting views on the issue of force and violence as a Party principle, and it also concedes that 'some Communist literature in respect of force and violence is susceptible of an interpretation more rhetorical than literal.'"

The Court took note of the fact the writings of Marx, Engels, and Lenin acknowledged that the peaceful achievement of socialism depended on the circumstances, and specifically quoted Lenin: "In order to obtain the power of the state the class conscious workers must win the majority to their side. As long as no violence is used against the masses, there is no other road to power. We are not Blanquists, we are not in favor of the seizure of power by a minority."

Then came the blockbuster!

Justice Murphy wrote: "A tenable conclusion from the foregoing is that the Party in 1927 desired to achieve its purpose by peaceful and democratic means, and as a theoretical matter justified the use of force and violence only as a method of preventing an attempted forcible counter-overthrow once the Party had obtained control in a peaceful manner, or as a method of last resort to enforce the majority will if at some indefinite future time because of peculiar circumstances constitutional or peaceful channels were no longer open.

"The judgment is reversed and the case remanded to the Circuit Court of Appeals for further proceedings in conformity with this opinion." (Signed by Justices Murphy, Douglas, Black, Rutledge, and Reed.) The dissenting opinion was signed by Chief Justice Stone, Roberts, and Frankfurter. (Justice Jackson had disqualified himself from voting.)[6]

Even in his dissenting opinion, Chief Justice Harlan Stone hinted at some doubt about the decision of the trial judge. Although holding that the finding of the lower court as to evidence was binding on the Supreme Court, he added, "even though, sitting as trial judges, we might have made some other finding." (And although he also signed the dissenting opinion, one might wonder what the now silent Frankfurter would say about this heretical thought.)

But this momentous decision, crucial as it was to my own status and the legal status of the Communist Party, had even greater importance than the fate of Communists alone. Justice Rutledge, in an opinion concurring with the majority, summed it up as follows: "Immediately, we are concerned with only one man, William Schneiderman. Actually, though indirectly, the decision affects millions. If, seventeen years after a federal court adjudged him entitled to be a citizen, that judgment can be nullified and he can be stripped of this most precious right, by nothing more than re-examination upon the merits of the very facts the judgment established, no naturalized person's citizenship is or can be secure. If it can be done for Schneiderman, it can be done for thousands of others. . . .

"No citizen with such a threat hanging over his head could be free. If he belonged to 'off-color' organizations or held too radical or, perhaps, too reactionary views, for some segment of the judicial palate, when his admission took place, he could not open his mouth without fear his words would be held against him. For whatever he might say or whatever any such organization might advocate could be hauled forth at any time to show 'continuity' of belief, from the day of his admission, or 'concealment' at that time. Such a citizen would not be admitted to liberty. His best resource would be silence or hypocrisy. This is not citizenship. Nor is it adjudication. . . .

"It may be doubted that the framers of the Constitution intended to create two classes of citizens, one free and independent, one haltered with a lifetime string tied to its status. . . . The danger, implicit in finding too easily the purpose of Congress to denaturalize Communists, is that by doing so the status of all or many other naturalized citizens may be put in jeopardy."[7]

We lived from Monday to Monday, when the Supreme Court decisions were handed down. From week to week the tension grew, as the calendar approached June, when the Court normally recessed. The important decisions were usually handed down by the time of the summer recess; if not, then we had a reprieve till the October term. Ironically, I was awaiting induction into the army. Would I go into the army as a citizen, I wondered, and then be yanked out if I lost the case? "Not on your life," I would solemnly tell anxious inquirers, "would they pull me out in the midst of battle, and thus deprive themselves of my valuable services? No, they'll wait until the war is won, and then democratically decide what to do with me."

My cynicism might be understandable in view of press predictions of an adverse Court decision. On a Sunday night radio broadcast the Washington columnist Drew Pearson predicted that the Court would rule against me. Friends of ours who heard the broadcast decided not to call us in order to spare us the bad news.

Wendell Willkie must have had his doubts about the outcome; he wrote me on June 10, in reply to a letter of thanks I had written him: "It has been a great satisfaction to me to represent you in the Supreme Court. I think the decisions of the lower courts were outrageous and I will still think so whatever the decision of the Supreme Court happens to be." None of this "we're going to win" pose. He seemed to be preparing me for a possible adverse decision. Actually, up until then I had been cheerfully optimistic about the outcome. How much of this was wishful thinking, and how much a realistic estimate of the chances, I cannot say. I did not believe that the war situation had swung the scales so much in our favor; but at least they were not weighted so heavily against us as they were at the trial. So Leah and I waited—and sweated it out.

Monday, June 21, 1943, was the final court session before the summer break. We knew that a decision was likely. We waited for the morning news broadcast, but before it came on, the phone rang. Someone had heard it earlier and called. Leah and I barely had time for an exuberant embrace when the phone started ringing, and it rang all day. A telegram from Willkie and Carol King: "Congratulations." By nighttime our one-room apartment was in pandemonium, and it was impossible to believe how many people had crammed themselves into it, far into the night.

At a Civic Auditorium mass meeting we held later, I told an audience of 8000: "The Supreme Court in their decision acted in the best traditions of Jefferson and Lincoln. What was at stake in this case was not only the rights of citizenship for Communists. There are eight million naturalized Americans who know now, by this decision, that their citizenship rights are inviolate, that no arbitrary court or authority can re-examine their citizenship status at any time, years after they were naturalized, that they are not on probation. Thus, in reaffirming the fundamental American right of freedom of political opinions and free political association, the Supreme Court has done a great service to our country at a moment when we are engaged in a life and death struggle against fascism to preserve those very rights. Now let us demand that the Attorney-General drop his persecution of Harry Bridges."

The picture was not as rosy as I painted it that day—not for thousands of Japanese-Americans put away in concentration camps, not for Blacks and other minorities, not for the Native American Indians—and I regret to say that in my exuberance I did not make that point. But the decision was nevertheless a historic landmark and set a precedent in the fight for civil liberties and strengthened the fight against fascism. After the war, however, it did not prevent the Supreme Court from a regression to McCarthyism during the cold war, in its decisions upholding the Smith Act and the McCarran Act. But as we came out of the McCarthy period, the "Schneiderman case" became an important legal weapon in the fight to reverse or nullify those decisions.

For myself, there was an anticlimax to the happy outcome of a tense and exciting period. I was due to be inducted into the army in two weeks, but after a round of parties which were combined victory celebrations and farewell parties, I didn't pass the physical examination because of a bad back and was classified 4F. For me it was not a cause for rejoicing, but an embarrassing letdown. I resumed my political activities, but I had a guilty feeling for being safe at home while others, including many Communists, were risking their lives on the battlefields. Some of my comrades had already been killed or wounded in action.

Two of them, Bob Thompson and Herman Bottscher, were cited for heroism. Captain Bottscher was later killed in action in the Philippines. Thompson, who had fought in Spain against Franco with the Abraham Lincoln Brigade, received the Distinguished Service Cross for his role in the South Pacific. (Three years after the war, a grateful government indicted him under the Smith Act and sent him to jail for three years.)

We were proud of the role that Communists played in the war, and attributed it to the fact that we understood the meaning of fascism better than most. Communists had vowed never to support an unjust imperialist war, but we were never pacifists. In World War II we saw American democracy, limited as it might be, threatened with destruction by fascism, and therefore gave our utmost in its defense.

Postscript: The government had not given up on me. They filed a petition for a rehearing in the Supreme Court. More waiting. On October 11, Carol King sent us the following telegram: "Petition for rehearing denied." Across the face of the telegram I wrote in large letters: "Finis." But that was only Round One.

9 Hot War and Cold War: From Stalingrad to Fulton, Missouri

The opening of the second front in Europe brought nearer the prospect of victory, and the conference at Teheran of the anti-Hitler alliance opened up discussions of postwar perspectives. Euphoria was in the air when the Americans and Russians met and embraced at the River Elbe, and we were deceived by it. After the Teheran agreement reached by Roosevelt, Stalin, and Churchill, the leader of the Communist Party of the U.S., Earl Browder, propounded a thesis of permanent postwar peace between the war-time allies, the United States, Britain, and the Soviet Union, which would lead to cooperation between capital and labor.

Browderism was a theory which denied the class struggle, the very foundation of Marxism. It visualized imperialism as disappearing, which rejected the main foundation of Leninism. In this new age, Browder argued, Communists would have a different role, although still espousing socialism, and so Browder proposed the transformation of the party into a Communist Political Association. It was the tremendous authority of Browder, who had led the Party through its most eventful period, that made it possible to foist such a theory on the Party. Looking back, it seems incredible now that he was able to win its acceptance by most U.S. Communists except for Foster and a few others (including Archie Brown, a San Francisco longshoreman).

Once before in its history the Party had fallen victim to opportunism, when Lovestone promulgated the theory of "American exceptionalism" in 1929 (over Foster's opposition), and won the majority of a split party for his position. He had argued that American capitalism was so strong at that time that it was immune to the contradictions and crises which Marx had analyzed. A debate in the world Communist movement ensued, and the repudiation of his theory ended in Lovestone's removal and expulsion. Shortly thereafter, the outbreak of the economic crisis put an end to his rosy view of a golden era of capitalist prosperity.

I had opposed Lovestone and his theory, and I wish I could say that I showed the same perspicacity when Browder advanced his thesis. I accepted it with the rationalization that if the capitalists failed to cooperate, the workers could always revert back to a policy of struggle. But beyond that, I had no reservations about believing that we were entering a period of peace and cooperation among the powers that had been wartime allies, with profound and unprecedented domestic consequences.

Even before the aftermath of the war shattered our illusions, the French Communist Party, through an article written by one of its leaders, Jacques Duclos, opened fire on Browder's doctrine. This attack triggered a discussion in the Party which had not really taken place when the new line had been adopted. Foster's position was presented for the first time, and won overwhelming support. Browder was defeated and the Party was reconstituted (an act which was used by the goverment three years later to indict the Party leadership for "organizing" a conspiracy).

The episode brought home to me a great flaw in the decision-making process in the Party. Had a discussion taken place, with Foster's opposition throughly aired (he had not stated his views publicly), we might not have been so easily persuaded. But with the Party constantly under fire, the membership had accepted the necessity of discipline and unity, sometimes at the expense of democratic discussion. The principle of "democratic centralism" became distorted when it was so rigidly applied. I resolved that I would never again accept an analysis handed down from above without thoroughly examining all the pros and cons. I could not guess how soon this resolve would be tested, nor the desperate circumstances in which my vow would present me with a fateful decision.

With the war over, there was not much time for introspection. The problems of reconversion to a peacetime economy soon revealed that the big-business interests, who had waxed fat on profits during the war, had not changed their stripes. The dislocation during the transition period brought rising unemployment and bore down most heavily on the conditions of the workers, and strike struggles flared throughout the country.

The expectations of an era of peace when the United Nations was formed were rudely dashed. After Roosevelt's death, events moved quickly in another direction. Truman ordered the dropping of the atomic bomb on Hiroshima and Nagasaki and began to talk tough to the Russians. We had entered the nuclear age.

The origins of the cold war lay in the fact that the United States and its allies never became reconciled to the changed relation of forces in the world, when American imperialism was no longer the kingpin. Half of Europe was socialist, and the colonial world was swept by movements for national liberation and independence. World imperialism was losing its base for exploitation, and the hunger it had caused was now sparking rebellion against its rule.

The signal for the cold war was given when Winston Churchill, at the invitation of President Truman, came to Fulton, Missouri, to make his "Iron Curtain" speech. Churchill had fought against the Second Front in Western Europe. He proposed in its place an invasion of the Balkans in order to "contain" the Soviet Union within its borders, instead of a nutcracker operation from East and West to crush Nazi Germany. He had failed in his attempt to set up his own iron curtain, but his new strategy to "contain communism" was a continuation of the old. Soviet "intransigence," which was the harsh accusation made by Churchill and Truman, was a logical reaction to the new "get tough" policy of its one-time allies.

A destitute Europe swung to the left. Britain voted Churchill out of office and elected a Labor government; and in France and Italy, where the Communists had led the antifascist underground resistance during the war, the postwar governments chose Communist vice-premiers in recognition of their role and mass influence.

It was in this "alarming" situation that the United States marshalled its vast resources for economic aid to Europe through the Marshall Plan. It was not an altruistic venture. It was aimed at saving Europe for capitalist and American domination; and it had strings attached which would guarantee that the economies and political direction of the countries aided would be under the tutelage of the United States. Simultaneously, American policy toward Germany was helping to bring back into power the same industrial and financial interests which had backed Hitler's rule. But the Soviet Union, which had lost twenty million people and suffered vast devastation over its land, did not receive any aid because it would not subject its socialist economy to the terms demanded of it.

The intensification of the cold war and the left's opposition to the Marshall Plan brought about a rift in the old Roosevelt coalition. Disagreement with the "get-tough-with-Russia" policy

led Henry Wallace, former vice-president under Roosevelt and
now secretary of commerce under Truman, to resign from the
cabinet and become a third-party candidate for president. Foreign
policy was not the only issue. The Taft-Hartley Law had been
enacted against labor and other major issues were jobs and the
economy.

At the time of Wallace's declaration, there appeared to be a
groundswell of opposition to Truman and support for a third
party. In California, where getting on the ballot faced enormous
obstacles, the left was instrumental in launching the Independent
Progressive Party with nearly half a million signatures. But
progressive Democrats were split on the issue of supporting
Wallace or Truman. Even a staunch progressive like Bob Kenny
balked at breaking with the Democratic Party. He had been
attorney general in the Warren administration when Earl Warren
was governor, the only Democrat elected in a Republican sweep.
Under strong urging from the CIO unions he had run for governor
against Warren, with whom he had close ties, and had been
defeated. I had many discussions with Kenny in which he showed a
keen interest in the possibility of a third party, but in the end his
instinct for remaining with the mainstream prevailed.

By election time the "lesser evil" concept, coupled with
Truman's "give the Republicans hell" oratory, won out with the
electorate. Labor stayed with the Democratic Party. The Progressive Party ticket of Henry Wallace and Senator Glen Taylor of
Idaho received only about a million votes. The voters were not
ready to swing to a ticket that had been redbaited and appeared to
have little chance of election. As usual the electorate was trapped
in the two-party system, and will continue to be so until those who
are seeking to escape it abandon the "lesser evil" trap and make a
breakthrough for a meaningful alternative.

The disappointing vote for Wallace and the evaporation of the
Progressive Party made some people question whether there
should have been a third-party ticket. The alternative would have
been to leave the dissatisfied hundreds of thousands no choice but
to support with their vote the Truman foreign policy, his antilabor acts, and his persecution of the left. It may have been
premature to organize a whole new party, instead of limiting the
effort to an independent presidential ticket. Such a ticket could
have appealed to voters who were turning away from the Truman
policies but were not willing to break completely with the
Democratic Party. But it is not at all certain that the results would
have been much different. Without labor's support, it did not
represent a broad enough breakaway to challenge the two-party
system.

As cold-war tensions grew, the drive against the left intensified. Communists and other militant workers were screened off the waterfront by "security" regulations and "loyalty" oaths were required of all city, state and federal employees. Repressive legislation to register Communists and left organizations which were "Communist dominated," and to bar Party members from holding trade union office, went into effect and were challenged in the courts. The "Hollywood Ten" were jailed for defying the House Un-American Activities Committee and exercising their First Amendment rights, and hundreds more lost their jobs, victimized by a purge of the movie industry. Indictments under the Smith Act were obtained by the Justice Department against twelve Communist leaders. Deportation proceedings against foreign-born radicals were stepped up. When the Korean War broke out, attacks were launched against a growing peace movement that had rallied around the worldwide Stockholm Peace Petition and had gathered millions of signatures.

The CIO leadership, which had been moving to the right with the times, was coming into even greater conflict with the eleven CIO unions which were under left leadership. The left-led unions followed a more militant policy on economic issues than the Philip Murray leadership. The 1948 Pacific Coast maritime strike, in which the longshoremen supported by the seamen fought a three-months battle against the shipowners to win their demands, was an example of the solidarity and militancy which had marked the earlier battles of the thirties.

But it was not just on the domestic economic front that the divergences occurred. The CIO leaders supported the Truman foreign policy and began to come closer to the position of the AFL leadership. The left-led unions, on the other hand, opposed the Marshall Plan and called for a policy of reviving friendly relations with the Soviet Union, and abandoning support for Chiang Kai-shek, who had just been repudiated by the Chinese masses and driven from the mainland.

The clashes of policy inevitably led to the expulsion of the eleven unions from the CIO, and it was not too much later that the CIO leadership carried its abandonment of its earlier traditions to its logical conclusion and merged with the American Federation of Labor.

The expulsion of the left marked the closing of an era in which the new currents in the American labor movement had made a profound impact on the economic and political life of the country. The organization of the unorganized in the basic industries and the establishment of industrial unions rather than craft unions changed the face of the labor movement, and its new militant leadership turned it into an instrument of struggle in place of the old collaboration with the bosses. On the political front these new forces had a progressive influence within the Roosevelt coalition at every level.

Perhaps the most lasting change that it brought about was the breaking down of the Jim Crow barriers, and the entry of masses of Black workers into the unions of the basic industries and eventually into many of the old craft unions of the AFL. It introduced a new element of unity, the solidarity of Black and white, and a new spirit of militancy to the ranks of the workers. While racism was not eliminated by far, it was a big first step in breaking down the barriers set up by a racist society, and gave a firmer working-class base to the movement for equal rights. (The civil rights movement of the sixties could not have taken place without this earlier breakthrough in the trade union movement.)

The alliance of the left with the Lewis-Murray forces in the CIO is a classic example of the problems that arise in a coalition of this sort. The common immediate interests may be temporary, and the conflicting goals and objectives of diverse elements may create strains which inevitably lead to breakup when a changed situation leaves no basis for a continued agreement. The fact that the coalition does not last does not in any way minimize its validity for the period in which it is able to hold together. Hindsight can point to flaws and mistakes in the implementation of a coalition policy, but no one can argue convincingly that if only things had been done differently, the alliance of the left and center would not have come apart. In my view the rupture was inevitable.

The polarization that began with the tensions of the post-war period radically changed the situation and undermined the basis for the left-center alliance. Under such circumstances, the left in the CIO unions could only have maintained the alliance by abandoning a principled position on matters of peace and the economic struggles of the workers. The Communist Party has been reproached for demanding an intransigent stand of its members in the unions on issues that were labled left; but what we sought to do was to stand firm on issues of principle and be flexible on tactical and peripheral questions. Where mistakes were made, it was in sometimes failing to make a distinction between the two. Furthermore, neither the Party nor the left union leaders, those who were Communists and those who were not, made sufficient efforts to educate the workers in the unions on the issues that we believed to be paramount.

Then there are those who say that the left gave up too much in an effort to maintain unity with the CIO top leadership in the period of mutual cooperation. But this approach would have risked an earlier break in the coalition when the basis for unity was stronger than the points of disagreement. Furthermore, it overlooks an important factor that cannot be ignored: that the membership of the left-led unions was not always ready to take the same positions that its leaders took on various political issues. Members supported the basic economic programs of the unions and their democratic procedures, but many were closer politically to the position of the center forces. The occasions when the Communists in the unions failed to take this into account fed ammunition to the right-wingers and the redbaiter for disruptive purposes.

The purge of the left by the Murray leadership robbed the CIO of a vitality which it has never had since. It became so much like the AFL that a merger was natural, and occurred soon. The left injected a policy of struggle into the unions. It introduced democratic procedures which were a far cry from the dictatorial rule of the old-line leadership of both AFL and CIO. It sought to organize more independent forms of political action within the coalition, and it challenged the cold-war foreign policy of the Truman administration. The nearly two decades in which it played such an influential role saw the trade unions make giant strides forward and point the way to the kind of labor movement the working class needs to be effective in defending its interests.

10   McCarthyism on the Rampage

The McCarthy period of the early fifties is looked back upon as one of the darkest periods of American history, but it did not begin with Senator Joe McCarthy's witch hunts. It goes back to a congressman from Whittier, California, named Richard Nixon, who together with the ultraconservative senator from North Dakota, Karl Mundt, authored the Mundt-Nixon Bill in 1949, aimed at suppressing dissent under the guise of outlawing Communists. It goes back even further than that, to the dropping of the atom bomb on Hiroshima, which ended the hot war and launched the cold war. For President Truman's decision to use the bomb was as much a warning to our wartime ally, the Soviet Union, as it was an ultimatum to our wartime enemy, Japan.

The anti-Communist war psychosis reached its crescendo after the Chinese Revolution had triumphed and the Korean war was drawing to a close. Truman, in recently revealed private memoranda written between 1945 and 1953, considered threatening "all-out war" against China and the Soviet Union and "dropping one (an atomic bomb) on Stalin" in order to "eventually set up a free world." He also wrote, "It seems to me that the proper approach now would be an ultimatum with a 10-day expiration limit, informing Moscow that we intend to blockade the China coast from the Korean border to Indo-China, and that we intend to destroy every military base in Manchuria, including submarine bases, by means now in our control—and if there is further interference we shall eliminate any ports or cities necessary to accomplish our peaceful purposes. . . . This means all-out war. It means that Moscow, St. Petersburg, Mukden, Vladivostok, Peking, Shanghai, Port Arthur, Dairen, Odessa, Stalingrad and every manufacturing plant in China and the Soviet Union will be eliminated. This is the final chance for the Soviet government to decide whether it desires to survive or not."[1] Hitler could not have said it better, except that he did not have the atomic bomb. (It is no wonder that Truman is much admired these days, and there is a revival of Truman lore among the war hawks.)

All the cold-war rhetoric which conditioned the American people to look upon the Soviet Union as "the enemy" crystallized into the hysteria which reached its peak with the McCarthy witch hunts, which pictured Communists as "spies" and "saboteurs," anti-fascists as "fellow travelers" and "fronts," and all others who failed to be stampeded by the Red scare as "dupes" of a vast "Communist conspiracy."

Most liberals were silent or ran for cover, competing with the redbaiters as to who could be more loudly anti-Communist. The liberal Senator Hubert H. Humphrey fought the longest and hardest to enact a law to ban the Communist Party, a law which could never have been constitutionally enforced. The supreme irony came when General George C. Marshall, who has since been acclaimed as having "saved Europe from Communism" with the Marshall Plan, was called a "dupe" of the Communists; yet so poisoned was the atmosphere that Eisenhower, a protegé of Marshall's, not only failed to rebuke McCarthy for . this nonsensical tirade, but rode on an election campaign train with him through Wisconsin during the presidential campaign.

McCarthyism was not simply the aberration of one fanatic or a group of fanatics who had momentarily swayed public opinion with their intimidating tactics. It was a useful tool of the cold war of which it was the product, to suppress dissent and switch our alliances; wartime allies became "enemies" and wartime enemies became "friends." So while our political leaders may have clucked their tongues at its most extreme manifestations (even Dean Acheson, Truman's Secretary of State, later expressed "regrets"[2]) they accepted the Red-scare technique to convince the American people that the Soviet Union was our enemy (as do the opponents of detente today). To achieve this objective, the rule was "anything goes!" (as later revelations—much later—about the "excesses" of the FBI and the CIA so amply demonstrated).

It has been customary for historians to limit their laments about the "excesses" of that period to the injustices done to the many innocent victims who were not Communists. It would seem, then, that had the violations of constitutional rights been confined to the Communists alone, they would not have been considered "excesses" and the McCarthyites might have been viewed as true patriots; few historians have said that hunting down Communists was bad in itself.

The Truman Doctrine to "contain Communism" in Europe was proclaimed in 1947. The Taft-Hartley Law against labor was passed in the same year. And it was in the same year that the Justice Department placed before a Federal Grand Jury in New York the task of returning an indictment against the Communist Party on charges of acts of "espionage" and "subversion." After months of fruitless investigation, the Grand Jury could not find any evidence to return an indictment. 1948 rolled around, and resistance was beginning to form against the cold-war policies, highlighted by Henry Wallace's resignation from the Truman cabinet and his third-party candidacy for president. By this time the Justice Department came up with a new formula for the Grand Jury.

Since no acts of espionage or subversion could be presented to the Grand Jury's satisfaction, the Justice Department asked for and got an indictment on "conspiracy" to violate the Smith Act—a charge that did not require the kind of hard evidence it was unable to find. The "overt act" of organizing the Communist Party in 1945, when it was reconstituted, was a "conspiracy to advocate the overthrow of the U.S. Government by force and violence," and the Party's activities in organizing the unemployed, organizing the unorganized into trade unions, fighting Jim Crow segregation. and even participating in election campaigns and challenging American foreign policy, were alleged to be additional "overt acts" in furtherance of that "conspiracy."

Eleven national leaders of the Party went on trial in New York in 1949 on a wave of unprecedented hysteria.[3] (William Z. Foster, also indicted by a federal Grand Jury in July, 1948, had been severed from the case because of poor health.) They sought to present a defense of their views, but Judge Harold Medina time and again refused to allow them to present their defense, while paid informers were allowed to "interpret" the case for the Government.

The numerous clashes between the hostile judge and the defendants, who together with their attorneys fought valiantly to be allowed to present an adequate defense, resulted in defendants and attorneys alike being sentenced to jail for contempt of court. It was a foregone conclusion that the verdict would be "guilty," and ten of the defendants were given the maximum sentence of five years. The eleventh, Robert Thompson, received three years; ironically, this generous concession was due to the fact that he had defended his country heroically during World War II, for which he had received the Distinguished Service Cross from the same U.S. Government which he was now accused of conspiring to overthrow.

The appeals against the verdict dragged through the courts until 1951. By this time the Korean War was on. The cold war approached hysteria. Against this background the U.S. Supreme Court in June 1951 upheld the Smith Act convictions, with Justices Douglas and Black dissenting at this blow to First Amendment rights. To many it appeared that fascism was just around the corner, and that the Party would have to go underground. On July 2 seven of the defendants went to prison. Four did not surrender, and became political refugees.[4]

The debate over the Party's going "underground" took place over a period of months in the National Board prior to the Supreme Court's final decision. I was a participant in these debates because I was being groomed to take charge of the National Office when the convicted defendants went to jail. I had thus been elected as one of the alternates to the National Board and was making more frequent trips to New York.

Our discussion centered around the question of whether fascism was imminent, and the majority of the Board was inclined to believe it was. During that period of heightened cold-war tensions amid the threat of a new actual war, it was hard to believe the wave of repression would pass and the Party be allowed to function. Powerful big-business leaders were fascist-minded, from the days of the Roosevelt-haters and the America First Committee, men who had only been stalled by the outbreak of World War II and U.S. participation in the war against Hitler. It was not far-fetched to believe that we were in for a long period of suppression of the Bill of Rights, in which the Communist Party would be one of the prime targets.

But the organizational results as carried out in most districts were devastating. Party leaders at every level were to make themselves unavailable; headquarters in many districts were virtually closed down; clubs were reduced in size. While some security measures were undoubtedly necessary to prevent the Party cadres from being decimated by the expected arrests, these measures were carried to extremes in many places.

A few of us on the National Board had reservations about the political estimate and the organizational results. We did not believe the U.S. ruling class needed fascism to rule as yet, because it had vastly more resources to deal with the postwar crisis than had Germany in the thirties. Nor did Germany have our background of democratic traditions. So while the rulers of Germany embraced fascism to deal with its crisis and to crush resistance, we had seen during that same period the most unprecedented democratic upsurge in the United States, brought about by the mass struggles of the working class against the effects of the economic crisis.

As a result of my reservations, most of the California Party leaders—perhaps too many—remained at their posts and were caught up in the dragnet that followed. But headquarters remained open, and we did carry on activities throughout the period, and a fairly effective defense campaign after we were arrested.

It was in the midst of these climactic events that I flew to New York in response to an urgent summons. The eleven convicted national leaders were due to surrender, and I was to take my assigned post in the National Office. I had unwelcome company on the plane to New York. The FBI presence had been conspicuous for some time wherever I went. Although my movements were quite open and I made no secret of my plans, they must have thought that I, too, would become a fugitive.

I had no such intentions, but to my astonishment I was informed by Gene Dennis, the General Secretary, on my arrival that I was to remain in the National Office about two weeks and then "take off." I strenuously opposed this proposal. It would have meant virtually closing down the functioning of the National office as an operating center. (William Z. Foster was too ill to function; Elizabeth Gurley Flynn was still there, but although she was an eloquent representative of the Party as a speaker and writer, she had not served in the organizational operations and in any case was herself facing a prison sentence soon. The *Daily Worker* was also without an editor.)

I wrung from Dennis before his surrender a concession that I was to use my own judgment as to when would be the best time to leave, but I told him frankly that my present inclination was "never." I was determined that the Party should have a public presence as long as possible. I had no illusion that I would be able to avoid arrest, but the National Board had been free on bail for three years till their court case was finally decided, and so I believed that I would be able to function even after an indictment.

Foster, Flynn, and I met as a makeshift Secretariat, and Foster proposed that I should be the Acting National Secretary. He urged that we immediately make a public announcement to that effect in order to demonstrate to the Party and the public that the national center was still functioning. However, we decided against it, as we all agreed that such a public announcement would probably invite an immediate crackdown.

In the end, however, our decisions came to naught. Smith Act indictments were being prepared in every major state, and the Justice Department had no intention of allowing me to stay in New

York, with or without bail. The hysteria created in the media by the failure of four of the eleven National Board members to surrender in court made it clear that the Justice Department was going to take advantage of the situation to speed up its timetable. During the next ten days I was calling the districts, urging whomever I could reach to keep their headquarters open, and to have at least one party official in each city remain at his or her post. If only we had a little time, I thought, some of the damage could be undone. But time was one thing that the witch hunters were not going to give us.

11   Presumption of Guilt

The blow fell on a hot summer morning in July 1951. I was spending the weekend alone in the Bronx at the home of one of the editors of the *Daily Worker*, who was out of town with his family at the time. He had left me a note to deliver to the city desk, which was in the same building as the Party's national office, where I was headed on that Monday morning.

As I stepped out of the house, someone called my name and three men rushed forward and surrounded me. One flashed his FBI badge, the other two grabbed my arms and hustled me into the back seat of a waiting car.

"We're taking you down to headquarters," I was told.

"What am I charged with?" I asked.

"You'll be told at headquarters," was the curt answer.

"I've not had breakfast yet. I demand you stop and let me get some breakfast."

"You'll get it later."

Perversely, I insisted, "I don't want to wait for the slop they'll serve me later."

"We'll get you some coffee and doughnuts at the office."

I settled back in the seat and closed my eyes. The agent on my right hand leaned over to me and said, "Are you feeling all right?" The idea that the FBI might be solicitous about my health made me grin. I just looked at him and didn't bother to answer. I settled back again.

I had been expecting my arrest, so it came as no great shock to me. In a way, it was a relief that the days of waiting were over. I knew it was getting closer when a tight surveillance was clamped on me in San Francisco before I left for New York. At least two cars followed me everywhere. My phone was monitored. Once an unsuspecting telephone repairman came to the house when the phone was out of order, and when he opened up the receiver and the box he looked rather strangely at me and summoned his superior. "Did you find the bug?" I asked innocently. He didn't answer.

On the plane to New York I had an escort. After my arrival I was accompanied to theaters, restaurants, and to the office. Undoubtedly I was guarded while I slept. But since we had more members than the FBI had agents in New York, their movements did not go unobserved. The spies were often spied upon. The night before my arrest while I was attending a meeting at Carnegie Hall, someone came up to me and said, "Comrade Schneiderman, do you know that you are being followed?" I replied that indeed I did. It seems that I was seen in a drugstore, sampling the magazines on the newsstand, with my shadower hovering nearby. (Would it give him extra points to be able to report what I was reading? Was it *Business Week* or *Nero Wolfe?*)

At FBI headquarters my captors showed a strange interest in an aspirin box they found in my pocket. What puzzled them was that the box was empty except for a slip of paper with some printed directions from the manufacturer. I had put it in my pocket to remind me to buy another box, but this explanation was too simple for the FBI when they questioned me. They looked it over carefully, minutely examined the printed slip of paper for some hidden message, and for some reason decided to keep it, because five months later the aspirin box was missing when my property was returned. ("It just goes to show," I told a fund-raising meeting later, "that the FBI probably has more headaches than we have.")

When I was allowed to make a telephone call, Elizabeth Gurley Flynn told me, "You're on a California indictment. Eleven other comrades have been picked up in San Francisco and in Los Angeles." It was the entire California leadership except for a few who were no longer living at home (three more were arrested later). The same pattern had been followed in New York with the district leadership, after the national leaders had been convicted, and was to be followed throughout the country in city after city. (In all,140 defendants were indicted in 14 cities.)

My first reaction was relief that I was to be tried with my associates in California. Most of the people I knew in New York were already in jail or in hiding, and the Party organization was reeling from the loss of both its national and district leaders. I had a base in California after being involved in the labor and political struggles there for over fifteen years. The prospects of mounting a defense campaign in my home state were much better than in New York, and the trial would take place in a less superheated political atmosphere, I thought. But my optimism faded quickly when bail was set at $100,000.

*   *   *

Some of the most distinguished men I have ever met were in the police van with me, all of us handcuffed in the cramped quarters of the vehicle carrying us to the Federal House of Detention on West Street, where federal prisoners were held awaiting trial or pending transfer to more permanent prison quarters after conviction. It was under these rather inauspicious circumstances that I met the four men in the van with me: Alphaeus Hunton, head of the Council for African Affairs; Dashiell Hammett, that great master of detective fiction; Frederick Vanderbilt Field, radical descendant of a famous family; and Abner Green, secretary of the American Committee for the Protection of the Foreign Born. They were the trustees of the Civil Rights Bail Fund, and had been cited for contempt of court the same day for refusing to reveal the names of contributors to the bail fund, for fear of subjecting hundreds of people to persecution. Meanwhile the bank had frozen the deposits of the bail fund at the behest of the Justice Department.

I remembered when I was a boy running around the streets of Chicago, we would chase after a police van, yelling, "There goes the paddy wagon," and try to peek inside at the unfortunates who were being hauled off to jail. And here we were, being given the same treatment for exercising our First Amendment rights.

Each of the four had come to this rendezvous with "justice" by a different path, but out of a common determination to fight the McCarthy repression that was sweeping the land.

Alphaeus Hunton, distinguished-looking and soft-spoken, was one of the first Black leaders in the United States to try to arouse interest in African affairs. (We did not meet him again, for he was immediately sent to the section segregated for Blacks.) Fred Field, spectacled and ruddy-faced, had eschewed the life of the idle rich and devoted his time to left-wing causes and defense of civil liberties. Abner Green, his deeply lined, Lincolnesque face always solemn looking, had long headed the fight against the deportation of radicals. His organization had conducted a campaign in my behalf during my citizenship trial and had sent its chief counsel, Carol King, to participate in the Bridges case and then again in my citizenship trial. (I learned later that he was suffering from a fatal disease, but he never talked about it.)

But none of the four attracted as much attention as Dashiell Hammett. The creator of *The Maltese Falcon* and other "tough" detective stories was mild-mannered and had a dry wit which enthralled the inmates. "All my life," he announced plaintively, "I never listened to my mother when she told me to keep my mouth shut. And the first time I obeyed her, I land in here." Some of the toughness of his fictional characters was present in this gentle-looking person. The playwright Lillian Hellman tells in her memoirs about their life together that when he was summoned before the House Un-American Activities Committee he flatly rejected her advice that he talk.

So the famous, the notorious, and the obscure swabbed floors together, shared the common showers and mess hall, and did their walking and exercising on the roof together in the brief time allotted for fresh air. I was placed in a huge cage which held a dozen or more prisoners separated by bars from a corridor running around three sides so that guards could keep a vigilant eye on us. I did not realize that I had attained a certain status among the prisoners because my bail was the highest of any of the inmates. (My status dropped abruptly toward the end of my stay when a hood was brought in who was being held for $250,000 bail—so much for fame!)

The jail conditions, according to some of the more knowledge-able inmates, were slightly better than at the federal penitentiaries in Atlanta and Leavenworth. "The food is not quite as bad as I thought it would be," I wrote to Leah. She did not believe me. We could supplement it with chocolate bars bought at the commissary. At night we had a special treat when a trustee came by in the corridor with a pail of hot water. We would reach through the bars to fill our tin cups, mix some of the chocolate into the water and imagine we were drinking hot chocolate.

Communists were the objects of great curiosity among the prisoners, often friendly, only a few hostile. The most popular of the Communists was the most unlikely one. V. J. Jerome, Marxist editor and scholar, was the epitome of the absent-minded profes-sor, both in the pedantic manner and fussy appearance, usually the target of jokes and jibes. (I, myself, was guilty of telling this story about him. He had left the National Office with his suitcase for an out-of-town lecture appearance. Half an hour later the phone rang and it was Jerome. "I'm down at Grand Central station. Where am I going?") But he was able to establish a special rapport with the inmates and would help to while away the hours by telling them tales of ancient times from his vast store of knowledge.

I shared a double bunk, upper and lower, with a Cuban charged with smuggling. He spoke very little English, but I gathered that he was a supporter of Batista. I had tried to pick up a little Spanish from a textbook, but when I tried it out on him, he only laughed and shook his head. It turned out that the textbook was a Castilian one, Spanish as spoken in Spain, and together with my fractured pronunciation, it was unintelligible to him.

One of my cellmates was a flamboyant young fellow from Brooklyn, who had tried to hijack a liquor truck. The dream of sudden wealth was too much for him to resist, but now the prospect of years in prison had disheartened an otherwise exuberant spirit, as he talked wistfully of the wife and child who were waiting for him. He was intrigued by the charges against me ("What are you in for?" is the first question usually asked of an incoming prisoner), and could not understand why I was not following a more lucrative profession. By his standard the risk should be measured against the possible profit. If there was no material reward, to risk arrest was foolish.

Another fellow prisoner was Morton Sobell, awaiting transfer to Alcatraz to serve a thirty-year sentence while his co-defendants, Julius and Ethel Rosenberg, were appealing their death sentence to the Supreme Court. (Their sentence and execution for alleged espionage shocked the world; subsequent revelations unraveled the sordid story of how the Justice Department, the FBI, and the courts used the climate of the cold war and the McCarthy period to orchestrate their destruction.)

I soon found how difficult it was during that period to get a lawyer to argue for reduction of my bail. (Our attorneys were either in jail for contempt or arguing other cases.) A young, inexperienced attorney was finally sent to see me. As we sat down to confer in the windowless "conference room," with the guard standing at the barred door, the young attorney kept looking nervously around the room and finally, to my astonishment, abruptly rose and exclaimed, "I'm sorry, you'll have to excuse me, but I've got to get out of here. I can't stand being closed in like this." He asked the guard to let him out. I muttered to myself, "You're sure in the wrong profession, brother." I have often wondered since how that young lawyer pursued his practice when he was so terrified of jails, unless he confined himself to civil cases. Our attorneys in those days had to be prepared to face jail themselves when they defended Communists. (The moral: If you have claustrophobia, don't practice law.)

I sent word to Elizabeth Gurley Flynn: "Don't send that scared kid around again. If you can't do better than that, I'll argue my own bail case." When Carol King heard of my predicament, she offered to represent me. "I'm only doing this for you. I don't take political cases," she told me. Her field was immigration and naturalization law, in which she was an expert.

When I appeared for my bail hearing before the U.S. Commissioner, Carol King argued that the U.S. Supreme Court had already cleared me of similar charges when Wendell Willkie represented me. Although little impressed by this argument, the Commissioner did reduce my bail to $75,000 pending my transfer to Los Angeles.

I was awakened early one morning, when most of the other prisoners were still asleep and told by a guard, "Get your things together. You're on your way." (California, here I come!) As I got to the door of the cell block, my young friend from Brooklyn called out "Wait a minute," rushed up with a cloth in his hand and to my astonishment dropped to his knees and began to shine my shoes. He was courting trouble just to be there. "What the hell has gotten into you?" I protested. "We can't let you go looking like this among all those Hollywood swells," he said with a flourish. (The view of Los Angeles from Brooklyn!)

Two federal marshals escorted me to Pennsylvania Station, handcuffed to one of them, where we boarded a west-bound train. They were to be my escorts for four days and three nights on the journey to Los Angeles. I had often traveled the same route by coach, but this time I was introduced to the "privileges" of a private compartment with two lower beds and an upper berth and a private toilet. With my ankles shackled with leg irons, I had to climb into the upper berth at night, and try vainly to find some comfortable position to sleep. "What if I have to get up at night to go to the toilet?" I inquired of my escorts. I had visions of them waking up startled and drawing a gun on me. "We're not worried that you will try to escape," one of them replied with a grin, nodding at my shackled legs.

On the long journey across the country we had no choice but to become better acquainted. They were two Irishmen who had lived through the wars of Tammany Hall politics in New York City. In describing one of the elections in the early 1900's, one of them chuckled, "That was the year-r-r the ballot boxes wur-r-r floatin' down the East River-r-r." As we talked their attitude thawed. How come a nice fellow like you got mixed up with those Reds, they wanted to know.

By the time we reached Wyoming, they had decided that I was not going to try to escape. When the train made a stop at Laramie, my leg irons were removed, and I was allowed to take a walk on the platform. And then occurred one of those rare coincidences which had unfortunate consequences. A train going in the opposite direction had stopped on the other side of the platform, and as the passengers were alighting, a stout, rosy-cheeked woman came up to me, exclaiming: "Comrade Schneiderman, what are you doing here?" With the shackles removed and the marshal standing some distance away, there was no visible sign that I was a prisoner. She was one of our members on her way from Los Angeles to the East, and the last she had heard about me was that I was in a federal prison in New York. When the marshals saw a strange woman approach me, they rushed up to me, seized my arms, hustled me back into the train and started to grill me, "Who was that woman?" Was this a rendezvous? Had she given me a message? They could not believe that it was not an escape plot, and they were worried that they would be called to account for letting me out on the platform unshackled. After that incident the leg irons were never taken off, and I was confined to the compartment the rest of the way. (I learned later that the woman was hounded for months by the FBI, who was convinced she was an accomplice in an escape plot.

The top floor of the Los Angeles County jail was reserved for "maximum security" prisoners. Female prisoners were placed in the women's section on another floor under slightly less rigorous supervision, but not in such "elite" company as we were. The men were mostly young, usually awaiting trial for such assorted charges as murder, drugs, or armed robbery, or pending their transfer to San Quentin or Alcatraz. One of the young drug addicts, son of a policeman who was one of our tormentors in the twenties, tried to commit suicide by slashing his wrists. In another cell block was the gangster Mickey Cohen, rumored to have the run of the floor, and a Yugoslav fascist who was wanted for mass murders in Yugoslavia. (His deportation case dragged on for years, but the U.S. government finally released him and allowed him to remain in the United States.)

The floors below were immeasurably worse than ours. The prisoners were confined in huge crowded cages. The heat was unbearable in the summer time. The arrangements for visitors were primitive. A heavily meshed wire fence separated the inmates from their families, and with the crowd all talking at once in half a dozen languages, the prisoners and visitors on each side of the screen had to almost shout to make themselves heard above the din. Many of the inmates dreaded the ordeal of seeing their families under such animal-like conditions.

I was more fortunate than most, due to the fact that Leah had to come from San Francisco to see me, usually at night, when visiting hours were over. Skilled union negotiator that she was, she persuaded the warden to let her see me in the lawyers' conference room. He offered twenty minutes. She demanded two hours, citing the 500 miles she had to come from San Francisco. They settled for one hour. The guard in the conference room was so confused by this unusual arrangement that he let us stay the full two hours till the lights finally went out. There was seldom anyone else in the room in the evening besides the guard at the other end of the room. We sat across from each other at a long table which had a barrier in the middle, to keep us from touching or passing anything to each other. But we were able to talk in comparative privacy.

She put on a cheerful face, but I could tell that behind that brave front was the strain that the burdens of a wife and mother in such a predicament imposed. Yes, Ellen was fine, but she didn't tell me that the child faced the taunts of her schoolmates when one of them said: "Your father is in jail." No, she didn't need anything; but she said nothing about the fact that she had to borrow money to live on and to pay her fare to visit me. In the disorganization that occurred after the arrests and the resulting pall of fear that was prevalent, it was hard to find anyone in San Francisco who was concerned about the families of the prisoners. (Nevertheless, she plunged into the campaign to raise bail, as did the relatives of all the prisoners.)

I, too, hid my anxieties from her. I assured her that the courts would not sustain the astronomical bail demanded of us. By this time my bail had been reduced to the same level as that of the others held in Los Angeles, which was $50,000, or a total of three quarters of a million dollars for all fifteen defendants. I did not anticipate that the fight for bail would drag on for nearly six months, and that it would take a decision of the U.S. Supreme Court and two decisions of the U.S. Circuit Court of Appeals before an implacable judge determined to keep us in jail was finally moved—oh, so reluctantly—to bow to a higher authority and grudgingly grant us a right which we should have had in the first place.

* * *

The children stand in the crowded hallway outside of the courtroom, waiting for a glimpse of their mother or father before the doors open. Presently there is a commotion down the hall as the federal marshals clear the way for the fifteen prisoners, the ten men manacled two by two, the five women with hands free (a touch of chivalry!) but accompanied by women deputies. As the line passes, the children would lean over to touch their mother or father or cling to their hand for a moment. Husbands and wives exchange a hurried greeting ("How are the kids?—" "I'm fine."—"Kiss the little one for me.") The prisoners invariably smile, and their spouses smile back, but the strain and worry is etched on many of their faces. What went through the minds of the children one can only guess.

When the doors to the courtroom open and the spectators are seated, the defendants are already seated in the jury box, with the handcuffs removed. The visible signs of their imprisonment are no longer there; thus is maintained the fiction of the presumption of innocence. Occasionally, during recesses or while waiting for the session to begin, a marshal relents and allows the prisoners to stand at the barrier and talk to their spouses and children and hold their hands. My seven-year-old Ellen climbs the railing so she can hug me. The marshal turns away.

The murmur of conversation ends abruptly when the courtroom is called to order, and the judge enters to take his place. His stern face never relaxes for a moment as he listens to the argument of counsel or engages in colloquy. He acts out the role of the chosen instrument of retribution, unrelenting in his determination to smite the evil before him. The arguments of counsel do not move him. The precedents of law do not convince him. Even the orders of the higher courts do not persuade him. The masquerade of dispensing justice goes on.

* * *

The surest way to become a media hero in the fifties was to ride the wave of anti-Communism. Witness Nixon, who rode the wave to finally become president, or Judge Medina, whose ruthless conduct in the New York Smith Act trial eventually elevated him to the U.S. Appellate Court bench. Judge William M. Mathes of Los Angeles must have seen himself as a candidate for similar honors as he presided over our hearings for bail. But whereas Medina used a sledge hammer, Mathes concealed a stiletto. His courtly manner cloaked his steely determination to keep us locked up.

The Eighth Amendment in the Bill of Rights reads: "Excessive bail shall not be required." What is excessive? the judge would inquire and listen carefully to counsel's arguments, giving all the appearance of an open mind. How far is the Mexican border? he would ask; or: how do we know that the defendants cannot raise that amount? When our attorneys pleaded poverty for their clients, the judge innocently observed: "This is my first experience with defendants charged with conspiring against the government and earning only $50 a week."

When the prosecution hinted at concealed riches and pressed the point that the bail set was not beyond the capacity of the defendants to pay, the judge ordered the defense attorneys to bring in their financial records so that the court could determine how much they had been paid by the defendants. Our attorneys were strongly inclined to refuse as a matter of principle, but a hasty meeting of the defendants overruled them. "Our main objective in this trial," I quipped, "is to keep our lawyers out of jail." Of course, the records showed that our attorneys had not been paid anything. (It took many weeks and months before enough money was raised to cover bare expense and court costs.) It helped to establish our contention that the $50,000 figure was the same as denial of bail.

But the most telling argument made by the defense was that in a political trial of this kind, with myriads of books as the main evidence, the defendants would be denied due process by being unable to prepare for trial. Preparing the defense would require a library and other facilities for research which would not be available to them in jail. Furthermore, the fifteen defendants, charged with conspiring with each other, could not prepare their cases individually, but would have to do it collectively.

This confronted the judge with a dilemma. He was determined at all costs to avoid prejudicial errors in his conduct of the case which might cause his ruling to be reversed on appeal. In order to maintain the fiction of impartial justice, therefore, he made an extraordinary ruling: The defendants would be given space in the Federal Marshal's office, where they would be brought every weekday. They would be allowed to confer with their attorneys and other visitors. They could bring in books and other material necessary for the trial, and they could make their own arrangements for having lunch and dinner there. (Now who could claim that we weren't going to get a fair trial?) But he was adamant in his refusal to reduce bail, and the lengthy process of appealing to the higher courts began.

Actually, the arrangement was not quite as magnanimous as it sounded. Each morning we were brought (the men handcuffed) across the street from the county jail to the Federal Courthouse, and each evening we were returned the same way. During the rush hour throngs would stand on the corner gaping at the sight of the notorious prisoners they had read about. (A story went around, which we could not verify, that on one of those occasions, as we were being returned handcuffed two by two, surrounded by marshals, an elderly couple stood watching us. The woman said: "I wonder who they are." "Why, don't you know, dear," the man answered, "that's the jury being locked up for the night.")

Our workroom was a cage in the Marshal's office ordinarily used for prisoners on their way to jail. We sat at a table piled with books and other material, which filled up most of the room. Into this cramped space our attorneys would come to confer with their respective clients, or with the group as a whole, and each defendant was assigned to do some research for the collective defense, in anticipation of the prosecution's expected presentation. Relatives were allowed to come and see the prisoners and talk to them through the bars. At least it was better than the bedlam at the wiremesh barrier. We were spared the indignities with which other prisoners were forced to see their families.

The most unusual part of the arrangement was the operation set up to feed us in our conference room. A volunteer committee of our supporters set themselves up as an amateur catering service, and undertook to prepare two meals each day that were more than an ordinary lunch or dinner, to make up for the deficiencies in our prison diet. Each ethnic group vied with each other in preparing their respective specialties. The word about this "special treatment" for Communists spread throughout the jail, but when any of the other prisoners would voice their wonder or envy, we would invariably reply: "We'll exchange it any time for freedom." Mickey Cohen, the gangster, angrily demanded of his lawyer why he couldn't be given the same "privileges" that the Reds were getting.

In our cell block we had no privileges. The only exercise we got was walking the narrow corridor in front of our cells. At night, standing on tiptoes at the window, we could see through the bars the lights of cars moving down the freeway far below. Occasionally we could faintly hear the shouts and chants of demonstrators circling the building, demanding our release on bail. This more than anything else heightened our spirits and also generated respect for us among the other prisoners in our cell-block. (Nothing helps the morale of prisoners more than the knowledge that on the outside there are people who are putting up a fight for them; and nothing is worse than knowing that they are alone and forgotten, as many of them are.)

Pinochle was the great time-killer. I envied those who could play. Their preoccupation and absorption in the game whiled away many long hours. At times we would listen to the life stories of some of the other inmates, some of them pitiful, some of them sordid. Many of them could not understand why we were considered dangerous criminals—we were such a peaceful-looking lot.

A handsome Black youth from the South cornered me once and began to ask questions about how we expected to bring about socialism. We always had to be on guard against a plant, but he seemed to be genuinely curious. (In any case, we had nothing to hide.) "Do you really think that you can bring about a revolution peacefully?" he asked. I replied that violence did not depend on us, but on whether those in power would accept peaceful change achieved democratically. He shook his head. "You ever been in the South?" he asked. "I'll never believe that you can change the South peacefully." During the sixties I often thought of that conversation when the struggles of the Blacks for the most elementary democratic rights met with violence.

There was a certain level of guarded camaraderie among us all that almost got me into a tight spot. Through the prison grapevine I heard that one of the prisoners who was awaiting a hearing planned to make his escape. He was going to try to make a break for it when they brought him to the courtroom. Slim as the chances were, the mood of desperation among those who had previous convictions and were expecting long sentences made the odds seem worthwhile. The prisoner wanted to conceal an extra shirt and exchange it for his prison garb when he made his escape. As luck would have it, Leah had just negotiated with the warden to send in a clean, white shirt for my courtroom appearances, and I got word that the prisoner planned to stop by my cell in the morning on his way to court and ask me for my old shirt. I had visions of headlines reading: "Convict escapes. Caught wearing Red's shirt," at a time when Judge Mathes was citing the closeness of the Mexican border to justify his bail ruling. What to do? I wanted to handle it tactfully, without an outright refusal, so early in the morning I threw the shirt into a sinkful of water, and by the time the prisoner came by it was hanging dripping wet.

My cellmate was Ernie Fox, a balding, rosy-cheeked, ex-seaman with a beer belly. This was not the first time he was behind bars. Of German nationality, he had been incarcerated during the war in a detention camp, with the added indignity of being held there with Nazis, although the immigration authorities were fully aware that as a Communist he wholeheartedly supported the antifascist war. On his release he returned to the sea until the cold-war screening barred Communists from getting seamen's papers. He was good company, but at night his snore-whistle-snore-whistle often kept me awake.

One night in my upper bunk I woke up with my heart pounding and my pulse racing. "Ernie," I whispered, "I think I'm having a heart attack." Startled out of his sleep, he leaped out of bed, grabbed a tin cup and raked it over the bars, creating a tremendous racket and shouting for the guard at the same time. Ordinarily, "racking the bars" could land a prisoner "in the hole," but when the guard heard "heart attack," he hastily took me down to the infirmary, where I was put under heavy sedation. In the morning my face was puffed up so badly that my eyes were almost closed.

When we reached the Marshal's office, I had one of the attorneys call a doctor I knew to tell him what had happened. And that's how I found out that I was allergic to penicillin. I had completely forgotten that I was given a shot of penicillin the day before for an infected toe, and the "heart attack" was really a violent reaction to the drug. Meanwhile, Ernie was warned, "Don't you ever do that again."

Our mood ranged from grim to boisterous. Some of us tried to maintain a cheerful outlook, but none had any illusion about our prospects. One of the defendants said to my sister, "Your brother is the only one who thinks we have a chance." We were all veterans in the movement, so all of us had known that sooner or later we might have to face the prospect of jail, but this did not mean that we were reconciled to it. Our chief concern was about our families. Those of us who were parents worried about the children. They were more vulnerable than our spouses, who had shared our struggle and were more prepared for adversity. But on the whole we were a resilient lot, and the work assignments preparing for the trial helped to distract our minds, at least in the daytime. The morbid thoughts came at night.

Our appeal for reduction of bail was turned down in the Appellate Court; as far as it was concerned, all the substantial issues had been decided in the first Smith Act trial in New York, and the bail issue was also clouded by the disappearance of four of the defendants in that case. The next step was the Supreme Court.

A piece of news came out of the Washington bail hearing, as surprising as it was unexpected. Justice Felix Frankfurter, hearing the case called "Schneiderman vs. U.S.," inquired: "Is this the same Schneiderman who was before us in the citizenship case?" When Margolis eagerly assented, Frankfurter said: "He may have grounds for res judicata" (the issue has been adjudicated). What gave us cause for jubilation was that if a finding was possible that the same issue had been decided in my favor in a previous case, it added a strong additional ground for granting us bail. Ironically, this bit of good news came from the very Justice who had fought so ferociously against the favorable verdict in my citizenship case. Furthermore, it gave us a clue to the strategy we could use in the forthcoming trial.

Our first concern was to try to avoid some of the pitfalls of the New York trial. While our national leadership made a courageous and principled defense of Marxism-Leninism, Judge Medina did such a hatchet job on them that it was virtually impossible in the atmosphere that surrounded the trial to make the issues clear, and the series of confrontations provoked by Medina proved disastrous to the defendants and attorneys alike.

We set as our goal to make clear that the issue in this trial was our *constitutional right to advocate* the Party's principles and program. We would try to avoid the kind of clashes in the courtroom which would divert attention from the main issues raised by the defense. We would strive to show what we had *done* as Communists, as a logical consequence of our ideology. And above all, we would endeavor to show that this was a trial of books and ideas, not illegal acts, and that what was on trial was the Bill of Rights.

On the legal side our attorneys set their sights on the facts in our case on which the government was most vulnerable, one of which was the question of the intent of each individual defendant. The conspiracy charge was a tricky way of getting around the fact that the government could not show any illegal acts by the Party or the defendants. We were *not* charged with teaching or advocating the overthrow of the U.S. Government by force and violence; we were indicted for *conspiring*, not to act, but to teach and advocate, with the Party as the instrument of the conspiracy. The overt acts charged in the indictment "in furtherance of the conspiracy" were innocuous listings of meetings where one or another defendant "did appear," or "did speak." In my case, they were usually public mass meetings, well advertised in advance, where I spoke on foreign policy or the economic situation, or at membership meetings on Party policy. One could well wonder: what conspiracy?

Finally, we decided to use to the hilt the Supreme Court decision in my citizenship case, in which the Court not only restored my citizenship but declared in effect not only that a Communist could be attached to the U.S. Constitution, but that it was a reasonable conclusion that the Party did not necessarily advocate force and violence except when violence was used against the majority. With that in mind, it was agreed that I should be my own counsel, so that I could address the jury and examine witnesses if necessary. Keeping in mind Justice Frankfurter's remark, we were going to throw that Supreme Court decision at the jury right at the opening of the trial, and keep reminding them throughout the trial, through the same defendant who had been cleared, that the same books and ideas were being tried again. *Res judicata*!

The Supreme Court acted swiftly on the bail question. The case was remanded to the lower court with an order to set reasonable bail. Then began an amazing filibuster. Judge Mathes was perplexed. He had pondered and could not decide what the language of the Supreme Court meant. What was reasonable bail? He asked the U.S. Attorney and the defense attorneys to enlighten him. He listened to their arguments, with head thrust forward as though he were anxious not to miss a word of advice. And then he announced that he could come to no other conclusion than the figure of $50,000.

Our attorneys wasted no time in appealing to the U.S. Court of Appeals in San Francisco, which handed down a decision ordering Judge Mathes to carry out the mandate of the Supreme Court. Again the judge went through the same comedy. He did not know how to interpret the language of the Supreme Court. Once again Ben Margolis flew to San Francisco, and the Appellate Court finally ended the charade by setting bail at $5,000 for some and $10,000 for the rest of us.

Once the long fight was over, the appeal for bail money met an overwhelming response. Most of it was from workers' savings, but there were some unexpected sources. A peach grower from Marysville, who had just sold a bumper crop, came down to Los Angeles with his pockets bulging with greenbacks. A Midwest banker who had married a distant cousin of mine contributed $1,000 and came to the trial on his vacation. A building contractor of Yugoslav descent put up the $10,000 for my bail. All the other defendants had similar experiences.

But we were not through with Judge Mathes. He put each donor on the stand and grilled him. Did he know that he was responsible if the defendant escaped? Was it his own money? Did he have the consent of his spouse for putting up this money? This led in one case to an amusing incident, unbeknown to the judge but a matter of great merriment for those in the know. The stepfather of Al Richmond was on the stand, being grilled after putting up the bail for Al, whose mother sat in the visitor's section. The judge, unaware of the relationship, sternly asked him, "Does your wife agree to this?" The stepfather, in what could be ranked as the understatement of the year, replied with a straight face, "She has no objection." It was one of the few times we had something to smile about in that courtroom.

And so, after five long months, from July to December, our fight was won and we were released. A triumph for "justice" on a charge which should never have been made in the first place for a "conspiracy" that never existed. We had little time for either celebration or rest, however, for the trial was less than two months away. Leah and Ellen moved with me to Los Angeles, so they could be with me during the trial, and we rented a house in Boyle Heights, where I had spent most of my boyhood. This East Side district had been Jewish when I lived there, but now was a mixture of Jewish and Mexican-American. We were impressed by the warmth and sympathy we encountered everywhere we went. The corner druggist refused to accept money for a medicine for Ellen, a Mexican-American restaurant owner told us lunch was on the house. People would stop us on Brooklyn Avenue and wish us luck. After one such incident, when a passerby stopped to tell Ellen "We're with your daddy," she exclaimed, "Gee, Mommy, everybody in Los Angeles is for peace!" Not everybody, of course. McCarthyism was still rampant; and then there was Judge Mathes.

12 "Ladies and Gentlemen of the Jury"

The trial opened with a great deal of fanfare—a real "show trial" for press and radio—before a packed courtroom on February 5, 1952. The defendants included all but a few of the Party state and county leaders.[1] All were from San Francisco and Los Angeles except Albert "Mickey" Lima, a former fisherman and longshoreman, who headed the Party in Oakland. Two of our Black comrades who were in the state leadership, Bill Taylor and Hursel Alexander, were never arrested; they were among the "unavailable," although Hursel was harassed by the FBI while he lay ill in a hospital. Two others, John Pittman and Pettis Perry, were in the East at the time. The defendant who was to become the central figure of the trial and the main target of the judge's vindictive vengeance was Oleta O'Connor Yates. Of Irish background, she had a frail and demure appearance which gave no clue to the strength of her character and will power, no hint of the moral courage she was later to show on the witness stand.

We had assembled an impressive team of attorneys: Ben Margolis, veteran of the labor wars and the defense of the "Hollywood Ten"; A. L. Wirin of the American Civil Liberties Union, known in Los Angeles as "Mr. Civil Liberties"; Norman Leonard, San Francisco attorney for the International Longshoremen and Warehousemen's Union; Leo Branton, a young Black attorney (later to become famous in the Angela Davis trial); and Alexander Schullman, counsel for several A.F. of L. unions in Los Angeles. They were backed up by a team of lawyers doing research headed by Sam Rosenwein; Benjamin Dreyfus and Doris Walker were in charge of our legal defense office.

One of our prospective attorneys was conspicuous by his absence, however. Leo Sullivan was a criminal lawyer whom we had picked because he was well known in Oakland, where one of our defendants, Mickey Lima, lived. When he failed to show up at the pretrial hearings, he kept telling us that he was delayed and promised that he would show up in time. On the day before the trial he had still not shown up. Increasingly worried, I asked one of our attorneys to telephone him and give him an ultimatum that we were dropping him from the case unless he was present when the trial opened. After a few moments of conversation, our attorney motioned to me to get on another line; and then I heard an extraordinary story. His voice choking with emotion, Sullivan described how the FBI had approached him to enter the case as an informant. He was to participate in the defense, but was to report regularly to the FBI so that the prosecution would know everything being said in the defense strategy councils.

He begged us to release him from his commitment, so that he would not have to be a spy for the FBI. We assured him that we understood his predicament. It was the usual story. The FBI may have had some information about him that they thought could be used to put pressure on him, as they did with all of their victims, more often innocent rather than guilty. Only this could explain how they could bring this man so close to cracking up as he was then. I know nothing about Leo Sullivan's doings, but it is to his everlasting credit that in his own way he found the courage to defy his tormentors and refuse to stoop to the despicable role of informer. But it gave us a taste of what was to come. (When he died, I was strongly tempted to go to his funeral and tell this story.)

The prosecutors at the government's table were U.S. Attorney Walter B. Binns and two assistants, Norman S. Neukom and Ray S. Kinnison. From Washington the Justice Department (not taking chances with the local talent) sent a special assistant to the Attorney General, Lawrence K. Bailey.

The jury was swiftly selected and was probably as good as could be expected from a federal jury panel. Although we took as much care as possible in the selection, we knew that our problem was not so much the composition of the jury as the pervasive political atmosphere, the anti-Communist hysteria, and the prejudices which had been so deeply imbedded in the minds of a large part of the American public. Even though the jury included a sprinkling of wage earners and lower middle-class people, including two Blacks, we knew that the majority might be swayed by the prevailing climate of fear. As we anxiously scanned the jury panel we wondered if somewhere behind those impassive faces one or more government plants were concealed. Among those housewives and employees of big corporations, was there anyone who could stand up to the pressure? (I personally put my faith in a woman juror who was a writer of children's books.)

The United States Attorney, Walter Binns, in his opening statement to the jury, outlined the government's case: the defendants were engaged in a "conspiracy to teach and advocate the overthrow of the United States government by force and violence as speedily as circumstances would permit"; for that purpose they had organized the Communist Party and had committed a number of overt acts to further the conspiracy. Thus were summed up a hundred years of some of the greatest contributions in the field of philosophy, political science, and economics by some of the greatest minds in human history.

Our task was to try to demystify the myths about Communists and defuse, if possible, the type of onslaught we knew was coming in the prosecution's parade of witnesses. In their opening statements, the defense attorneys before me, after outlining the biographies of their clients and the overt acts charged against them, would focus their remarks to the jury mainly on the legal aspects of the case. By previous agreement it was left to me to present to the jury, within the limits allowed in an opening statement, the broader political aspects of the case; to explain the Party's theory and practice within the context of what we intended to prove, and to keep reminding them of the Supreme Court decision in my citizenship case.

As I waited my turn, I let my mind drift, and it seemed to me that all of my political life had pointed to preparing me for this moment. From the window of the courtroom to the north you could see the Plaza where an agonized youth tried to speak up for Sacco and Vanzetti twenty-five years before, when my journey began. Only a few blocks away to the south, was the hotel where in the same year the American Federation of Labor convention leaders had stripped me of my delegate's credentials because I was a Communist. Down the street was the meeting hall where I had stood with Upton Sinclair before an overflow crowd so long ago, waiting to debate the merits of socialism with a high school championship debating team that never showed up.

Together with my codefendants, I had trudged on hunger marches, walked the picket lines, endured clubbings by policemen, exhorted thousands at mass meetings and demonstrations, and defied the witch hunts. We had a vision of social justice and equality, and it was because we were striving to make that vision real that we were in the dock here.

A liberal president had intervened to deprive me of my citizenship, and by an unusual converging of circumstances his conservative rival for the presidency unexpectedly rose to challenge that attempt. A Supreme Court Justice, the "liberal" of yesteryear, had engaged in a personal crusade to oppose the high court's ruling in my favor, and yet the same Justice had inadvertently thrown us a lifeline to use that ruling in our present defense. An attorney general whose office filed the denaturalization suit against me became the Supreme Court Justice who only a few years later wrote the majority opinion restoring my citizenship.

As I mused over these strange quirks of history, I focused my gaze on my favorite juror, the woman writer. Was it possible, I wondered, for our defense to penetrate behind the scare words "conspiracy" and "revolution"? In a trial of witches, how do you go about showing that there are no witches? That is what I was asking myself as I took a deep breath and stepped to the rostrum to address the jury.

"Ladies and gentlemen of the jury: My name is William Schneiderman. I am one of the defendants in this case, and I am here representing myself as my own counsel. I think you are entitled to an explanation why, with the able lawyers we have here, I choose to represent myself in this trial. I do so because I feel that not only my political beliefs and ideals by which I live, but the meaning of my whole life is on trial here, and I must defend it myself. I also feel that I, myself, can best defend my party, the Communist Party, of which I am state chairman in California, against the false charges in the indictment.

"Our contention is that there was no conspiracy . . . and we shall show that the prosecution's charges constitute what amounts to a political frame-up to outlaw a minority political party that has sought to bring its platform to the people by democratic process. We will tell you what the theory known as Marxism-Leninism really is, not what the prosecution distorts it to be. . . . And the evidence will show that my intent, as revealed by my political beliefs and actions, was not what the indictment charges, but it was to work for peace and democracy in our country, and to win the majority for socialism, and that is why we are being tried here. And the evidence will not be the usual type of evidence in a criminal case, but books and ideas, for that is what is being tried here.

"I am well aware that none of you may agree with the views or activities of my codefendants and myself, but of course you understand that the merits or demerits of our views and activities are not the issue here. All we are asking is that you keep your minds open to what is the issue—when you hear what we do advocate, whether we have the right to advocate these views as Communists, or whether a working-class political party such as ours is to be penalized for these views and in effect barred from American political life, and prevented from submitting its program to the judgment of the people. . . .

"I began at a very early age to question why there should be so much poverty in the midst of plenty, as I saw from my own experience. I tried to find the answer in my studies of political science and history, and in the labor movement, and this led me to investigate what the writings of Marx and Lenin had to say about existing social conditions, their causes and cure. . . . And some of the very writings that the prosecution announced its intention to introduce into evidence, I found in the Los Angeles public libraries in the twenties and they were being discussed and debated in the schools and in the unions of those days. And I came to the conclusion that . . . the only way to eliminate the slums in which I lived, the sweatshops in which my father worked, the discrimination I saw practiced against the Negro people and the Jewish people, and the only way to end devastating war, was by socialism.

"I have always believed that my Communist principles and activities were consistent with my understanding of the American democratic tradition as I learned it from the study of Jefferson and Lincoln and Frederick Douglass, and from some of the early American labor leaders who were also Marxists. And I joined a union and participated as a Communist and a union man in campaigns to organize the workers into trade unions, and in strikes for higher wages. I took literally what I had read about the right to petition Congress for the redress of grievances, and helped organize delegations of unemployed workers and farmers during the Depression years to the State Capitol, when I lived in Minnesota, to petition the legislature for relief.

"And the evidence will show that I advocated no doctrine of force and violence, but that I learned who really advocated it when I saw violence used against these lawful activities, and that meetings to hear lectures and open forums were unlawfully broken up, and books and pamphlets were seized and destroyed."

As I was outlining the expected "evidence" against me and contrasted it with my actual activities, I found I was not as nervous as I thought I would be. Standing at a rostrum and addressing an audience was nothing new to me. Still, it was an eerie feeling to know that this time my audience was not the usual kind I was accustomed to, but one that had the power to send me and my co-defendants to prison for five years.

"This trial is not the first time that my intent, as revealed by my conduct and beliefs, was tested in the courts. The evidence will show that I was the defendant in a case which became known as the

Schneiderman case, in which I was represented by Mr. Wendell Willkie, without fee, before the United States Supreme Court.

"Some of the very same books which the prosecution has announced its intention to introduce into our trial here, were before the Supreme Court when it acted on my citizenship; in fact, nearly all the main theoretical works on which the prosecution appears to be relying in this present trial to show that there was a conspiracy to advocate doctrines of force and violence against the United States Government—these same works—were before the Supreme Court when it handed down its decision."

As I came to the key quotation, I raised my voice to make sure the jury was listening. I thought I detected some of them leaning forward ever so little as I went on.

"If I may quote from the Supreme Court decision on this point:

> A tenable conclusion from the foregoing is that the Party in 1927 desired to achieve its purpose by peaceful and democratic means, and as a theoretical matter justified the use of force and violence only as a method of preventing an attempted forcible counter-overthrow once the Party had obtained control in a peaceful manner, or as a method of last resort to enforce the majority will if at some indefinite time in the future, because of peculiar circumstances, constitutional or peaceful channels were no longer open.

"There was another occasion when my intent, my conduct and beliefs, and those of the Communist Party, were tested to show that we constantly sought to follow democratic processes. . . . When a bill was introduced into the California State Legislature in 1940, ruling the Communist Party off the ballot, where it had been since 1934, on the grounds that the Party advocated the overthrow of the government by force and violence, I went to Sacramento to testify against the bill and at the invitation of the State Assembly I addressed that body, sitting as a Committee of the Whole; and I denied the charge and testified as to our beliefs. When the bill was passed, I filed a suit which became known as the *Communist Party vs. Peek*, and the State Supreme Court declared the law unconstitutional and restored the Communist Party to the ballot in 1942."

It was time for the noon recess, and as we were waiting for the jury to file out, I asked Frank Carlson, the most pessimistic of my codefendants, "How did it go?"

"I'd like to have it submitted to the jury right now," he grinned, "it's our best chance."

"Yes," I replied, "but unfortunately we still have the prosecution's witnesses to hear from."

The United States Supreme Court decision had given the jury something to ponder. The key paragraph which I had quoted was a reasonably accurate summarization of the Party's position on the question of force and violence. But from the experience of past trials, we knew the type of "evidence" the government's informants were prepared to present, and the judge would be more than willing to accept.

Ben Margolis had urged, and I had agreed with some misgivings, that I must give an explanation of our theories so as to prepare the jury in advance with a definition of our terminology. We wanted them to hear their scientific meaning before they heard government prosecutors and witnesses try to equate words like "revolution" with guns, and "class struggle" with blood in the streets. It was going to be heavy going for most of the afternoon session.

"The principles of scientific socialism on which we base ourselves are known as Marxism, because they were first developed by its founder Karl Marx and his coworker, Frederick Engels. They were the authors of the first *Communist Manifesto* in 1848, a historic document issued in London, which has become world-famous for the past hundred years. They drew on the best thought from England, France, and Germany in political economy and philosophy to shape their theory. When Engels wrote his work on *The Origin of the Family*, he quoted extensively from an American's book, Morgan's *Ancient Society*. Marx also corresponded with Lincoln, and while a European correspondent for Horace Greeley's *New York Tribune*, wrote extensively on the Civil War in the United States. Lenin, the founder of the Soviet State, developed Marx's theories further, and so Marxism became known as Marxism-Leninism. So you see why we look upon it as a science so universal in scope that no single country can lay claim to it.

"Marxism looks upon the history of society as a history of change from one mode of production to a new and more advanced mode. We see the mode of production, or the way men make their living in a particular period, as determining the political forms and ideas and culture of that period. . . . When the economic relations change, the political forms and ideas change accordingly. This has been the history of society's development as it went through the various stages of primitive communal life, chattel slavery, feudalism, and capitalism. And now we believe that the transition from capitalism to socialism is just as inevitable.

"Each stage of historical development has its own form of political and social institutions, which are replaced by a new form when the economic system changes. . . . This law of change is a fundamental law of historical development, and takes place independently of man's will or desires. In other words you cannot change an economic or political system simply by wanting to; such a change only comes as a result of a historic process when the social conditions are ripe for it. . . .

"Society in each stage is divided into classes, with the class that owns or controls the means of production being the dominant or ruling class. The state is an instrument of that class which exploits those who do not own or have control of the productive machinery. In this sense, every government is a dictatorship to a greater or lesser degree. . . . Under modern capitalism the big capitalists control the state machinery to rule over and exploit the working class, that is, make profit from their labor. . . . The conflict in interest between the exploiting class and those exploited by it results in a class struggle. . . . This inevitably results, when social conditions are ripe, in a new class coming to power, introducing a new and higher economic and social system, and new political forms. . . .

"We regard the capitalist economic system as outmoded, even though in its early days it was the most advanced and progressive system of its time, and it introduced the most advanced political democracy of its time. In the present phase, modern capitalism has developed into imperialism, which if it can be described in a phrase, means the rule of monopoly capital, that of the big trusts and banks and corporations, which has destroyed the free competition of early capitalism, oppressed colonial countries . . . and breeds fascism and wars.

"In the evolution of society, revolution is that stage of the historical process when political power is transferred from one class to another, and society is transformed from one mode of production to a more advanced mode. Thus the English Revolution of 1649, the French Revolution of 1789, the American Revolution of 1776 represented the coming to power of a new and progressive class and the rise of capitalism. The Russian Revolution of 1917 represented for the first time the working class coming to power and the establishment of socialism.

"Revolution is the inevitable result of social forces at work, and not the brain child of individuals or groups. It is not the mere replacing of one government by another, and does not necessarily denote the use of force and violence. Revolutionary social changes can take place by peaceful and constitutional means. The frequent reference of Marxist classics to the use of force and violence is because historical experience has shown that no privileged class has ever given up its power without resistance, and has frequently used force and violence to prevent the democratic will of the people from being exercised peacefully. From this, Marxists draw the conclusion and predict that violence may be used by those in power against any attempt at fundamental social change, not because Communists or the people desire it or advocate it, but because history has taught that this usually happens. There is a great difference between such a prediction and the advocacy of the overthrow of the United States Government by force and violence.

"Marxist predictions regarding force and violence are based on two types of historical circumstances: one, when a majority was suppressed by a tyrannical dictatorship, violence occurs when the people no longer have any peaceful constitutional means open to them, as in the case of the French Revolution, the American Revolution, the Russian Revolution and the great colonial revolutions sweeping Asia. Second, when a new democratic government uses its constitutional powers to introduce sweeping social changes which encounter the resistance of former ruling classes or parties, this resistance may take the form of illegal violence when the classes or groups being deprived of their former privileges defy the constitutional authority of the new government, which then is compelled to use force. This is approximately what happened in our own Civil War and in the more recent Civil War in Spain in 1936. . . .

"Everything I have said about our teachings summarizes what I testified to in my citizenship trial as to my beliefs and my understanding of the principles of Marxism-Leninism. . . . We taught that as long as democratic processes are open, force and violence is against the interests of the people, because it is used against the people, and being a working-class party, we seek to avoid it because workers would be the first victims of such violence. . . .

"One of our fundamental principles is that we distinguish between democracy and fascist rule. Even though under capitalism the real power is in the hands of big capital, and democracy for the people is limited in a hundred different ways, we teach the necessity to defend a form of government where democratic rights exist against any attempt to overthrow it by force and violence. We teach that such a threat comes only from fascism, which means the open terrorist rule of the most reactionary sections of big capital.

"Ever since the coming of Hitler to power, we have warned that the danger of fascism might come to our country, too, and overthrow American democracy. We will show that we are pledged to defend the American form of government against any such threat should it come, and that there is no conflict between such a pledge and our fundamental criticism of the government, and our desire to bring about fundamental changes in the economic and social system."

I turned to the question of our attitude to war, anticipating that the prosecution would quote Lenin's slogan "Turn the imperialist war into civil war" in Czarist Russia. We were still in the midst of the Korean War, which, unpopular though it was, was able to generate enough jingoism to feed the anti-Communist crusade.

"We have always taken the position that we would defend the United States from aggression and attack, but that in the event of our engaging in an imperialist war, we would exercise our right to express our opposition and work for a just and democratic peace, as Abraham Lincoln did when as a Congressman he spoke up against the Mexican-American war.

"Marxism-Leninism distinguishes between just and unjust wars. We regard a war for national independence, as when a colonial country seeks its freedom from an imperialist power, as a just war. We regarded the Second World War as a just war to defend democracy against fascism.

"But we would oppose an imperialist war, whether waged by our nation or any other, as an unjust war that is waged for profit and conquest. . . . The Communist Party of the United States, at the outbreak of the Korean war and since, expressed our opposition to this war as an unjust war; we used the democratic process to oppose our involvement and to call for the withdrawal of our troops; and from the beginning we have demanded a cease fire pending peace negotiations by the big powers through the United Nations."

The judge was getting impatient and inquired how much longer I would take. I could see that the jury was getting weary, and so was I. But there was still the question of the Party being named as an illegal conspiracy, the matter of the underground, and what was taught at the meetings which were charged against me as overt acts in the indictment. I hastened on.

"We will establish that the Communist Party is a working-class political party that has carried on public activities for over thirty years, and that its roots go back to the early socialist, trade union, and abolitionist movements in our country. We will show that this party is guided by its own understanding and interpretations of the principles of Marxism-Leninism, and their application to the specific situation in the United States. . . .

"We will prove that although Communists of all countries have a common world outlook and learn from the historical experiences of all countries, we proceed from the belief that some nations may follow different paths of historical development than others; and we are also guided by our own American history.

"We will show that we taught that concern for our country's welfare is not in conflict with our feeling of international solidarity with the workers of other lands, as expressed in the following words of Lincoln in a letter to Karl Marx: 'The strongest bond of human sympathy outside the family relation should be one uniting all working people of all nations and tongues and kindred.'

"We will show that we were not engaged in an illegal conspiracy as charged when the Communist Party pioneered in organizing workers into trade unions; or when during the Depression it was the first party to put in its platform the demand for unemployment insurance; or when it raised sharply to the attention of the nation the whole question of equal rights for the Negro people; or when we first sounded the alarm against the danger of fascism and war.

"We will establish, through the specific overt acts charged against me, that during the period from 1940 to 1945, the Communist Party followed a policy which we believed would defeat fascism and avert war, and when war could no longer be averted, supported the war as a just war and did everything in its power to help win it. . . . The essence of our program was to support President Roosevelt's policy based on the friendship and cooperation of America, Britain, and the Soviet Union to guarantee the defeat of the German Nazis and the Japanese militarists. . . .

"We will show that others of the overt acts . . . consisted of meetings where there was a discussion to the effect that since the death of President Roosevelt there was a danger that his war policies and his postwar aims would be abandoned by the Truman administration; that this would result in an appeasement of the German and Japanese fascist leaders, and the preservation of their trusts and war industries for future war-making.

"The evidence will show that a further overt act charged against me is a convention in July, 1948, of the Communist Party of California, to which I delivered a report in my capacity as State Chairman. The platform adopted by the convention characterized the policies of the Truman Administration and of both major parties as war policies dominated by big business. It warned against the abandonment of the Roosevelt concept of American-Soviet friendship as the way to world peace. It opposed our playing ball with the very fascist elements who were so recently our mortal enemies in the last war. The convention declared that war and fascism are not inevitable, and that the central task of the Party was to fight for peace, and against the revival of fascism. It outlined an election policy to form a people's coalition for peace and urged support for the newly formed third party, the Progressive Party, in the 1948 election. . . .

"The indictment referred to meetings in '49 and '50 where the decisions were to build a united front with others of different parties who advocated peace as we did, and who opposed repressive legislation. . . . These meetings adopted a policy of forming election coalitions with independent Democrats and Republicans who opposed the administration's foreign and domestic policies, went on record against proposed repressive legislation aimed at outlawing the Communist Party, and took note of the fact that even the attorney general's office expressed doubts as to its being constitutional. And the evidence will establish that in my speeches at these meetings I stressed that the Communist Party would fight against being driven underground, but would fight to retain its legal status and its constitutional rights as a political party. . . .

"The evidence will establish that the latest overt act charged against me in the indictment was a meeting of the Communist Party on April 6, 1950, which devoted itself largely to a discussion of the Party's policy on the Negro question. We condemned the national oppression of the Negro people, which subjected them to discrimination, disfranchisement, and lynchings. We raised among the main demands in our 1950 election platform: passage of a Fair Employment Practices Law; for the abolition of poll taxes; for the passage of federal legislation to punish lynchings. But the basic question of policy that we raised was that the Negro people were entitled to representation in the government at all levels; and that, therefore, a number of Negro candidates, regardless of party affiliation, should be supported for the state legislature and for Congress.

"That was the essential character of the overt acts charged against me; they were the actions of the Communist Party, and my actions; they were what I advocated, and what the Communist Party advocated. They were the actions that flowed from the principles of Marxism-Leninism that we taught.

"Now, these actions dealt with everyday immediate issues. The prosecution charges that these everyday activities were for the purpose of shielding and preparing an alleged conspiracy to achieve our ultimate goal. We will prove this charge false. We will show that we taught that socialism could only come to the United States when the majority of the people wanted it; that while our country is economically ready for socialism, the majority of the people do not yet accept it; and that until they do, we do not see socialism as an immediate issue. Rather we see our task as education to explain what socialism is, and it is our belief that in the course of economic and political struggles the working people would come, from their own experience, to understand the need for socialism, provided there was a Communist Party to lead the way . . . . The danger of force and violence comes not from the Communists, but from the advocates of fascism and atomic war; what we advocate is that the American people use their constitutional and democratic processes to save our country from such disaster; and this is the real issue for which we are being tried. . . .

"And may I conclude with one final word to you. Since as the court told you we are presumed to be innocent unless proven guilty, you must bear in mind that when the prosecution comes before you and speaks in the name of the United States government, this should not weigh against the defendants; this is not the first time in a trial, from my experience, that the prosecution, speaking in the name of the United States government, has been proven wrong, and the defendants vindicated. The decision will be in your hands."

13 Trial by Fury

As we waited for the prosecution to bring in its first witness, we wondered: which trusted comrade would they spring on us? What horrendous tales would he tell? What nonexistent "secrets" would he reveal? What did the FBI have on him? The pattern had already been established in the first Smith Act trial, and in numerous sessions of the House Committee on Un-American Activities. A discredited method, but unfortunately it still worked in political trials of this kind. The first two witnesses, however, were innocuous; The fireworks were to come later.

David "Butch" Saunders was a seaman first-class, a former waterfront organizer of the Party in the thirties, blacklisted from working on ships when the cold war broke out. After agreeing to testify, he received clearance, was reinstated, and was now a ship's officer (a position he could never have dreamed of achieving when he was organizing seamen).

A short, balding man with a cocky manner and a defiant air when he glanced at the defendants, he testified about a number of meetings which various defendants attended, so that the prosecution could establish their membership in the Party and their titles. He was also used to identify a number of Party books and articles which the prosecution wanted to introduce into evidence, including an article of mine on "The United Front Against Fascism."

So eager was he to earn his pay that he identified the defendant Ben Dobbs as having attended the 1945 State Convention of the Party, and he was quite positive about it until Dobbs's attorney, Leo Branton, brought out on cross-examination that his client's discharge papers from the army showed that he was stationed in Europe until 1946.

From the very beginning, Judge Mathes intervened repeatedly to protect the witness. He complained that the cross-examination was going too slowly, telling Norman Leonard: "Speak faster, like a radio commentator." Leonard, who conducted his cross-examination in a sharp incisive manner, retorted: "I'm not speaking on the radio. I am defending my clients on a serious charge."[1]

At another point, when Saunders named a nondefendant as "known to be a Communist," Ben Margolis objected to the prosecution introducing hearsay evidence against people who would then be characterized by the government as "unindicted co-conspirators"; the judge overruled the objection.

But it was against Leo Branton, the Black attorney, that Mathes showed his most blatant bias. He repeatedly mispronounced his name, variously calling him "Bratton," or "Brayton"; it was only after Margolis protested against this arrogant behavior that the judge subsided.

Lloyd Hamlin was an FBI agent who was in the Party for seven years, his primary income being $250 a month as a "confidential informant." The government introduced a number of additional pieces of Marxist literature through him, which he testified he had bought while in a Party club. The prosecution then proceeded to read selected passages dating back many years, containing such ominous-sounding phrases as "overthrow all existing social conditions" in the *Communist Manifesto*, or "revolutionary overthrow" in *Foundations of Leninism*.

But while the judge permitted the prosecution to repeat the same quotations from Marxist classics three or four times, his demeanor managed to convey to the jury that the questions regarding these passages put by the defense on cross-examination were a waste of time.

Attorney Al Wirin opened his cross-examination by asking Hamlin about a number of party documents dealing with the current campaigns and activities of the Party over the past few years, but the witness, who showed a remarkable memory about all the government exhibits, suddenly found his memory failing him.

LEONARD: Directing your attention to the article Mr. Binns (U.S. Attorney) made reference to: Do you remember that being discussed when this article was distributed? (Reading) "Defense of the Party," by William Schneiderman, *Political Affairs* magazine, October, 1946. "It has demonstrated that the Party teaches and advocates not force and violence but principles in keeping with the most advanced thought and aspirations of mankind and with the best American revolutionary tradition."

A. I do not remember the article.

WIRIN: The only documents you remember are the documents which were offered in evidence by the government? You have no recollection of a single document circulated in 1948? Will you tell us just one, not every one, just one, please?

A. No. At the present time I don't remember.

COURT: Do you propose to go into everything in all these campaigns?

WIRIN: Not at all, Your Honor. It is important that we show that these defendants as Communists were engaged in seeking or opposing legislation . . . the same as is done in every other political organization. . . . Here is the problem. The government talks about force and violence, and picks out a few catch phrases here and there, out of context, and hopes to give the impression that that is all this organization did was preach force and violence. It is our function to attempt to demonstrate that is a distortion, and we can do it only by showing what the defendants really taught.

While Margolis was cross-examining, testing Hamlin's understanding of *Foundations of Leninism*, about which he had elaborated, Mathes interrupted:

COURT: What difference does it make whether this witness understands it?

MARGOLIS: I want to find out if he understands the subjects that are covered here . . . .

COURT: He does not claim to understand it.

MARGOLIS: He says he does in part, Your Honor. He testified . . .

COURT: Well, I do not want you to be making your own resumé of the witness's testimony.

When Branton objected to the prosecution's reading to the jury from government exhibits after the witness had left the stand, Mathes inquired, "What difference does it make whether the witness is on the stand or not?"

BRANTON: It makes a great deal of difference to us because we might want to examine the witness from the very testimony which is read from the books. . . . I can hardly imagine a document introduced through a witness which I would not like to have the privilege of examining the witness upon that particular document.

COURT: Objection overruled.

Alexander Schullman, whose practice consisted of respectable labor unions, and who thought that, therefore, the judge might look more kindly on him, rose on one occasion with Webster's Dictionary in his hand.

SCHULLMAN: I want to read from the word "revolutionary."

COURT: No, I won't permit that, Mr. Schullman.

SCHULLMAN (to witness): Let me ask you this. You had a specific job you were doing at the behest of the FBI, for which you were paid, and which you desired to do?

COURT: Are you testifying?

SCHULLMAN: No, Your Honor, it is preliminary.

COURT: Just ask him the questions and move along, Mr. Schullman.

SCHULLMAN: . . . Then as a matter of fact you were deliberately falsifying on these occasions?

COURT: No, you do not need to go any further than that. Now, I will limit you on that type of examination.

John Lautner, a former New York Party functionary who had been expelled two years before as a stool pigeon, was the next witness. Since his expulsion he had been traveling around the country testifying at various anti-Communist hearings, and was a star witness before the Subversive Activities Control Board in Washington. His ambition, he was forced to admit in cross-examination, was to write a book exposing the "Communist conspiracy," an enterprise which promised a great deal of profit to stool pigeons. (The FBI agent Philbrik, for example, had received $75,000 for his book *I Led Three Lives*.)

Lautner's testimony about a national Party school did not appear to involve any of the defendants, and when queried about its relevancy, the government prosecutor tried to justify it by saying that the New York school was an "arm" of the National Committee of the Party, and one of the defendants, Schneiderman, was a member of that same National Committee. By this strained reasoning and such remote connections was the web of "conspiracy" woven!

We were puzzled about the purpose of the prosecution in bringing him into this trial, but we soon found out. Lawrence K. Bailey, the special assistant to the attorney general from Washington, was examining him about one instructor, an assistant professor at Columbia University, who was teaching general science at the Party school.

LAUTNER: He was supposed to give a lecture one Saturday in the Museum of Natural History in New York, and he couldn't make it because, he said, he was going to Schenectady that weekend to the General Electric laboratories there to smash atoms.

MARGOLIS: The obvious purpose of this is just to create prejudice, (it has) no relation to any issue in this case, and we therefore move to strike the volunteered statement of the witness.

BAILEY: Your Honor, I intended to ask him about this conversation he just now volunteered.

COURT: Motion denied.

BAILEY: I ask the court to take judicial notice that the first notice that the American people had of the atomic bomb was at the time of its dropping on Hiroshima on August 6, 1945, a period of four years later, Your Honor.

MARGOLIS: We object to this on the ground it is immaterial, and it points up the immateriality of the last answer, Your Honor.

COURT: It is an historical event.

MARGOLIS: But this whole thing is an attempt to create bias and prejudice and has no other purpose.

WIRIN: Are we going into the whole question of the atomic bomb?

COURT: No, it is an historical event of which the court is asked to take judicial notice. Is there any dispute about that?

WIRIN: There is not, except, Your Honor . . . .

COURT: I do not know whether it will relate to anything in the progress of this trial.

MARGOLIS: But our reason is that there is an attempt to throw out inferences having no relevancy to any issue in this case, it seems to me, and the court should keep it out.

COURT: Gentlemen, let's proceed.

SCHULLMAN: May I address the court to add, also, that judicial notice be taken that the bomb was dropped by the United States and not by any of these defendants or anybody connected with the defendants. As long as we are getting some immaterial matter in . . . .

COURT: I don't know. This event is that it was dropped by the United States Air Force.

SCHULLMAN: May I ask now that the court also take notice of the fact that it was not dropped by, or at the instance of, these defendants.

COURT: Are you testifying, Mr. Schullman? I don't want any more voluntary statements of that character from counsel. Your request is denied. The jury will decide.

Only a year before our own trial, the Rosenberg case was making sensational headlines about "atom spying," which were still fresh in most people's minds, and the appeal was still pending in the appellate courts. Although Lautner's testimony on this matter was to be stricken from the record at the end of the trial, with instructions to the jury to ignore it, we knew the damage had been done. As Al Wirin reminded the court, quoting Supreme Court Justice Jackson on conspiracy and prejudicial effects: "The naive assumption that prejudicial effects can be overcome by instructions to the jury, all lawyers know to be unmitigated fiction."

Norman Leonard also asked the court to take judicial notice that, according to the *World Almanac* of 1941, the world premiere of the splitting of the atom took place in 1940, a full year before the incident which Lautner related, so the "secret" was well known. But we had no illusions that the members of the jury would wipe it out of their minds.

Lautner served another purpose for the prosecution. In order to bolster their "conspiracy" charge, he was asked to testify about the Party "underground" as though it had some illegal purpose as outlined in the indictment. But on cross-examination his story fell apart.

MARGOLIS: Was the main purpose (of the underground) to fight its way back to legality?

LAUTNER: That was not the main purpose.

Margolis then read to the jury Lautner's testimony before the Subversive Activities Control Board, only a month before: "It was necessary to have a structure even if the Party is driven underground, to have an organizational force that can fight its way back to legality."

The witness had stated that part of the sinister scheme to build an underground apparatus was to have a number of small mimeograph machines placed in various members' houses. Wirin queried him:

Q. The purpose of having an inexpensive machine . . . was so that if Dorothy Healey's home were raided by vigilantes or storm troopers or political police and the machine was smashed, it could be replaced comparatively easily and at small cost?

A. That was not the consideration.

Q. The matter of raids on a home and seizure of the mimeograph machine or the smashing of it was not contemplated?

A. No. This is an over-melodramatization. That was not even considered.

Q. Didn't you have the understanding when this system was put into effect and was used in France, precisely that happened, namely, that storm troopers invaded a person's home who was suspect of being a Communist and mimeograph machines and printed materials were seized and smashed? Is that overdramatic and untrue?

A. That is right.

But after persistent additional questions on the subject, and after some hedging, Lautner finally admitted that Bob Thompson (New York Party organizer) had told him about the French experience. (We in California did not have to go that far afield; we could recite our own experiences in 1934, when vigilante raids smashed our printing presses at the time of the San Francisco General Strike.)

After the witness testifed that the Party would follow the example of the Russian Revolution, Margolis introduced Frederick Engels's preface to an edition of the *Communist Manifesto*, of which he was a co-author with Marx, and read the following: "The practical application of the principles will depend, as the Manifesto itself states, everywhere and at all times, on the historical conditions for the time being existing," and then asked the witness the following:

Q. Weren't you told that in the light of a study of Marxism-Leninism you had to draw your own conclusions about the problems of the Communist Party in the United States, and how socialism might be achieved in the United States?

A. That is what I was taught on the basis of my studies in the 1941 training school.

WIRIN: Do you remember (quoting the 1948 Party Convention resolution): "The special path along which the transition to socialism will proceed will be determined by the democratic choice and struggles of the American working class and its popular allies on the basis of the concrete conditions in the United States?"

A. I don't remember this exact clause.

But the political and moral deterioration of a stool pigeon was best exemplified when Lautner expressed his new assessment of fascism:

WIRIN: Today you believe that the statement that fascism is political banditry, provocation, and torture, and that it is barbarity and bestiality, is merely a figure of speech, is that right?

A. Today I believe that is a nice figure of speech.

Q. That is all it is?

A. Overemphasis, yes.

Q. How many Communists were fed into ovens in German concentration camps?

A. I don't know.

Q. Just two or three?

A. I don't know.

Q. What was your understanding when the underground system was being used by Communists in Germany as to the conduct of the Gestapo in the raiding of homes, in the seizing and smashing of mimeograph machines, and other printing equipment?

(Objection by the government attorney, Neukom)

Q. Was it your understanding that 25,000 Communists were murdered in France by the Nazis?

A. I have no recollection.

Q. Did you make a study of the persecution of the Jews in Germany under the Nazi regime?

A. No.

Q. Of the Jews in Spain during the Spanish Inquisition?

A. I have no recollection.

Q. Of the Underground Railway in the U.S.?

A. Well, that is historical stuff.

The courtroom was frequently so crowded that friends and relatives of the defendants could not get in to be seated. There was a special roped-off section, for which the court issued passes, supposedly for visiting lawyers and guests of the court. One day Ben Margolis noticed that in the roped-off section was sitting Norman Jacoby, editor of the notorious right-wing, redbaiting sheet *Alert*. Complaining angrily to the judge that relatives were unable to enter the courtroom, Margolis pointed at Jacoby in the roped-off section and asked, "How did he get in there?" "It's none of your business how he got there," Mathes replied.

It may well be that Jacoby had been tipped off to some juicy material for his red-hunting sheet that was anticipated from the next witness.

Daniel Scarletto was a study in the morality of a stool pigeon. He joined the Party as an FBI informant, he claimed, at a Party meeting. It turned out to be a wedding where he was a guest, and he turned in the names of the wedding party. Among others whose names he turned in were: an elderly lady, a Party member with whom he had struck up a friendship, ate free meals at her house, and who "treated him like a son"; Party members whom he had solicited for work on their houses (including the elderly lady's) for which they paid him; a neighbor, not a Party member, whom he persuaded to subscribe to the *People's World*.

Cross-examination further brought out that he had committed a falsehood on his voter's registration. According to his divorce papers, he was supposed to be suffering from a service disability, but he received no pension. He claimed to have been married to a woman in another state, but was not. One could only guess what the FBI held over his head.

When the defense attorney Leonard objected to Scarletto relating a conversation he had with an FBI agent, the United States attorney gave this explanation:

BINNS: This is being offered as evidentiary fact and not for the truth of anything that is said in any of these conversations.

LEONARD: If it is not offered for the truth of anything being said, then it is obviously irrelevant. . . . If the truth isn't relevant, then why is it being offered?

COURT: Objection overruled.

The witness had a convenient memory for what the prosecution wanted, but occasionally it tripped him up. When asked to identify a "Walter Martin" as having attended a Communist meeting in Los Angeles on May 1, 1950, he pointed to a spectator in the courtroom who turned out to be a Reverend Turner of the San Francisco Baptist Church, who was visiting the trial for the day with a delegation of observers from San Francisco.

He stated positively that Rose Kusnitz, one of the defendants, was at a Communist meeting in September 1951. Defense attorney Branton asked the court to take note of the embarrassing fact that the defendant Kusnitz was in jail at the time, from July to December 1951, fighting for bail before Judge Mathes. Branton turned to Scarletto:

Q. So, as a matter of fact, you know that you did not see Mrs. Kusnitz at that meeting, isn't that true?

A. I have letters from her. I saw her there.

But this sorry figure had been brought in by the prosecution for a purpose—to bolster Lautner's testimony about the "underground." When asked about when he had last met with the "underground," Scarletto replied dramatically, "Last night." When Margolis questioned him, it turned out to be simply a club meeting for which members had been cautioned to make sure they had not been followed. Cross-examination further brought out that his club was concentrating on the Mexican-American community, and its activity consisted of helping to fight cases of discrimination and fighting for jobs, housing, and against police brutality in the community.

His memory went conveniently blank on cross-examination. He did not remember a widely publicized incident in which a young Mexican-American boy was shot in the back by a policeman; but when cornered, he struck back.

MARGOLIS: It is a fact, is it not, Mr. Scarletto, that this club at practically every meeting discussed one or another aspect of the problems, such as housing, police brutality, playgrounds, things of that kind that affected the Mexican-American people, and tried to work out ways and means of doing something about it?

A. Along with sabotage (of) American airplanes . . . . I was told there was no need for sabotage while there was no war going on.

Now, such sensational testimony would surely have been brought out by the United States attorney in his direct examination if there were any truth to it. He must have been as startled as everyone else was when this extra little bonus was off-handedly

tossed into his lap, but strangely enough, he never pursued it on re-
direct examination. But Margolis did.

Q. Did you tell the government about this before you took the
stand?

A. I certainly did. It was in my report.

Q. And Mr. Binns (U.S. attorney) knew all about it when he put
you on the stand, is that right?

A. If he read my reports, he did.

Q. What else was there?

A. I had been on aircraft mechanical work in the Navy Air
Corps, and I said: "I really could keep a lot of planes on the ground
that should be in the air."

Now it was clear why Binns had asked nothing about this incident. If the incident happened at all, it was not any Communist in
the club, but the FBI agent, who had raised the question of sabotage and played the role of agent-provocateur.

MARGOLIS: Did you sabotage any airplanes?

A. You bet I never did.

Q. Do you know anybody in the Communist Party who ever
sabotaged any airplanes?

A. No.

Q. Isn't it a fact that their activities consisted of things that I
have enumerated, such as distributing leaflets, getting petitions
signed, getting delegations, sending letters, and doing things of
that kind?

A. Yes. It was everything to sway the masses.

The sensational items about atom bombs and sabotage were
featured in the press, and the atmosphere in the courtroom,
marked by frequent clashes of the defense with the prosecution and
the court, became highly charged. It did not reach the volatile level
of the first Smith Act trials, but in a more subtle way the judge was
able to do almost as much damage to the defense as Medina did
more blatantly in New York.

Mathes refused to strike this highly inflammatory testimony
from the record at the time. At the end of the trial, however, he
thought better of it. Always careful to avoid errors which might
lead to a reversal on appeal, he agreed to strike it out, but the
prejudicial effect on the jury could not be entirely rubbed out.

To prosecutor Neukom, who was reading to the jury
voluminous extracts from writings by Lenin and Stalin, the judge
said: "There is no suggestion here that anyone has indicted the
Communist Party as such . . . . There is no evidence suggesting that
any of these defendants taught them."

Nevertheless, Mathes accepted into evidence all the books and quotations introduced by the prosecution through its "expert" witnesses, which pointed, not to the defendants' opinions or activities, but to the conclusion that because it distributed this literature, the Communist Party itself was a conspiracy and that membership alone warranted prosecution, a conclusion that even the judge stated was not a valid one.

Often one paragraph from an entire book was read out of context, as when an Australian Marxist's book was quoted on the "seizure of power." When defense attorney Schullman protested that the book and the quotation had no relation to the United States, but referred to the French Revolution of 1789, and objected to reading one paragraph out of a book as misleading, the reply was, "The court will later instruct the jury"; but the desired effect on the jury was already achieved. On another occasion, the defense had to protest that this quotation, which the prosecution evidently thought was especially telling, was read four or five times from other books under different pretexts.

All the prosecution had to do to introduce these books as evidence was to prove that the witnesses, although ignorant of Marxist theory, had bought the books at a Party bookstore or club, or had used them as historical reference material in a class, and then proceed to read extracts from them. It counted on the cumulative effect of these references to historical revolutionary experiences to give the impression that the Party or the defendants were plotting revolution.

On the interpretation of this literature, the defense frequently sparred with the court.

MARGOLIS (to court, quoting Justice Murphy in the Schneiderman case): "Political writings are often over-exaggerated polemics bearing the imprint of the period and the place in which written."

COURT (to Margolis): That statement in the Schneiderman case is but a specific application of the time-honored rule that when two interpretations can be given to a state of facts, one innocent and one other guilty, the innocent interpretation should always be placed on it.

To bring the true interpretation of the Party's objectives into focus, the defense was able to introduce through the prosecution's reluctant witness an educational outline which showed what was really taught at the Party classes. The judge inquired as to its purpose.

MARGOLIS (to court): The outline says, we want a peaceful change. (The witness) Hamlin says a person in his class (said)

"We ought to stand them up against the wall and shoot them." (It) flies in the face of official declarations. . . . The government has no intention, no plan to producing this kind of proof (that) that person in San Diego may have ever talked to any of the defendants, seen them, been aware of each other's existence. The statement is not binding on the defendants. . . . In the Dennis case the Communist Party was not outlawed. It is a question of individual intent (as the judge himself stated in an amendment to the indictment).

. COURT (to Margolis): I don't think the government is suggesting these defendants be convicted just because they are members of the Communist Party or any other group. . . .

The educational outline in question contained quotations from William Z. Foster's *In Defense of the Communist Party*: (The Russian Revolution) "is not a blueprint or model for revolution in this country. . . . The Party seeks the most peaceful and democratic means for the ultimate achievement of socialism. . . . Marxism, as Lenin pointed out, is not a dogma, but a guide to action. . . . The classics are scientific guides. They must be read, however, in the light of actual situations. . . . Much new Communist theory is developing . . . American writings on Communism, if produced before the change in the world situation and in our political tactics, now have little more than historical value. . . . We cannot be judged fairly except upon the basis of writings and political activities that truly reflect the present line of the Party in relation to the political situation in the United States. . . .

"The Communist movement, in this country as well as abroad, has been going along on the practical working theory that in this period it has become possible in a whole number of democratic countries, including the United States, legally to elect democratic governments, which could, by curbing and defeating capitalist violence, orientate (sic) in the direction of building socialism."

The story that Timothy Evans, the next witness, told was a pathetic one. Under the gentle cross-examination of Leo Branton, the sordid methods of the FBI in using and exploiting the victims of racism came more fully to light. A Black, born in the South, Evans was a college graduate with a physical-education major, but couldn't get a job except as a laborer. After applying at ten or twelve schools, he worked one short semester as a coach at a Negro high school for $50 a month. He worked as a warehouse laborer for 35 cents an hour, and when there were no more jobs available, he moved to California, where he took odd jobs as a carpenter and milk-wagon driver.

He was unemployed when the FBI called on him in February,

1948. After agreeing to become an informant and joining the Communist Party, he was employed the same month by the State Department of Architecture.

Q. Did your employer know that you were a member of the Communist Party? (Objection by the prosecution sustained by the court).

Although the FBI told him he was doing this for his country, they still treated him as an inferior. They gave him only $10 a month at the start, but gradually increased the amount as he rose in the Party and produced more material for the FBI, until his incentive pay reached $125 a month plus expenses. (Hamlin received $250.) Evans paid no income taxes on these earnings, reporting it as "expenses"; when queried, he said the FBI had no objections to his not reporting his income.

He joined a Party club in the Black community of Oakland. A victim of racism himself, he showed no compunction about turning in the names of Black Party members to the FBI. He obtained subscriptions for the *People's World* in the Black community, and turned in the names of subscribers, some of whom lost their jobs.

In discussions in the club relating to discrimination, during which he related some of his own experiences in the South, it was brought out that 62 percent of the homes of Blacks were without running water. Among the activities in which the club participated or supported were: a tenants' council to fight for rent control; a fight for jobs on the Key (transit) system, which resulted in twelve Blacks getting jobs; the defense campaign for Jerry Newson and Willie McGee, frame-up victims; picketing of the Bank of America, which hired no Blacks; picketing of a minstrel show at a public school, as a result of which the school board agreed to withdraw the show. It supported a Black candidate for the Senate running on the Progressive Party ticket; circulated a petition against the extradition of a Black citizen wanted in Mississippi; and gathered signatures on a petition to the United Nations charging genocide against the Black population.

Although the witness denied turning in the names on the petitions, one of the signers by the name of Batista was visited by the FBI and warned to "be careful," following which he withdrew his name.

When a Black veteran by the name of Gary moved into a white neighborhood in Richmond and was threatened by a mob, the club helped mobilize 2000 people to surround and guard the home until the danger subsided.

All of these facts were drawn out of the witness on cross-examination. His direct testimony dealt again with Marxist classics and classes. When Norman Leonard took up the questioning, he asked:

Q. The instructor said that whenever the experiences of other countries do not fit the conditions in this country, we don't use them, didn't he say that?

A. Probably did.

Only once did he involve a defendant. He said that in a speech at a public meeting, Loretta Stack, speaking about discrimination against women, spoke to the effect that "women should take up arms side by side with the men . . . and bring about the dawn of socialism." Why didn't he report this on direct examination? he was asked. Didn't he say on direct that he recalled nothing further about the meeting? Was his memory "refreshed" after talking to the government attorneys the night before? Was he urged to volunteer this statement when the defense took him on? Despite Evans's denials, re-direct examination by the United States attorney revealed that during the recess they had discussed his previous testimony, and matters which the witness couldn't recall earlier were then elaborated in detail to patch up the story.

Stephen A. Wereb, the next witness, was asked by the FBI to join the Party in 1944. He received no salary as such, but received expenses up to $125 a month, no questions asked, including a $75 "anonymous" donation he claimed to have given at a meeting. He started out jauntily enough, but under the defense attorney's hammering he went to pieces, until he finally said to the court, "I don't feel very well," was excused from the stand, and a doctor was called.

Through him the government brought into the record some of Lenin's thirty-year-old writings on the Communist International, dealing with the postrevolutionary period in Soviet Russia and Europe in 1919. Aside from the fact that the Communist International itself was dissolved in 1943, the revolutionary phrases which the prosecution dwelt upon had no relevancy to the present situation in the United States. Margolis's objections that they were introduced solely to create bias, prejudice, and hysteria were denied.

After numerous objections, prosecuting attorney Neukom admitted: "That has been read many times (before)." When the defense was told by the court to wait till later to make motions to strike such testimony, defense attorney Schullman exclaimed: "You cannot strike from the jury's mind everything like that." (Much later, nineteen pages of testimony were struck from the record by the court, but it was a meaningless gesture as far as erasing the prejudice; in fact, it only served the purpose of reading the same objectionable material to the jury for a second time.)

Reporting about a 1945 convention of the Party, Wereb said that one delegate had spoken about revolution and "overthrow" of the system. (Motion to strike, as not binding on the defendants, denied).

Loretta Stack made a "fiery" speech. (The word "fiery" was stricken by the court.) Dorothy Healey spoke about the need for demonstrations, picketing of Congressmen, recruiting trade union members, and the re-education of Marxists. Schneiderman said, "he was willing to lead on to a more militant party."

Wereb was told in a class: "We should start a movement whereby we would bring the boys home, to demobilize fast, and do not interfere with the Chinese affair and the Chinese political activities by the assistance of U.S. troops."

Regarding a speech by Schneiderman in 1946 on foreign policy, prosecuting attorney Neukom used both fractured logic as well as fractured English.

Q. Was the A-bomb discussed?

A. Yes, and he said that the A-bomb policy of the Truman administration could only lead to the road of disaster.

(Motion to strike by the defense.)

NEUKOM: I think it ties in with being able to accomplish the ultimate goal (of overthrow) as speedily as circumstances permit. . . . It shows that they would describe certain wars as being just or unjust wars. . . . It, like the element of a strike, comes into the picture of this case when we note that catching the American people off-guard, such as no longer helping our allies, is going to have a tendency, maybe in degree, to overthrow the country . . . . This is not mere political discussion; this, we contend, is direct advocacy.

COURT: The jury must not be led to believe that some person's opinion on foreign affairs has anything to do with this trial.

NEUKOM: But, Your Honor, this is advocacy: Get out of China, don't let them have any more supplies, send them no more weapons. . . . They are not political discussions. They are advocacies. They are telling us "get out." They are characterizing in the wrong fashion, and even the Chiang Kai-shek case, many people believe that this war in China was wrong; that we should leave our ally China stranded at the mercy of the Communist hordes that were coming upon them. . . . And I think, Your Honor, that that testimony is part of this case, because inevitably as we lose an ally, just more speedily does this country become susceptible to this overthrow. . . . (quoting a government exhibit on the question of just and unjust wars) They italicize "just" and "unjust" wars.

SCHNEIDERMAN: (It was) 1946, we were not in the war, as the government misrepresented. . . . Ever since the end of the war there has been considerable public debate on the question of our policy toward China . . . and some pretty sharp characterizations of what the Chiang Kai-shek government was, as to its reactionary character. . . . Not only Communists but large sections of the American public and members of the State Department themselves participated, and very often our views even coincided. Now, to come before the court here and state that this evidence is to be admitted in order to impute disloyal motives (to the Communists) completely misstates the facts. The theory on which the government is trying to get this evidence into the record here is · based on misrepresentation.

NEUKOM: My representation of whether we were at war or not cannot now be misrepresented.

SCHNEIDERMAN: 1946, 1946, Your Honor.

COURT: One at a time, gentlemen.

SCHULLMAN: I think, Your Honor, we can take judicial notice that VE Day was in 1945, and VJ Day was the same year.

MARGOLIS: I think that the government's theory of this case is now fully revealed . . . that anybody who disagrees with the foreign policy of the United States is subject to being prosecuted under the Smith Act; that anything which is labeled "Communistic"—and what is it that has not been?

COURT: Let us save that argument for the jury.

Although the motion to strike the testimony was denied, the court deleted it later in the trial.

The witness also told about a strike at U.S. Motors Corporation, and that an appeal for pickets was made by the defendant Connelly at a Party club meeting, although the number of pickets was limited by court order. In answer to an objection by the defense that this was purely a trade union matter, the prosecutor explained its bearing:

GOVERNMENT ATTORNEY: I think it ties in with being able to accomplish the ultimate goal (of overthrow) as speedily as circumstances permit.

MARGOLIS: The position that because the Communist Party supports the strike, that strike can be used as evidence under the Smith Act, is the first step to outlawing strikes altogether and again is an indication of where this leads—that evidence of support of a strike is to permit the utilization of this case to begin with the destruction of all trade unions.

U.S. ATTORNEY BINNS: I think the government is entitled to show that these people intend to bring about the things they are teaching. . . . The same thing with the Chinese situation. A citizen of the United States can express himself on the China situation. Nobody questions that. But these people do it very peculiarly. They call it an imperialist war . . . that means start the revolution.

SCHNEIDERMAN: Even if the court should instruct the jury to disregard that (testimony), without showing to the jury that Connelly was there as a CIO official, it seems to me that going into the question of the picket line any further would be highly prejudicial to him.

COURT: What does the government have to say to the observation of Mr. Schneiderman?

NEUKOM: We will confer on that.

The court granted the motion to strike the testimony.

On cross-examination, Wareb began to stumble almost immediately. He tried twice to point out and identify the defendant Lima and failed.

NEUKOM: May the record show that he did not identify Lima?

MARGOLIS: May the record also show that he first identified the bailiff (as Lima)?

COURT: That is a matter of argument.

As the defense proceeded, he became more unnerved. He admitted that in addition to running a typewriter service, he took a second job as a policeman in 1946, and carried a gun. He would sell used typewriters to Party members, and turn in their names to the FBI. He gave different dates for alleged meetings and classes than he did on direct examination. He said he "drifted out" of the Party, but actually he had been asked to leave.

When asked if his alleged $75 "anonymous" contribution to the Party had been reported as an expense to the FBI, he answered it was in an "oral report." (Up to that point, all reports had been "written.") He was evidently wary that the defense might demand to see the written report.

The United States attorney became nervous and complained that the defense had spent half an hour on these questions. Defense attorney Schullman retorted that it was a matter of testing the credibility of the witness. As the latter got deeper into trouble, the court intervened and sharply upbraided the defense.

COURT: Don't spend time with this sort of matter.

SCHULLMAN: I submit this is very relevant and pertinent.

COURT: I don't care to have you waste time on trivial matters.

BRANTON: I would like to object to Your Honor's characterization of this as a trivial matter. Mr. Schullman is attempting to impeach the witness by showing prior inconsistent statements . . . and has shown they are of consequence.

COURT: Please be seated. You have stated your objection, Mr. Branton.

BRANTON: May I state my objection for the record, Your Honor?

COURT: You have stated your objection. I don't care to hear any argument.

Wereb had spent two hours the night before with the prosecutor Neukom going over his testimony. He then tried to explain why he pointed to the bailiff, and then to the defendant Lambert, and identified each of them as Lima.

WEREB: I pointed to the top of his head.

MARGOLIS: Were you relying on your best recollection?

WEREB: I have tried to.

MARGOLIS: In the same way that you relied on your best recollection when you testified concerning conversations of others that occurred five years ago?

COURT: You know better than to ask that kind of question.

The witness for some reason insisted on placing me at frequent meetings in Los Angeles. (Being stationed in San Francisco, I visited Los Angeles for a meeting only three or four times a year.)

Q. When is the next time that you recall having seen Mr. Schneiderman (at functionaries' meetings)? He appeared there and spoke seven or eight times?

A. He appeared everywhere and he spoke everywhere, sir.

Q. What other occasions do you recall?

A. Mr. Margolis, I am only a human being. I wouldn't know how often Mr. Schneiderman popped up at every functionaries' meeting.

COURT: Let's don't spend any more time on this sort of thing.

MARGOLIS: I have a reason for it.

COURT: You may have, but I am going to limit the cross-examination if you keep it up. Proceed.

MARGOLIS: Can you recall one meeting (in 1947)?

A. Not 1947. I wouldn't right at the present moment unless I had some way to refresh my memory, sir.

Q. Did you have anything to refresh your memory yesterday (on direct examination)?

(Objection by the prosecution)

MARGOLIS: Yesterday he remembered the date. Today he does not.

COURT: I don't care to hear any more argument from either side.

Q. Did Mr. Schneiderman speak at that meeting?

A. Mr. Schneiderman spoke at every meeting. He appeared everywhere and he spoke everywhere.

Wereb remembered classes where revolution was taught, but could not remember the quotation from a government exhibit of the Workers' School which read:

"At the same time the Communists of the capitalist countries must never overlook the fact that they have to fight under other historical concrete conditions than those obtaining in Tsarist Russia. For all these reasons, the Communists in the capitalist countries must not blindly follow the experiences of the Communist Party of the Soviet Union when solving their concrete political tactical and organizational tasks, must not apply these experiences mechanically to the conditions of their countries and their labor movements."

LEONARD: Do you recall what outline was used in the Workers' School?

A. May I, with all apologies, state, sir, that it was all way over my head. I did not even know what a Communist looked like actually until I met one.

Q. You mean now you can tell a Communist by looking at him?

A. Oh, you bet.

Q. And you attended these classes solely for the purpose of obtaining the names of people who attended those classes and for solidifying your position in the Communist Party?

A. Well, first to solidify—pardon me. First to get all the information for the interest of the government of the United States.

Q. All the information that the FBI asked you to get?

A. To find who those persons were, what did they say.

Q. How did you decide what to listen to and what to report?

A. I have been an American for fifty-five years, sir, and I know Communist Bolshevik talk, anti-American talk, and I don't believe that any of those are part of the system of our government.

Q. You are opposed to everything that the Communist Party stands for?

A. Not exactly.

Q. As a matter of fact, (at) those classes you listened hardly at all?

A. I listened to everything whereby a point was driven home.

Q. The fact is, however, that you just listened to points that were being made, and other things you didn't listen to, is that right?

A. Some points I did not deem that it was anything more than the same hash over and over.

Q. What was the general subject matter of this series of classes? Can you give any indication of what subject matter was covered?

A. With all apologies to you, Mr. Margolis, I never knew and I still don't know a darn thing about Marxism and Leninism, and I pray that I never do.

MARGOLIS: That wish will probably be granted.

COURT: Proceed, Mr. Margolis. I care for no further comments of that kind on the witness's testimony. That last remark will be stricken from the record.

Q. Do you recall a class about revolution?

A. I do, sir.

Q. Can you fix the time to the best of your ability?

A. To be sincere with you, at this time, Mr. Margolis, I don't believe I could.

Q. Do you recall fixing the time of that yesterday (on direct examination)?

A. Your Honor, I just don't feel well.

NEUKOM: Your Honor, this witness has a bad heart. May we have a recess?

MARGOLIS: I am sorry. I certainly—

COURT: You may step down. You are excused for the day, Mr. Wereb.

When the witness took the stand again, the defense returned to the 1945 Party convention, where he said a delegate had talked about revolution.

Q. Directing your attention to the statement made at the convention by Mr. Goldstein, he urged that there should be a revolution of the workers in the United States and the overthrow of the government?

A. That is the exact wording, sir.

Q. Did he say that that should be done immediately?

A. He didn't specify a date, sir.

Q. He didn't say when it should be done?

A. No, sir, he did not.

Q. Whether in the remote future or now, is that right?

A. He didn't say that, sir.

Q. Did he say what method should be used to accomplish that?

A. I don't recall him telling the method, sir.

Q. I will ask you whether or not it is a fact this Mr. Goldstein about whom you testified . . . was not thereafter expelled from the Party.

A. It will be an affirmative answer, yes. He was expelled for left sectarianism.

The witness then gave a bizarre description of the discussion.

Q. Nobody at this convention spoke of socialism?

A. No, sir. The theme of each one's speech was never emphasis on socialism . . . it was all communism or bolshevism. Those are the words that were the most popular. Socialism was quite taboo, because they might confuse it with Trotskyism, sir.

Q. So that it was your understanding of that convention that the people were opposed to talking about socialism, because that would get them into Trotskyism?

A. Yes, I believe that's it, to a certain extent . . . . if you were married to a non-Communist, they put the pressure on you, that you either divorce the Party or divorce your wife. In fact, I was given that choice, one of the two.

Q. Was your wife a member of the Communist Party?

A. No, sir.

Q. Were you ever expelled from the party because your wife was not a member?

A. No, sir.

NEUKOM: Would Your Honor inquire if the witness feels all right?

COURT: Are you feeling all right?

WITNESS: Fine, sir, never felt better.

COURT: Suppose you sit up, then, in the chair and we won't be so worried about you.

When Norman Leonard took over the cross-examination, Wereb continued to founder on his contradictory testimony.

Q. Isn't it a fact that in November 1946 at the Embassy Auditorium, Mr. Schneiderman wasn't there at all?

A. I didn't exactly—I don't recall stating a month. . . . I might have.

LEONARD: If Your Honor please, I would like to read from the *People's World*, November 16, 1946, to the jury: "Citizens of Los Angeles today are being alerted to fight against the threat of a Republican drive to eliminate all rent control, following a resolution unanimously adopted at the . . . rally held last night. Approximately 1500 persons had heard the resolution read. Chief speaker of the meeting (was) Oleta O'Connor Yates."

Q. When was the meeting at which Mr. Schneiderman spoke? . . . Can you give me an approximate date?

A. It was in the fall of 1946. Will that be closer, Mr. Leonard?

Q. Actually, wasn't it March of 1947?

A. No, sir.

The witness stumbled into a new field of malfeasance when he was being questioned about a member who he said was running for the Party's state committee, but the convention ballot showed no such name.

Q. So he did not run for the state committee at that time?

A. If his name was not on there, Mr. Leonard, evidently he didn't.

Q. What did you do with the ballot after you voted on it?

A. My original ballot I turned over to the agent. . . and turned it back to the Party.

Q. Didn't you have to return these ballots to the Party?

A. Some of it I did and some of it I filched.

Q. That might have been one of those that you filched?

A. It may have been.

NEUKOM: Oh, Your Honor, we object to the characterization.

LEONARD: It is the witness's, Your Honor, not mine.

Q. During the time you were working for the FBI did you filch other papers?

A. Well, shall we say I forwarded other papers, then? Whenever I had a chance I did, sir.

Q. You had not received permission from the Party or from any of them whose papers they were, to take these papers did you?

A. I certainly did not.

COURT: Let us have the witness tell us what he means by "filched," and then we will know what he is talking about.

A. I meant by taking them on the sly, keeping them in my possession long enough for them to be turned in to the FBI.

Q. Is it your testimony that you took the document, wrote some notation on it, had it photographed, erased the written notation, and then returned it?

A. I believe that is what happened, Mr. Leonard.

Q. You gave these documents to the agent with whom you were working, and you told him, of course, how you had obtained them?

A. Well, that was no secret to them.

Q. He knew it?

A. Yes, he did.

Q. As a matter of fact, he suggested that this was a method in which you could get papers?

A. I don't believe anyone suggested anything to me, Mr. Leonard.

Q. At the time you were engaged in this process that you have told us about, you were an authorized representative of the FBI, is that right?

NEUKOM: Your Honor, that is objected to

SCHULLMAN: May I ask, Your Honor, a stipulation from counsel to the effect that he was an authorized representative of the FBI. There is a serious legal question.

COURT: Proceed.

LEONARD: Did you steal any papers while you were in the Communist Party?

A. Officially, I would not say steal them, sir.

SCHULLMAN: At this time we move to strike each and all of the government's exhibits introduced through the witness . . . on the grounds that the manner of acquisition as testified to by him is within the constitutionally proscribed area of unreasonable search and seizure.

COURT: Motion denied.

William Foard had been a clerk in a steel company warehouse when he joined the Party in 1945. He belonged to a club dominated by ultraleftists who were in constant disagreement with party policies and its interpretation of Marxist-Leninist theory, who were eventually expelled for their extreme leftist position.

When he dropped out of the Party in 1948, the FBI sought to get him to testify at the New York Smith Act trial.

LEONARD: When were you first approached (to testify)?

A. In about November or December 1951. I was approached by an FBI agent.

Q. Where did he approach you?

A. On my job.

Q. As a matter of fact, you were approached by agents of the FBI back in 1949 to testify in the New York trial, isn't that correct?

A. Right.

Q. And at that time agents of the FBI told you that they knew that you were on the outs with the Communist Party and wanted you to testify against the New York defendants, and you told them you would not testify, isn't that true?

A. That is true.

Q. And you had several conferences with the FBI. They even came to your house in an effort to get you to testify?

A. Yes.

Q. And they told you that if you did not testify, that you would be caused a lot of trouble?

A. That is not true.

Q. You discussed this matter with Jack Olson, and you told him that time that you were very much afraid of the FBI, isn't that true?

A. That is true.

Q. At that time you were not a member of the Communist party?

A. I was not.

Q. And you refused to testify, didn't you?

A. I did.

Q. Did your employers know that you had been a member of the Communist Party?

A. They did. They did.

Q. Between the 1949 conversations with the FBI and November

or December of last year, did they ever contact you at any time?

A. Every two or three months one of them would call up and ask if I knew a certain person during the time I was in the Party; if I knew where he was at present or where he worked.

Q. Would you answer those questions?

A. If I knew the correct answer, yes, I would.

Q. And you told Jack Olson at that time that you were considering testifying, doing what the FBI wanted you to do because you were afraid that your wife might be hurt?

A. That is true. My wife had reason to be afraid. I had to consider my wife's feelings.

Q. And you also considered your wife's feelings when you agreed to appear as a witness in this case, isn't that true?

A. That is true . . . . I didn't want the publicity that was entailed with it. He (Olson) said, "Well, you were right, but these men will not leave you alone. They will undoubtedly contact you again and again. I am going to make an appointment for you with one of the union attorneys."

It is on this background, with the FBI agent sitting in the courtroom, that the credibility of his testimony should be weighed. The prosecution opened the questioning about a meeting in February 1947 at which Foard claimed I spoke.

Q. Will you give me what Mr. Schneiderman said at that time?

A. He wanted to assure the members that the Party was still on a Marxist-Leninist line, that the left sectarians who had recently been expelled from the Party were like the horse that was too far ahead of the cart; . . . they wanted the Party to embark on adventurous campaigns that would lead to the destruction of the Party; . . . that revolution means violence and bloodshed, and he doubted if many of the Party members themselves were ready for revolution; . . . that it meant the loss of our own lives, and of course, these were expendable to achieve the ultimate goal of socialism, but the Party was just not prepared for revolution. . . . Those may not be the exact words, but they were words to that effect.

Q. Did Mr. Schneiderman say anything with regard to the ultimate goal of socialism?

A. Yes, the ultimate goal was the establishment of socialism and that socialism would only be established through violent revolution.

Up to this point, the quotations about violence and revolution had been brought in by the prosecution through the classics of Marx and Lenin, some of them going a hundred years back, generalizing the revolutionary experiences of a number of countries. The prosecution considered Foard's testimony of crucial importance because for the first time he was attributing the quotations about violence and bloodshed to a defendant in reference to the United States. But alas! his story was torn to shreds by the defense. First of all, was there such a meeting where this alleged speech was made?

MARGOLIS: It is a fact, is it not, that the only meeting held by the Communist Party in January or February of 1947 in that hall was this Williamson meeting?

A. It is not.

Q. This Williamson meeting was a public meeting?

A. That is a fact.

Q. It is a fact, is it not, that the speaker at this meeting was Mr. Williamson (of New York), not Mr. Schneiderman?

A. At the public meeting, yes.

Q. It is a fact, is it not, that the main subject of Mr. Williamson's discussion was the problem of the American labor movement?

A. I believe so, yes.

Q. Was the meeting which you testified Mr. Schneiderman attended and spoke at in February of 1947 held before or after the Williamson meeting?

A. I do not recall definitely, but it was held in January or February of 1947.

Q. Do you recall whether it was held about the same time within a week or two?

A. I believe so, yes, within two or three weeks.

Q. And it is your recollection that it was held in the same hall as the Williamson meeting? Is that true?

A. Yes. It was a second meeting held in January or February.

In spite of repeated questions, Foard stood firm on the date and place. But the records of the building, which we introduced later in the trial, showed that aside from the Williamson meeting, there was no other meeting booked by the Communist Party at that address for the entire year of 1947, and most of 1946. (As I told the jury in my summary, over the objections of the judge, this showed that no such meeting had taken place.)

Furthermore, cross-examination by the defense attorneys about discussions in Foard's club revealed that it was the super-leftists, later expelled for opposing the Party's policies, who raised the question of violence.

LEONARD: Were these two paragraphs (from the discussion of Lenin's *Revolution of 1905*) discussed in this club meeting?

A. Yes, I recall the one about the making of bombs and rifles. There was a humorous incident that took place at the time. Some of the members asked what we were going to use to make bombs with—ash cans and thermos bottles, and fountain pens and things of that nature? Of course, it was mostly in jest.

Leo Branton rose to object. These statements were made by third party declarations, with no defendants present, he told the judge, and would do "irreparable harm" if left in the record. The objection was denied, but the testimony was stricken from the record at the end of the trial. (Whether it was stricken from the jury's minds was another matter.)

Norman Leonard's cross-examination brought out that the only speech I made, at the address where Foard insisted he heard me speak about violent revolution and bloodshed, was a year earlier than he had placed me; and that, contrary to the witness, I had engaged in polemics at that meeting against the leftists' contention that war was inevitable and against their opposition to the Party's united front policy. It was a San Francisco general membership meeting at which their position was heatedly debated for two or three hours.

Q. What was the action of the group?

A. They voted overwhelmingly to expel the persons that were charged with anti-Party activity.

Q. The left elements that were expelled said a coalition was impossible because they conceived that the immediate task facing the American people was the overthrow of capitalism rather than the building of antifascist coalition, isn't that true?

A. True.

Q. The people who were expelled took the view that the Party should not participate in such election campaigns?

A. Correct.

Q. There came a time in the machinists' strike, when the men had been out six or seven months, the Communist Party urged that there be a settlement?

A. I believe so, yes.

Q. And the leftists who were later expelled urged, instead of settling the strike, that it be extended to become a general strike, isn't that true?

A. I believe so, because the strike had been lost.

Q. Another issue upon which the Communist Party and these leftist members differed very sharply was the settlement which the maritime unions made in June 1946, isn't that true?

A. I believe so, yes.

Q. The Communist Party supported that settlement?

A. True.

Q. But the leftist elements who were expelled differed and didn't support the settlement.

A. Right.

Q. They claimed that the strike in fact was political and it should have been pushed for political reasons?

A. I believe so.

Q. And the Communist Party took the view that since the economic demands of the workers had been satisfied, the Communist Party would support that settlement?

A. That's right.

The witness had close friends among the leftists, but claimed he dropped out of the Party in 1948 because he resented the fact that Ernie Fox, a defendant, had castigated him in the warehouse union for opposing the holding of a Labor Day parade. His own state of mind which led him to testify was indirectly revealed in the following exchange:

Q. You were told that frequently people who had been expelled became bitter enemies of the Communist Party; and there was a danger that this might lead them into becoming informers against the Communist Party; and for your own safety, so that you should not be informed against, it would be desirable for you not to have association with people expelled as leftists; that because some of them might have had loose moral character or some of them might have had arrests, they were more susceptible to pressure to turn informers, isn't that true?

A. Yes, that is true.

Q. And that because they fell out on a line of policy and because they might have become embittered, these other considerations then become important because they were points at which pressure might be put against those people to testify and to turn informer; and that such people could not be trusted and there was a danger that they might say anything that the authorities wanted them to say?

A. That is true. Right.

While the prosecution was trying to attribute the leftist's rhetoric to the Party and the defendants, the defense was able to show just the opposite, from literature acknowledged by the witness to have been discussed in the club. William Z. Foster was quoted as saying, "We are not getting rid of Browder's right opportunism to fall into a swamp of 'left' sectarianism."

MARGOLIS: You were told, were you not, that Mr. Foster had reached the conclusion that it appeared there were several paths leading to socialism, not just one path?

A. That is right.

Q. Isn't it a fact that you were told that Mr. Foster said that each country must take its own special circumstances into consideration in determining the character of the road to socialism?

A. Yes, I have heard that many times.

Q. Isn't it a fact you were told in these discussions that Mr. Foster said you find socialism being advanced by strengthening the democratic process?

A. I believe so, yes.

Q. Weren't you told that it was necessary, if socialism was going to come to the world before there was a catastrophic war, for the United States and the Soviet Union to agree upon a way of living together and to continue to be allies rather than enemies?

A. Yes, that was pointed out, but many of the members of the branch claimed that it was impossible.

Q. But there were other members of the branch who said to the contrary, isn't that right?

A. I think so, yes.

Q. And what did you say?

A. I wasn't much interested.

Q. Didn't he (Foster) say that it was a different pattern than the Soviet pattern that was contemplated in the United States?

A. I don't recall.

Q. Isn't it a fact that you were told in connection with the discussion that took place that the Communist Party took the position that in order to obtain the power of the state it had to first win the majority to its side?

A. Yes, there were words to that effect.

Q. Weren't you told that . . . socialism, because of the difference of development of production here, the different conditions (and) traditions which existed here, would be quite different than it was in the Soviet Union?

A. Yes. We were told that after the revolution, that the recovery to a socialist state would be much more rapid because we had greater natural resources, a greater development of industry, we had more trained workers.

Q. And you were told that there was a difference between building socialism in a country which had just been devastated by a war, as Russia had been, in which 95 percent of the people were illiterate, than building socialism in a country with great productive capacity, a much higher degree of literacy, and education of the people, isn't that so?

A. Yes, sir.

Q. As a matter of fact, Mr. Foster said, did he not, that any change from capitalism to socialism was a revolution, no matter how it was accomplished, isn't that right?

A. It was a revolutionary change, yes.

But did the club spend all its time discussing revolution? The witness reluctantly admitted that most of its activities were campaigning for price control and low-cost housing; that it fought for jobs for Blacks, and as a result forced the Woolworth stores and the National Dollar stores to hire blacks for the first time in the Fillmore district; and engaged in numerous legislative and electoral activities.

But this was dull stuff. To liven things up, the prosecution had attempted to introduce discussions about the 1905 revolution in Russia, and the Paris Commune in 1871, as though it applied to current events and the activities of the club.

MARGOLIS: Was "The Revolution of 1905" (a government exhibit) used as the subject of educationals?

A. No, as a guide to action.

Q. You were told that what the Communist Party was interested in doing was not simply talking about making the world better, but to do something about it, isn't that right?

A. Right.

Q. Did you make any notes with respect to what was discussed in 1946, six years ago (regarding a discussion on the introduction to the "Paris Commune")?

A. Yes, I did.

Q. Did you keep those notes?

A. No, I did not.

Q. Have you had anything to refresh your recollection concerning what happened six years ago?

A. Yes, I have. Last October or November, when I turned over some of the literature to the government, they asked me questions concerning some of the pamphlets.

Q. Is this a meeting that you just recalled, but weren't able to remember earlier in your cross-examination?

A. Yes.

Q. Something happened to refresh your recollection between today and yesterday about additional meetings you had?

A. No, nothing happened. It just arose now.

Q. Do you recall now that yesterday you were asked to identify passages in the Introduction to the "Paris Commune," that you said that discussion was with relation to imperialism?

A. I do.

Q. Do you recall that when Mr. Kinnison (government attorney) read a portion of the same passage a few days ago you said that the discussion was with relation to the 1934 strike?

A. I do.

Q. Is your memory better, Mr. Foard, as to what happened six years ago than it is as to what happened a few days ago?

U.S. ATTORNEY BINNS: I object to that, Your Honor.

COURT: Sustained.

Q. The fact is, Mr. Foard, that the Paris Commune, to your knowledge, does not relate in any way to the relationship between the day-to-day activities of your club and the question of revolution, isn't that a fact?

A. It may be a fact that it does not relate to the day-to-day activities of the club. Perhaps he just isn't as good a Marxist as you, Mr. Margolis.

Q. Did somebody suggest to you that you refer to me as a good Marxist?

A. They did not.

Q. Or was that your own idea?

SCHULLMAN: With permission of the court, I ask that the remark made by the witness with reference to any counsel, and particularly the counsel conducting the examination, be stricken as prejudicial to the defendants in this case.

COURT: Which remarks? The witness, as I understand it, said "perhaps."

SCHULLMAN: I ask that it be stricken.

COURT: Very well. Motion granted.

Judge Mathes was growing increasingly impatient as the defense hammered away at the witness. After further questions about "The Paris Commune," he broke into the questioning.

COURT: What difference does it make whether he remembers it or not?

MARGOLIS: I object, Your Honor, to that statement, because we think it goes to the question of credibility of the witness.

COURT: I must limit your cross-examination, Mr. Margolis, if you keep up on this subject.

Q. You were told (in Foster's *New Europe*) that private ownership generally was being abolished in a series of stages in these various countries of (Eastern) Europe, that is, private ownership of the means of production.

A. That's right; but that the Soviet Union may again, with their armed might, stand by and assure the abolishment (sic) of private ownership in the United States.

Q. As a matter of fact, you made that up sitting right there on the bench, on the witness stand, didn't you?

A. That is not so.

Q. Did you know that this discussion had taken place when you were on the stand testifying on direct examination?

A. That is right.

Q. Did you forget it at that time?

A. No, I did not. I intended to inject it at the same time, but there was some inter-squabble here among the counsel and I didn't manage to get it in.

Q. I am going to show you pages 4479 to 4481, and will you please point out in the record what squabble there was by counsel which prevented you completing your answer.

U.S. ATTORNEY BINNS: I object.

COURT: Sustained.

Q. What was the squabble between counsel which prevented you from completing your answer?

A. I wouldn't remember.

Q. But you definitely remember there was a squabble?

A. Not definitely, no.

Q. As a matter of fact, you did not bring it in, Mr. Foard, because it never happened, isn't that right?

GOVERNMENT ATTORNEY: I object to that line of questioning, Your Honor.

Q. Did anyone point out that what the leadership of your branch was saying about the inevitability of war was a direct contradiction to what the leadership of the Communist Party was saying?

A. No, I don't believe they did.

It was obvious to everyone, even to the prosecution, that they had blundered. They had attempted to attribute to the Party and the defendants the bombastic rhetoric and ultraleft line of a few people with whom the witness associated. By giving us an opportunity on cross-examination to contrast the Party's united front policy with the "instant revolution" ideology of the leftists whom the Party expelled, we not only destroyed the credibility of the prosecution's witness, but refuted the prosecution's charge as to what we advocated.

But they hoped to recoup by the cumulative effect of a list of additional witnesses. And they were saving the blockbuster for the last.

14 False Witness:
"Bombs and Booby Traps"

There was a welcome break in the trial during a long holiday weekend, but for some of us it brought no respite. Our national chairman, William Z. Foster, who had been severed from the New York trial because of heart trouble, and the only one of all the leaders who was free, had sent word that he wanted to discuss our trial policy with us. Since we had to consult with some New York attorneys on trial matters, we received the reluctant permission of the court for members of the Trial Committee to fly to New York for the weekend.

We outlined to Foster our position: we considered it crucial to bring out to the jury and the people at large that the issue was the right of advocacy, not the correctness of our views. We insisted that we would conduct a militant defense, despite Judge Mathes's provocations.

The Justice Department was determined to wipe us out. By the summer of 1952, Smith Act trials in fourteen cities with 140 defendants were on its agenda. While we had no illusions, we felt we had some advantages which the national leaders of the Party did not have in the first trial, not the least of which was the Supreme Court decision in the case of U.S. vs. Schneiderman. If anyone had a chance to win a victory, we had it—if not in the lower court, then on appeal. After hearing our first-hand report of the trial, Foster fully approved our policy. We heaved a big sigh of relief, and headed for home.

The prosecution continued its practice of introducing testimony about inflammatory statements allegedly made by individuals not on trial, when none of the defendants was present, without any foundation or corroboration beyond the word of a stool pigeon. When the witness Howard Charles Litt quoted somebody as saying "blood would flow in the streets," the defense objection that this constituted prejudicial error was brushed aside by the judge. His alert ear spotted what he thought was a defendant's involvement.

COURT: Was there any of the defendants present at that time?
A. No, not at that time.
COURT: You mentioned a woman by the name of Stack?
A. That is not the defendant Stack.

SCHULLMAN: We have reached a stage where we must know the ruling of the court. We cannot go until some further time to strike this out. . . . Because we may have witness after witness who can be the conduit for which words are placed in third parties . . . it is not due process when you cannot cross-examine a third party who is not here, who has made a statement. I think it is the rankest kind of evidence, and I submit it should not be permitted and should be expunged from the record and the jury admonished that it be disregarded.

LEONARD: May I add one thing, that something new in the last couple of days has been added to the total in this record; but it is perfectly obvious from the testimony of the government's last witness, Foard, that third party declarants at Communist Party meetings do not outline the official position of the Party. . . . That lends substance to the argument that we have been making for weeks, that in no way can these defendants be bound by anything that the third party declarants have said. . . . It is perfectly obvious that this cannot be expunged from the minds of the jury, that irreparable prejudice which cannot be erased is being committed.

COURT: Gentlemen, I have nothing further to add at this time. I do not know that the jury will bind these defendants by this evidence or not. I am not making a decision. I have great faith in the jury.

SCHULLMAN: I have a cartoon from the *New Yorker*. One juror said: I am blank, blank if I can strike it out of my mind.

MARGOLIS: We are getting into here statements . . . without any showing that these defendants even knew that such a statement had been made. . . . Under the law, they cannot be bound by that kind of a statement. . . unless they knew and subscribed or in some way were a party to the statement. It has been shown here, Your Honor, by defense cross-examination of government witnesses. . . that they disagree with reports made from officers, that some of them do not accept what the head of the Communist Party or what a functionary report, and they say something else which has blood running in the streets which calls for force and violence. . . the jury is getting the impression that what people say in disagreement with what the leadership of the Communist Party says can be admitted, can be admitted against people because they follow the

Communist Party. It seems to me it is standing the rules of evidence on its head to admit this evidence. . . (by) permitting a statement of any person who might even be subject to expulsion for his views because they are so basically opposed to those of the Communist Party, as being binding on these defendants. . . . The appellate court establishes the rule that even single statements can be so prejudicial that even where there is an order (to strike) immediately that it is reversible error if the jury should happen to convict in that case.

Again, Mathes refused to act on the prejudicial testimony, but at the end of the trial he prudently had it stricken from the record. He continued to harrass the defense's cross-examination testing the credibility of the witness.

COURT: Can't we move on to something else? It is such a waste of time.

MARGOLIS: Your Honor, I object to that remark. I have reason for going into this.

COURT: Proceed and let us see it.

Schullman, whose experience had been with more conventional cases and not with political trials of this kind, was getting an education in "equality before the law."

SCHULLMAN: We would like to request the court not to characterize, in the presence of the jury, cross-examination or the effect of cross-examination. . . . It has occurred on many occasions—there is a cumulative effect. There has been no characterization in the record of direct examination (by the government), and therefore the weight with which it may be accepted by the jury. . . would cumulatively tend to prejudice our case. The jury may say, "he has never said it to the prosecution."

Judge Mathes was understandably impatient with the defense attorneys' probing of the witness. Litt first stumbled when asked to identify the defendant Frank Carlson. He was unable to do so, but when asked again later he pointed him out.

NEUKOM: May the record show he has identified Frank Carlson.

LEONARD: I will (so) stipulate, if you will stipulate that is the same defendant Frank Carlson he said fifteen minutes ago he couldn't recognize.

NEUKOM: I will abide by whatever the record says.

When it was shown that the witness identified Carlson as being in Los Angeles in 1948, at a time when the defendant was actually in San Francisco, working as a shipfitter and warehouseman, Leonard said, "I move to strike the prior identification of my client Frank Carlson." The motion was denied.

Litt had agreed to inform for the FBI in 1947, after several unsuccessful business ventures, and after three attempts to pass the bar examination, each of which had failed. He said he did so, however, out of reasons of patriotism. But this eagerness to serve his country got him into trouble on the witness stand, and at times the court had to help him out.

At one point Litt was quoting the defendant Dorothy Healey on the subject of recruiting.

Q. Just what was said?

A. She wanted people who were the leaders of unions and the important element. In other words, not the mass proletariat, the rabble, the workers.

COURT: Is that what she said, or is that your statement?

A. No. . . . Maybe I should have eliminated the word "rabble."

COURT: You move to strike the remainder of the answer?

MARGOLIS: Yes.

COURT: Motion granted.

The prosecution's favorite term was "blood will flow," and the witness Litt repeated it as having been said at one of the 1947 classes he attended. The defense probed persistently.

Q. Is that the only thing that you remember about those three sessions?

A. No.

Q. Other than the one or two you have identified, you can't think of a single piece of literature that dealt with war and peace, or peaceful co-existence, of the between 500 and 1000 that you turned over to the Bureau?

A. I don't think of a single title.

He could not remember the Constitution of the Party, of which the following section was read: Section 2. "Adherence to or participation in the activities of any clique, group, circle, faction or party which conspires or acts to subvert, undermine, weaken, or overthrow any or all institutions of American democracy, whereby the majority of the American people can maintain their right to determine their destinies in any degree, shall be punished by immediate expulsion."

Judge Mathes intervened again.

COURT: Proceed, gentlemen: We have spent too much time on this already.

MARGOLIS: Your Honor, I object to that remark. I think that the jury should be instructed to disregard it.

COURT: The jury will disregard the comments of counsel and the court. Please proceed, Mr. Margolis, as quickly as possible.

Q. You were told in a beginners' class that blood would flow in the streets?

A. No.

LEONARD: Don't you recall a special article in *Political Affairs* pointing out that taking quotations from Lenin out of context destroys their meaning?

A. I have no recollection of it.

COURT: Let's don't have any more questions on that subject, Mr. Leonard.

Q. You never read in any Party literature that it was necessary to examine the historical background of a quotation in order to understand it?

A. I can't recall a statement like that, no.

LEONARD (quoting an article in *Political Affairs* by V. J. Jerome): 'Let us examine the basic meaning of the statements quoted from Lenin. In the first place let us establish the historical context in which they were uttered. It was the period of civil war, blockade, and foreign military intervention against the young Soviet Republic . . . fighting the invasion forces of Britain, France, Japan, and the United States as well as the counter-revolutionary White Guards financed and equipped by the Entente (Allied Governments).'

Q. Do you recollect Dennis (General Secretary of the Party) saying at the convention: "We believe that social change can take place not alone when the historical objective conditions exist for such change, but also and only when a decisive majority of the most exploited class in society is convinced that this change is necessary and is prepared to act unitedly to enforce its democratic will and aims."?

A. No. I didn't hear him say that. I recollect very little.

COURT: Let's proceed to something else.

LEONARD: I would like to have this marked for identification.

COURT: Let's proceed, gentlemen.

LEONARD: Counsel was examining the document.

COURT: Let's proceed.

LEONARD: May I read from the flyleaf of the pamphlet?

COURT: Put your next question.

When Leo Branton took up the cross-examination, it was revealed that charges had been brought against Litt in the Party, that he belonged to a religious cult and was using drugs. As for the written reports he made to the FBI about the "blood will flow" statements, he denied that he had seen them recently.

Q. As a matter of fact, the only reason you haven't seen those reports is because no such reports exist, isn't that true?

A. No, that isn't right. That is a distinct lie.

BRANTON: I think the jury will determine who is lying.

(Court admonishes Branton).

Q. You were already in the Communist Party when you were first contacted by the FBI, isn't that true?

A. That is not true.

Q. It is also true that you contacted the FBI and the FBI didn't contact you?

A. That is not right.

Q. It is also true you contacted the FBI because you thought it would clear you in your efforts to pass the bar examination, isn't that true?

A. That is not true.

On re-direct examination, the prosecuting attorney attempted to press upon his battered witness the role of giving "expert testimony" on Marxist theoretical material he had never even read.

NEUKOM: Did you ever arrive at an opinion as to whether the Communist Party, the members you knew, advocated the overthrow of this government by force and violence? (Objections).

SCHNEIDERMAN: I would like to know in what manner the intent of myself or my codefendants could be determined by this witness—after he has stated his antipathy to the Communist Party, (and) the reason for which he joined the Party—as to what the Party advocated, and inferentially what the defendants advocated (on) the question of force and violence. To come in at this state of the trial and inquire of this type of witness (for) an opinion and conclusion is highly prejudicial. . . . Many opinions and conclusions of witnesses have been stricken on minor and unimportant questions; I cannot conceive how an opinion and conclusion of a witness on this basic, key, crucial question can be sustained by this court.

A long colloquy ensued before the court finally conceded to the defense on this matter. A final note on the witness Litt doing his patriotic duty: When a Party member sent a gift for his newborn baby, he accepted the gift, and then turned in the member's name to the FBI.

One of the crudest examples of FBI tactics was revealed in the case of Leonard Patterson, most of whose testimony was stricken from the record. He had been brought in from the East to testify against the defendant Loretta Stack. At the time he was interviewed by the FBI, his license to drive a cab had been suspended. Following the interview, his license was restored, and he started a career in which he testified at government hearings in ten cases, for which he was paid $34 a day, plus expenses.

In each case he fitted his testimony to the needs of the prosecution. At a previous government hearing he had stated that he joined the Party in New York in 1935; but this time he said that it was in 1930, so that he could go into Party matters which allegedly took place in 1932. At an earlier government hearing he had admitted that he had been charged with adultery, but Mathes sustained the prosecution's objections to questions about this matter. Caught in numerous discrepancies in the stories he told at different hearings, he got increasingly belligerent, and claimed that the transcript was in error, although he had made no previous attempt to point out the errors and make corrections. He remembered clearly what happened in 1932, but could not recall a conversation with the FBI only two years ago. He explained this by saying that he had kept notes of the earlier events; but at a previous government hearing he had stated that he kept no notes. Pressed by the defense, he exclaimed: "Well, I don't want to make a positive statement yes or no. This will bounce back some other time."

Nevertheless, he was forced to admit under cross-examination that Communist Party members were sincere in fighting for the unemployed and for homeless youth, and that there was no color line in the Party.

Before the next witness was called, the defendant Bernadette Doyle became seriously ill. Judge Mathes was torn between his desire to get on with the trial and his reluctance to sever her from the case. He kept insisting that she remain in the courtroom, even though she felt so faint she could barely sit in her seat. A motion by the defense to sever her from the case was denied. On the second day her illness became worse, and it was obvious that she would pass out if she had to stay much longer. But it was only after a long argument with the defense counsel that the judge finally granted a motion for severance. (Thus we lost an opportunity to present a defense witness who had received nearly 500,000 votes as a candidate for State Superintendent for Public Instruction in a remarkable election campaign.)

Louis Rosser, the next prosecution witness, had been a Party member in the Los Angeles Black community. He had been expelled for misappropriation of funds, drunkenness, and contact with the FBI. When cornered he proved to be particularly belligerent, hostile, and abusive under cross-examination. He testified that he received training in "street fighting," but it turned out that he was referring to demonstrations attacked by the police. He was questioned about "underground" meetings he claimed he attended.

WIRIN: Is it a fact that the police department did not allow open meetings of the Communist Party?

A. That is a fact.

Q. Is it a fact that the police of the city of Los Angeles resorted to tear gas in order to prevent meetings which the police department considered Communist meetings?

A. That is a fact.

Q. Were persons arrested at meetings scheduled by the Communist Party, put in jail, and then released without any charges?

A. Yes.

Rosser said he had never heard of Captain "Red" Hynes, who had unleashed a wave of terror against radicals in the twenties and thirties. Wirin then read to the jury the following account which had been entered into evidence: "It was a common thing in those days for comrades to reach their homes at three and four o'clock in the morning, covered with blood, nursing broken arms, jaws, and noses. Sometimes comrades did not return at all. . . . In October 1931, 10,000 people, including 26 unions of the A.F. of L. turned out to hear William Z. Foster speak on the Tom Mooney campaign. By the time the "Red Squad" had charged the crowd a few times and the barrage of tear gas wafted into the Biltmore Hotel and down Fifth Street, the *Los Angeles Record* estimated that 'nearly 50,000 people had assembled, hundreds of them in evening dress.' "

The attorney asked the witness if he remembered a discussion about the following headline in the *Los Angeles Examiner* of June 28, 1932: "Officer Slugs Foster as He Tries to Speak."

ROSSER: I don't remember.

COURT: It does not matter, Mr. Rosser. He might ask you about whether Noah's ark was discussed at a meeting.

Further evidence was introduced to show that a municipal court had awarded damages against Hynes for illegal search and seizure at Communist Party headquarters on October 5, 1933; that a district judge had issued an injunction against Hynes to prevent him from interfering with the Party or its members, or the general public, from entering the premises of Party offices and halls; that the Los Angeles Bar Association had obtained a judgment against Hynes; and that a sound truck driven by Rosser advertising Party candidates had been held by Burbank police, and released when the city attorney admitted there was no legal basis on which to hold the truck.

The witness struck back.

ROSSER: I remember you, Mr. Wirin, around the Communist Party a long time.

Q. Was I a member of the Communist Party?

A. I couldn't say, but I saw you in meetings at the CIO Building with nothing but top Communists.

Q. Did you know that I was attorney for the CIO? And that makes me a Communist?

A. I said you were associating with them. I mean you are getting rough with me.

Q. Did you ever hear of me as an attorney for the American Civil Liberties Union?

A. Yes.

Wirin established that in 1933, three injunctions had to be obtained against the mayor to prevent police interference with three different public meetings of the Party in a downtown auditorium. The court stated: "It has been well settled by our Appellate Court that mere membership itself in the Communist Party is a violation of no law . . . . However, contrary to the plain import and terms of these provisions of our Constitution, it is not unusual or an uncommon practice for officers, both federal and state, in some instances acting under bigoted conceptions of their power and in other instances under coercion of organized groups, to violate both provisions of the state and federal constitutions, presumably acting also on the theory that might makes right and the end justifies the means. A plainer set of facts or circumstances violating both the above provisions of the state and federal Constitutions could hardly be conceived."

Rosser gave his version of what constitutes a conspiracy.

Q. Did the Communist Party distribute a leaflet against the Criminal Syndicalism Law?

A. Yes, I am going to tell you what they did. . . . They had demonstrations and hundreds of thousands of unemployed people all over this country, and they tried to lead these people into a revolution. . . . They distributed leaflets and put out petitions.

Q. Were there any meetings that you attended, in which people went in one door and went out of another?

A. Yes.

Q. And they did that because they were afraid of the police, didn't they?

A. That is what they said. Not because of the police, because there was a secret organization underground conspiring at that time.

Q. Did anyone tell you to make that statement in the course of this testimony, Mr. Rosser?

A. No, Your Honor, I think—.

COURT: What do you mean by security reasons?

A. Because some of them worked for the gas company, some were truck drivers in the unions, some of them might have been social workers, and some were students, and they didn't want the people to know that they were Communists, and they were part of this conspiracy.

SCHULLMAN: Your Honor, I ask that the last part, as being a conclusion of the witness, be stricken.

COURT: The portion "and they were part of the conspiracy" may be stricken and the jury is instructed to disregard it.

WIRIN: With respect to those who attended the meetings, who worked for the gas company, they did not want their identity known because they might lose their jobs, isn't that correct?

A. No.

Q. Was there a discussion at any meeting you attended in 1942?

A. I don't remember.

Q. I haven't finished my question. What is it you don't remember?

The court was getting impatient with the length of the cross-examination. Schullman protested that it was unavoidable "if the witness is going to be recalcitrant, if he is going to volunteer, if he is going on ad infinitum with snide remarks, made for one purpose, to prejudice the jury."

When Leo Branton took up the questioning, he explored the many times that Rosser was in contact with the FBI and the House Committee on Un-American Activities.

Q. It is a fact, isn't it, Mr. Rosser, that during the two years you were in contact with the FBI, the FBI has been bringing various kinds of pressure against you to get you to testify, isn't that true?

A. No. I found out I was part and parcel of a plot to prepare a revolution.

He then went into a long harangue, until the judge interrupted, "You don't need to go into that"; (later in the trial his whole answer was deleted).

Q. And you remained in (from 1938) until 1945, knowing that the Communist Party was using Negro people?

A. Because I couldn't quit.

Q. And it took you four years after you got out of the Communist Party to get up enough nerve to go to the FBI, is that right?

A. Yes, that's right.

Q. Did you ever tell anybody, Mr. Rosser, that the FBI was bringing pressure against you to testify in this case?

A. I talked out (of) two sides of my mouth.

Q. How long have you been talking out of two sides of your mouth, Mr. Rosser?

A. Just like you.

Q. How many conversations have you had with the FBI in the last two years?

A. I don't know.

Q. As a matter of fact, you have had over a hundred conversations with the FBI in the last two years, isn't that true?

A. Mister, what is your name? . . . I don't remember.

Rosser went into another long tirade, uninterrupted by the court.

Q. When did you find out. Mr. Rosser, that the Communist Party was using the Negroes?

A. I was with this man right here, Schneiderman, coming from a meeting, and we stopped over here in a place and they wouldn't serve us, and . . . .

COURT: Who is "they?"

A. Mr. Schneiderman and these people. We didn't have time to stop and file a suit and fight for Negro rights here. We had other things to do.

SCHNEIDERMAN: May we have a date on that, Your Honor?

A. I don't remember the date.

SCHNEIDERMAN: May we have a place fixed?

A. I don't know the name of the place.

COURT: Were there other persons present?

A. I don't think there were. And then, again, in San Francisco during the war when we had the explosion in Port Chicago (California), and the next day they put fifty Negro sailors in jail because they refused to load the ammunition, and I went to their leader and said, "Why don't we go and fight to get these guys out of jail?" And they told me, "What is more important, loading the ships for the Soviet Union or fighting for these men?" These things began to open my eyes.

Q. Is it your testimony that the Communist Party did nothing about it?

A. That is my testimony. I went to Mr. Schneiderman and the leaders of the Communist Party in San Francisco, and they didn't do anything about it.

Branton later introduced into evidence an account of the Communist Party campaign in behalf of the jailed Black sailors and of the callous disregard for the safety of the workers at Port Chicago, in editorials and in an article in the *People's World* appearing on July 20 and September 22, 1944, which belied Rosser's statement.

The defense attorney also elicited from the witness a statement about his frame of mind when leaving the Party, which contradicted what he had previously said on the stand.

Q. Isn't it true, Mr. Rosser, that shortly after you left the

Communist Party you caused a public statement to be (inserted) in one of the local Negro newspapers on leaving the Party?

A. I had a statement to be printed in the *California Eagle* saying I was no longer a member of the Communist Party, and that I admired their fight against fascism, something like that.

The excerpt from the *California Eagle*, a Black community newspaper, was then read: "I resigned from the Communist Political Association in December 1944. I make this public announcement in order to relieve the CPA of any responsibility for my actions and activities. I respect the CPA and the program it is promoting to wipe out fascism throughout the world, and to build true democracy in America with freedom and equality for all people." (Signed Lou Rosser)

Q. Isn't it true, Mr. Rosser, you told somebody that the reason you were testifying in this case was because the FBI was holding something over your head . . . in Arizona?

A. No. That I did in Arizona?

Q. Yes.

A. I was a great football player in Arizona.

COURT: You weren't asked that.

Rosser's letter was published after charges had been brought against him in the Party for drunkenness, misappropriation of funds, and contact with the FBI. He admitted that after his resignation he appealed for another hearing, but when he went into a long, rambling explanation that went far afield, Branton moved that the answer be stricken as totally unresponsive.

COURT: Don't you interrupt, Mr. Branton, sit down.

BRANTON: I want to make a motion, Your Honor. May I make a motion?

COURT: No. Have you finished your explanation?

ROSSER: Yes.

COURT: You may make your motion. Please stand at the lectern, Mr. Branton. I ordered you to sit down so you would not interrupt the witness.

Branton then made a motion for a mistrial by reason of prejudicial error and interference with his right to conduct the cross-examination, citing the judge's hostile conduct toward him. The motion was denied.

COURT: I will not permit you to interrupt me, Mr. Branton, or any other counsel. This trial must proceed in an orderly fashion.

BRANTON: Your Honor, I want the record to be clear that I at this time desist from further cross-examination of the witness, and I do so because of the court's limitation which has prevented me from carrying on adequate cross-examination.

COURT: You may be seated, Mr. Branton. . . . He (Rosser) was entitled to explain why he asked for a hearing, not as a supplicant, but as a person who felt his record (of) service entitled him to better consideration than this exhibit gave him. . . . They (the witnesses) have to sit up there and just take it one after another.

Judge Mathes's touching concern for the witness came after Rosser's credibility was further battered when he placed the defendant Steinberg in Los Angeles at a time when he was living in St. Louis. He placed a CIO official at a local strike committee meeting when the latter was in Washington, D.C., and he identified another trade unionist at the same meeting, when the records of the draft board showed him to be out of the state at that time. He also reported a meeting eleven years ago with the defendant Philip Connelly, the CIO secretary in Los Angeles, which strangely enough had never been reported to the FBI.

SCHULLMAN: When did you report this meeting of March 1941 to the FBI?

A. The FBI heard it the first time yesterday, when I discussed it in this courtroom.

Q. Prior to testifying in this case, did you report the meeting to any representative of the U.S. attorney's office?

A. I did not.

Q. Did you make any notes of that meeting?

A. I did not.

By this time the rambunctious witness was a little more subdued in bearing.

MARGOLIS: I would like to know what your best recollection is now as to when you attended the school.

A. Mr. Margolis, I have been on this stand all day yesterday and today, and I am a little tired.

COURT: Please speak up, Mr. Rosser. I wish you had saved some of that energy you were spending so rapidly yesterday and this morning. Please speak up so we can hear you.

As his stories fell apart, Rosser's answers became almost inaudible, and the court had to again admonish him, "I can scarcely hear you. Speak up so all the people can hear you. You have demonstrated you can speak louder than that. Pitch your voice higher.

Margolis pressed the witness about what he learned about war in a Party school, in the course of which he introduced an exhibit which struck a chord of memory in me. It was a quotation from a speech by President Woodrow Wilson, recorded in the *Congressional Record* of September 5, 1919, which read: "The seed of war in the modern world is industrial and commercial rivalry. . . .

This war was a commercial and industrial war. It was not a political war." (Over thirty years before, when I was still a teenager, that speech inadvertently helped to shatter the myth of World War I as a "war to make the world safe for democracy, to end all wars." It helped to clarify for me as a youth the difference between just and unjust wars, a basic Communist doctrine—a difference which gradually dawned on millions during the Vietnam War, and which led them to oppose it.)

The questioning turned to the Party's campaign against the shipment of war materials to Japan during the invasion of China.

MARGOLIS: You were told that if that scrap iron was shipped to Japan, it would soon be used against American boys?

A. But we were double-talking. . . .

COURT: Did anybody say that to you in words, substance, or effect?

A. I used the wrong word.

COURT: You still haven't answered the question. Did anybody tell you this in words, substance or effect?

A. No. (After another tirade by the witness, a motion to strike was granted.)

* * *

A colloquy occurred in the midst of Rosser's testimony which gave a revealing picture of the Justice Department's version of a "fair trial," as well as Judge Mathes's unctuous facade of judicial "impartiality."

SCHNEIDERMAN: Your Honor, I want to ask this court to take some action against the interference with our preparations for defense by the harassment and intimidation of the FBI. Last Sunday I went to San Francisco to speak at a meeting relating to our defense, in a hall at 321 Divisadero Street, and had also intended to interview a number of prospective witnesses there. When I arrived I found a movie camera was installed in a second-story window across the street opposite the entrance to the hall, taking movies of everyone entering and leaving the hall. Now I am sure that this was not a Hollywood production of "The Philbrick Story," because we have had plenty of experience of former practices of harassment and intimidation of this kind by the FBI. I had to abandon my plans to interview prospective witnesses as a result. And I say that especially at this time, this form of harassment and intimidation is an interference with our conducting our defense, is a denial of due process, and is a violation of our right to a fair trial. It will be impossible to properly prepare our defense if this practice or any similar practice continues during the course of this trial. Therefore, I ask for an order of this court that the Federal Bureau of Investigation be directed to cease and desist from the practice of taking photos and movies of meetings in which we are engaged, and other practices of harassment and intimidation which interfere with our preparing for our defense in this trial.

U.S. ATTORNEY BINNS: Your Honor, I do not feel that there is anything here for the court to act upon, unless Mr. Schneiderman desires to take the stand under oath, and lay some sort of foundation. I do not believe there are any facts before the court.

SCHNEIDERMAN: Your Honor, I could not go and break down the door of the building to ask the people their credentials as to who they were. But I think that in the pretrial proceedings Your Honor was made aware of the fact on several other occasions the attorney general of the United States and the Director of the FBI have publicly stated in articles and speeches that they were engaged in this and various other forms of surveillance of members or suspected members of the Communist Party.

COURT: How are we to know that it was addressed to you or to any of the defendants who are on trial? The Bureau might be engaged, assuming it was the FBI, in the surveillance of some other people wholly unrelated to this matter. Of course, there should be no interference, unnecessary interference, with the activities of the defendants in preparing for trial and in preparing their defense. But how can you say that it was directed to you or any of the other defendants?

SCHNEIDERMAN: Well, it happens I was speaking of one incident. But when in case after case we find that we are followed to private homes or halls, then surely it is not a coincidence, and surely there is no other agency that has the interest and the resources to continually harass and keep us under surveillance except the FBI. I believe it was brought to Your Honor's attention in the pretrial discussions that we have reason to believe that our telephones are tapped, that dictaphones are placed in offices and homes, and it is extremely difficult to expect that we can in any way engage in defense of our trial without reasonable knowledge that the FBI is intruding on our privacy in that way. Here you have a camera that is taking pictures of an entrance or maybe pictures of the windows of a room. I understood that the Supreme Court at one time ruled that it was an invasion of privacy to pump out the contents of a man's stomach. Here is a case of where a camera is being directed either at the entrance or the window of a room in which a meeting is taking place. The government has stated here that the identity of their witnesses is so sacred that they wouldn't reveal them in advance, yet we are expected to prepare our case when it isn't only a question of revealing the witnesses, Your Honor, but we find it extremely difficult to get any witnesses because this practice is so widely known that often people who have jobs or families to protect are unwilling to subject themselves to the kind of persecution and harassment that they know will follow. I must say to the court at this time that we have run into difficulty from the beginning, that the practice which I ran into Sunday is creating a situation that I think the court should take notice of—that we are finding it extremely difficult to prepare our defense at this time unless we can call witnesses.

COURT: Mr. Schneiderman, unless you have something definite to act upon, it is only surmise. It would be difficult to prove, wouldn't it?

SCHNEIDERMAN: I would suggest one way Your Honor could find out—that is, to place an FBI representative on the stand, and ask him under oath to state whether these practices are followed by the FBI or not in this case.

COURT: Let's assume that the FBI is following every defendant, following every lawyer; as long as there is no direct interference can the court assume that the FBI is not doing its duty?

SCHNEIDERMAN: What redress does a citizen have when his privacy is invaded in that way and his right to prepare for a defense is interfered with in that way?

COURT: It's an interesting question. Have you discussed this with counsel for the defense? It's an interesting legal question.

SCHNEIDERMAN: Could not the court elicit from the FBI through a representative of theirs on the stand as to whether they are interfering as I have stated? I believe if it was shown that the FBI is responsible for this camera that was placed at a meeting where I was discussing my defense and trying to interview witnesses, that this court would have to take some action to tell the FBI to cease interfering with my preparing for my defense. I was discussing the question of raising money for our legal defense, and at the same time, since I only had a few hours, I had intended to interview some people to discuss the question of coming down to be witnesses at the trial. When I found out what happened, I informed them through messengers, and in one case by telephone, that they were not to come down to the hall, because I did not want to subject them to that kind of surveillance—and those that did, their pictures were taken as they went in and as they went out.

COURT: If he was any good as a witness, and was useful at all as a witness, he would have to come here in open court and get on the stand and testify and if he would lose a job for being a witness, he would lose it then. . . . The presumption is in favor of official duty being properly performed. For all the court knows, assuming it is the FBI, they may have been looking for an immigration suspect, a narcotics suspect, or a counterfeiter, or a violator of a hundred other federal statutes.

MARGOLIS: We could find out by calling the FBI and asking questions.

COURT: If this were something in a private home or in a lawyer's office, it might present a problem, but here as I understand it was a public meeting.

SCHNEIDERMAN: Yes, it was a public meeting. It was announced in the press before the meeting took place, and I would say it was a very striking coincidence that that camera was there for any other purpose.

MARGOLIS: The incident Mr. Schneiderman brings to the attention of the court is one incident. I know that when this case first started, that two days before our case started, around our defense office, the office was literally swarming with FBI agents. When the attorneys came down out of the building they followed us across the street and followed us into the cafeteria where we had lunch, they followed behind us. We drove to the office we were going to interview witnesses and didn't go. I turned around and came back and parked the car, because I didn't want anyone to follow me to find out to whom I had possibly talked. I submit, Your Honor, that is a direct interference with the right of counsel to prepare their defense. There is no speculation about what happened, and there is no speculation about what was the purpose for which that was intended, the purpose of keeping the defendants under surveillance. Regardless of the purpose, it interfered with our preparing for trial.

SCHNEIDERMAN: May I inquire if the court would summon a representative of the FBI to testify as to whether these facts which I have stated had happened by their authority?

COURT: I do not see a sufficient standing, which as I understand it is mere photographing persons attending a public meeting, to warrant the inquiry. I suppose the problems are the same if the defendants are following the government's lawyers or following the Federal Bureau of Investigation's agents around to try to learn in advance what witnesses it intends to call.

SCHNEIDERMAN: I do not think that the same problem is involved, Your Honor, because the question of intimidation and harassment has an entirely different effect on the defense and the defendants, even if what you suggest may be true.

COURT: Of course, due process does not guarantee the defendant may prepare his defense totally free from the influences of everyday life.

With this bit of philosophic advice, the judge dispensed his even-handed justice. Margolis moved for the withdrawal of a juror and for the declaration of a mistrial. The motion was denied.

* * *

In contrast to the erratic bombast of Rosser, the witness Estrada was of a different stripe.

Paul Estrada's testimony threw a bombshell into the trial. He was a police officer from Milwaukee and a Marine Corps veteran. There was some question whether he had ever been a member of the Communist Party.

Q. Isn't it a fact the reason you have no Communist Party card to produce is because you never were in the Party?

A. I was in the Communist Party and I tore my card up.

Q. And it has been after Al (the FBI agent) told you to turn over to him every single piece of written information you could get your hands on, is that correct?

A. Well, the card wasn't important.

Q. Isn't it true that you went to Communist Party meetings in the 6th ward approximately 21 times without being a member of the Party?

A. Sure.

Q. And those meetings were open to everybody that wanted to come in, isn't that true?

A. Well, everybody excepting the newspaper reporters.

Estrada startled the courtroom after the defense vainly demanded that the government produce his reports, which he said he had used to refresh his recollection.

LEONARD: Can you state the name of one other document distributed while you claimed to be in the Communist Party in Milwaukee in 1947?

A. Well, I got a book on how to make bombs and booby traps from them.

There was a stir in the courtroom. The prosecuting attorney looked puzzled. The defense attorneys and defendants exchanged incredulous glances. The judge leaned forward, his face, usually looking bored or impassive, showing a glimmer of interest. Here was the first solid piece of evidence!

When Leonard further elicited from the witness that he had turned it into the FBI and made a written report about it, Schullman rose to address the court.

SCHULLMAN: I now make a motion for the production of a book entitled *How to Make Bombs and Booby Traps* from the United States attorney or the FBI.

Prosecuting attorney Neukom, "We have no such book here."

LEONARD: I will accept the stipulation of Mr. Neukom that he has no such book here, and I will proceed, Your Honor.

Q. And when he showed you these four books that you have identified, didn't you tell him that you had turned in a book, *How to Make Bombs and Booby Traps*, and why didn't the government have it here for you to identify?

A. No, I did not.

There ensued a long and bitter argument, which continued intermittently for days, over the missing reports. Neukom claimed he had never seen them. The prosecution was frantic in its efforts to prevent the reports from being released, claiming the need for secrecy to protect the country's security. Neukom, in his fractured syntax, alternately pleaded and threatened.

NEUKOM: The revelation of material which comes from informants of that character can be just that one additional little thrusting, thrusting, thrusting, nibbling, nibbling, nibbling that could be undermining the internal security of this country. If an informant believes that his personal notes to a security agency are going to be laid bare to the public, maybe the man is not the most intelligent type of person, maybe he does go off on tangents, maybe he is sketchy in his reports, he will be reluctant. . . . Then you will take a report which is somewhat sketchy, and you will put a witness on the stand, and you say, "You testify to this, Mr. Estrada; why isn't that particular thing in your report?" And what does the jury gather from that? Now, you may smile upon the proposition—there were titters in this courtroom when he said he had directed these reports to the Bureau—but it shows the inflection (that) has been put into this case. . . . It shows that the situation is one of endeavoring to embarrass the position of the government . . . . And I dare say if such a ruling is made, Your Honor, (to release the FBI reports to the defense) I believe you will regret it some day.

The prosecution finally produced a War Department manual on making bombs and booby traps, claiming this was the book in question, but insisted that there were no written reports on it. There was no indication where the book came from.

SCHNEIDERMAN: May I call Your Honor's attention to one further fact, since Mr. Neukom stated there were no written reports made of the book which was introduced here for identification, that the testimony of the witness states that he made such a written report to the agent.

LEONARD: That's right. That is a third element of direct impeachment.

Q. Did you make a written report on that one to Al (the FBI agent)?

A. Yes, I did.

So it was obvious why the prosecution was so anxious to avoid the embarrassment of releasing the reports. If the book was actually reported to the FBI, the government must have been so dubious about its genuineness that it did not produce it in evidence. (If they had believed Estrada's story, what a sensation they would have created by entering it into evidence on direct examination!)

Neukom invoked some cold-war rhetoric and fervently appealed to the judge's patriotism against releasing the documents wanted by the defense to impeach Estrada.

NEUKOM: You don't go and impeach a man by insisting that the government break down the security that public policy requires to be maintained, especially in times such as this. And these are, Your Honor knows—I need not call attention to the situation that prevails throughout the world—I know the position Your Honor is in. He does not want error to be committed, and as a good citizen, as a loyal judicial individual, you likewise do not want to rule in a manner which might establish a precedent that would harm the security of the country.

MARGOLIS: Are we in a position where we are required by indirection to concede the genuineness of the reports which we have never seen and which we challenge, and we have no way to disprove them?

COURT: You can tell the jury. . . whatever you feel about them.

MARGOLIS: When they produced the book, that War Department manual, he stated that he did so because the defense by demanding the book had insinuated that the witness was lying—I think I am using Mr. Neukom's exact words.

COURT: Let's keep that verb out.

MARGOLIS: I will use the word falsify.

COURT: You can say that he wasn't telling the truth.

MARGOLIS: That he wasn't telling the truth. Let me make the record clear, not by way of insinuation, but by way of an outright statement, that it is our position that the witness is not telling the truth. . . . We have also a question about protection of the internal security of the United States to keep the reports of all informants confidential, even though they may impeach the testimony of the witness. I submit, Your Honor, that it is not protection, it is not destruction of the internal security of the United States. It may be protection of the internal security of the FBI and the Department of Justice. But it is destruction of the democratic rights of the American people if a witness can make a report to the government, which the government admits impeaches him, and they say we are going to protect the witness, not permit him to be impeached.

COURT: Is there anything in these exhibits which the government opposes disclosure of upon the ground of the internal security of the United States?

NEUKOM: Yes, all of them, all of them.

COURT: Is there any other grounds? No ground of state secret, I suppose?

NEUKOM: No, there is no state secret.

Nevertheless, the prosecuting attorney continued his desperate efforts to prevent the defense from seeing the exhibits on the grounds of confidentiality.

COURT: Is there any claim that the exhibits involved a disclosure of identity of informants?

NEUKOM: No. The informant himself has already been identified.

COURT: Then, let us not confuse the issue with that. . . .

Eventually, the attorney general, who refused to release the FBI reports to the defense, allowed them to be turned over to Judge Mathes, who inspected them and ruled that they should be sealed. Estrada's bombshell remained a mystery; and although it had backfired, the question still remained, how much of an impact did it make on the jury?

But his bitter animosity toward the Party was made clear to them.

Q. Do you feel bitter about it (the Party)?

A. I am an American, and Milwaukee was a good city before the Communists came there. I grew up right there in the sixth ward, the ward that they destroyed. . . .

Q. Are you still answering my last questions? Have you completed it?

A. I wish I could go on . . . . I would complete it for you.

NEUKOM: May I call your attention the witness had to have a doctor last night.

COURT: Do you feel like going ahead, Mr. Estrada?

A. Yes, Sir. I mean I get to thinking about it. We had a good city. The Negroes were all right there. We never knew what the word "Jim Crow" meant until the Communist Party taught it to us. We never knew about "You can't live here" or "Fight for housing." I never knew what the word "nigger" meant. I wish I could get myself together. I would really preach. And you are an American, and you standing there—.

Neukom asked for a recess, which was granted. The agitated witness was placed under a doctor's care and excused for the day. When questioning of Estrada resumed, although he claimed membership in the Party, he couldn't name any of the officers of the Party, either state or national. He didn't know of a big public meeting for Gene Dennis, the general secretary of the Party, and he couldn't identify a pamphlet containing Dennis's speech.

Q. And the reason you didn't know Mr. Estrada, is because you were never in the Communist Party, isn't that true?

(Objection sustained.)

To counter the idyllic picture that Estrada painted of the sixth ward, the defense introduced the report of the Mayor's Housing Commission, which described it as a "blighted area," with a high percentage of the houses ready for condemnation. Although the witness said that the mayor "worked overtime" to build housing projects, the mayor's report showed that of 518 units, only 6 had Black tenants.

The court began to show increasing impatience with Leo Branton's cross-examination, which completely unraveled Estrada's rosy story.

COURT: Mr. Branton, I believe we have gone into that enough. What difference does it make whether the Negroes are well off, poor off, or medium off in Milwaukee?

BRANTON: I believe we have a right to attack the witness's credibility on those statements to show he was not giving truthful testimony.

The judge cut off Branton again when the latter introduced a report to show that the tuberculosis rate was sharply higher among Blacks than whites.

COURT: How is it material, Mr. Branton? It may be due to the climate for all we know.

BRANTON: Your Honor, this witness has given reasons why he was bitter with the Comunist Party, and has stated matters as a fact about there being no segregation and no discrimination among Negroes. I think we have a right to meet that.

Contrary to the witness's charge that it was the Communist Party which "stirred up trouble," the Mayor's Commission Report on Human Rights, in dealing with "tension situations" caused by efforts to desegregate discriminatory housing, said:

"This process sometimes seems like stirring up trouble, but the trouble is there already, and noticing it is not the same thing as stirring it up . . . tackling the issue and taking measures to alleviate it will prevent explosive consequences. . . . A Negro, regardless of his financial or educational status, finds it almost impossible to move out of the worst housing area in this city."

Other examples of discrimination revealed Estrada himself held only menial jobs till he became a policeman; that there were only two Black policemen in a police force of 1100 in Milwaukee; that there was not a single Black employed in the city's largest industry, the breweries; and that no Black bus drivers were employed there before the war.

ESTRADA: Perhaps the Negroes didn't want to drive buses.

The court would not allow further questions about Jim Crow in the Marine Corps, where Estrada had served, to test his statement that he had never heard of Jim Crow before the Party told him about it. As Branton pressed the witness further, Judge Mathes's impassive demeanor changed, and his hostility began to show through. His face reddened with anger.

COURT: Now, Mr. Branton, no more of that kind of thing. I am not going to permit that sort of thing. You don't need to make a speech with the question.

MARGOLIS: I want to object to Your Honor's ruling on the ground the question was perfectly proper and appropriate.

COURT: You are not examining, Mr. Margolis. Please sit down.

MARGOLIS: On behalf of my clients, I want to object that they are being injured.

At the recess, defense attorney Schullman rose to make a motion for a mistrial, which the judge denied.

SCHULLMAN: May I say this, Your Honor, any asperity—

COURT: What is asperity?

SCHULLMAN: A characterization by the court of counsel which a jury will gain the impression different than either the court or counsel—

COURT: I am not going to sit and listen to this. . . .

MARGOLIS: I would like to add to the grounds of the motion for mistrial, that the statement of the court was made in such a manner as to indicate the anger of the court at counsel, that questions of this kind had been previously allowed, and I was simply proceeding in accordance with the rulings this court has made.

SCHNEIDERMAN: May the record show that I join in the objections made by other counsel and join in the motion.

COURT: Motion denied.

At the conclusion of Estrada's cross-examination, the court relented and unsealed some of the FBI reports, which showed glaring discrepancies with the witness's testimony. The latter claimed this was due to the fact that he had given "oral reports." (This was a favorite device of several witnesses to explain away discrepancies.) As for the War Department manual, the court drew a careful line. While refusing to strike the exhibit from the record entirely, he agreed to strike some of the testimony regarding it and made the following statement to the jury:

"It was received, not for the purpose of binding these defendants as to its distribution; the book is not in evidence as having emanated from the Department of Justice or from any of these defendants. . . . It is received as bearing upon the credibility of the witness."

Before bringing in their star witness, which they had saved for the last, the prosecutors paraded seven more informants to the stand. In the main, it was more of the same. Occasionally a comic moment lightened the scene. A witness was asked to identify Al Richmond. She pointed to Norman Leonard, one of our attorneys. When informed of the mistake, she exclaimed, "It should be the man in the brown suit." (Both wore brown suits.) On further questioning as to whether she had been told to look for a man in a brown suit, she said, "My mind is going blank on me. I have got the shakes so bad I can't think." The government asked for a recess, which the court granted.

Then there was the elevator operator in the office building where the Party had its headquarters. Nicknamed by the defendants "Arsenic and Old Lace," Daisy Van Horn looked like a sweet old lady whom you would like to have for a grandmother. She addressed the United States Attorney as "Your Honor." She would turn to the judge when answering questions as though to confide in him. She didn't actually address anyone as "Dearie," but one felt it was touch and go. Her job was to inform the FBI as to who went into the building and came out.

She related how she had been invited to a closed, exclusive reception which she was told to keep to herself. The speaker was "Mother" Ella Reeve Bloor, a well-known Party organizer and orator in her seventies, famous among the miners, in whose struggles she had participated. A "Russian song" was sung, the witness said.

VAN HORN: She said: There will be blood flowing in the streets. She says it is going to be a wonderful revolution. Just to be a good Red and remember there are three r's—slick, sly, and smooth. Always be nice to people. Don't be rough. She said the day of the revolution was nigh; we were on the threshhold of this revolution. And she says: We are prepared to the point that we have arms awaiting for us.

On cross-examination by Leo Branton, it was revealed that it was a public reception, held shortly after the United Nations Conference in San Francisco, in the home of a prominent Black church woman, who was not a Communist.

BRANTON: Do you remember Bloor saying, "I am happy to have lived to see the eve of our great victory over fascism?"

VAN HORN: Yes, I do. Yes.

BRANTON (quoting Bloor further): "It is wonderful that all the peace-loving nations of the world are gathered here in San Francisco to form the United Nations, which should be the basis for a lasting peace."

VAN HORN: Yes.

BRANTON (quoting Bloor): "The forces of fascism are on the run, and you and I will live to see the final victory over these forces of fascism."

VAN HORN: Yes, that statement I remember.

She also quoted Bloor as speaking of the death of Roosevelt as a loss, and saying "We don't know about Truman; we'll give him a trial." Daisy made no attempt to explain how to reconcile this with her own bizarre account. It also turned out that the "Russian song" she mentioned was actually the "United Nations" song, for which song-sheets were passed out to the audience.

When she was shown a photograph of the reception, she looked bewildered. After identifying two different women as the hostess, she said, "It doesn't look to me like it is the same place, unless there were two receptions, or a lot of people came in afterward, and the music came in after (I) left."

Another startling bit of information was volunteered by the witness: that she had won a raffle on a book from the Soviet Union which had been smuggled into the country, which "was a very valuable book and it was the general outline of which the revolution was to be carried on." When the book was produced and shown to the court, it was found to be a *History of the Civil War in the U.S.S.R.*, one of the editors of which was Maxim Gorky. The defense asked for the court to take judicial notice of the fact that this "smuggled" book was in the libraries of UCLA, USC, and the Hoover Institution at Stanford University, as well as in the public libraries. Copies of the book were produced from the Los Angeles public library, which had been ordered from a London publisher. It was also sold at the Party's International Bookstore in San Francisco.

Confronted with this disconcerting information, Daisy prattled on and on, and the court and the prosecution became more bemused as they tried to stop the flow of chatter.

COURT: Just a moment, what was the question that was asked?

VAN HORN: I don't know, Your Honor. I was just telling him, elaborating on this.

A motion to strike the answer was granted.

VAN HORN: Are you afraid to have that come out?

COURT: Just a moment. Don't make any more comments.

The government attorney watched aghast as their witness fell apart. As her story was punctured full of holes, she babbled on with a flow of unrelated trivia which they were barely able to bring to a full stop. But they were taking no more chances with "written reports" to the FBI. Before she got off the stand, she had switched her story from "written reports" to "oral reports."

15 General Strike — "Dress Rehearsal for Revolution"

Up to this point, members of the legal profession who had been observing the trial marveled at the shoddiness of the government's case. A mountain of "evidence" had been built on a molehill of facts. The defendants had all been identified as members and officers of the Communist Party, engaged in its public activities. Voluminous extracts had been read ad infinitum from the Marxist classics. The few examples of inflammatory language attributed to Party members, with none of the defendants present, were made by witnesses whose credibility was shaky at best, and in most cases was completely shattered on cross-examination. The sinister purpose of the "underground" was demystified when the defense showed that security measures by the Party did not involve some secret plot, but were taken to protect its members and their families from loss of jobs, political persecution, and even physical harm. Where was the conspiracy? Could the government really outlaw a political party and jail its leaders on such flimsy legal grounds? Legal experts wondered.

We, of course, knew better from the long history of political frame-ups in our country. The Party at its outset was virtually outlawed for a time by state "Criminal Syndicalism" laws and its leaders prosecuted and jailed, until saner times prevailed. And now that the cold war and McCarthyism had created an atmosphere of political reaction in the country, the legal niceties were being swept aside, the boasted "protections" of the Constitution were conveniently ignored, and who but the bravest souls would come to the defense of the Communists?

It would be several years before the reaction to McCarthyism turned the tide. But in the meantime, not only Communists suffered, although they bore the main brunt of the attack, labor's rights were also attacked, Liberals lived in fear of being called Communists, and dissent was curbed.

No jury could be expected to stand up against the pressure of the times, given its own prejudices as well. The government felt perfectly safe in presenting the sorry parade of witnesses, no matter how vulnerable they were, by appealing to the patriotism of the judge and jury, and even by a veiled form of intimidation.

When, for instance, the prosecution needed a little more

ammunition, it asked the court to take judicial notice of the Korean war.

NEUKOM: We can call to the attention of the court matters which show the encroachment of the Soviet Communist influence . . . that goes to the intent of these people, their cognizance of these world events, which can be considered first by Your Honor in connection with the clear and present danger. . . . You take the Chinese situation, the Korean situation, our aid to Greece and Turkey. . . . The court can recall the ever-changing international situation . . . the picture of which is a greater threat from the Soviet Union. When we refer to the Soviet Union, we are referring to Communists. These books reflect that . . . . We follow the same theory in this case that was followed by Judge Medina (in the New York trial). . . . Mr. Schneiderman admitted in his opening statement that they did oppose the Korean situation. . . .

The prosecutor, warming to his task, got emotional, and at times almost incoherent.

NEUKOM: You take the Chinese situation. . . . Is there ever an American who but knows that gradually the Communist army was ever creeping, creeping, on the Nationalist army, that the Nationalist army is now on Formosa, and that is virtually the only place that they are? We all know the Indo-China situation. Aren't those signs of which a jury has a right to have called to their attention. . . . Your Honor can't close your mind, you can't remain blind, which I know you are not, to the ever encroachment of Communism. . . . This strike on the San Francisco waterfront in 1934 could be a dress rehearsal from which the revolution might start up.

Even Mathes, ever mindful of keeping the record free of prejudicial error which might help the defense on appeal, balked at this blatant appeal.

COURT: Is there an attempt to visit upon these defendants responsibility for conditions in other countries? They are not here.

NEUKOM: Aren't these things here, that we have lost some 55,000 American boys in Korea?

COURT: There is the danger of suggesting to the jury that in some way these defendants are on trial for that sort of thing.

With all that had gone before, the prosecution knew that it needed a knockout punch to cinch its case, and so it saved its star witness for the last.

Nat Honig was a newspaperman now working for the Hearst paper in Seattle, the *Post-Intelligencer*. I remembered him as a lanky, awkward figure resembling Ichabod Crane. He had now fleshed out, in keeping with his acceptance by William Randolph

Hearst, but he wore his new mantle of respectability uneasily, unable to look one squarely in the eye. He had been editor of a monthly magazine of the left in the trade unions, and for a short period in 1936 edited the *Western Worker*, a Party newspaper on the West Coast in the thirties, forerunner of the *People's World*. He had been in the Soviet Union in 1934 at the same time I was, when he was working in Moscow as a research assistant at the Red International of Labor Unions, a world-wide federation of left-wing unions.

The FBI contacted him in 1940, he testified, after I had told him he could not return to his old job, and after he had been fired from a trade-union paper which he edited. At first he refused to talk to the FBI, but they kept after him for many months, appealing to his "loyalty." Then occurred an incident which changed his mind. He was arrested at a Seattle department store for shoplifting. Either he or his employer then called the FBI to get him out of jail. A week later he agreed to testify for them. Subsequently he appeared as a government witness at the Harry Bridges deportation hearing, before a witchhunting committee in Seattle, and at hearings of the Subversive Activities Control Board.

At first he denied the arrest, but then admitted he was taken to the police station and fingerprinted. The government objected to further questioning about the incident.

COURT: A $5 book?

WIRIN: There are small thieves and large ones, Your Honor.

COURT: I do not care to hear any more of that.

But whether small or large, it was not the only case of thievery reported. The Washington *New Dealer*, a weekly, reported that he had stolen books on other occasions and was followed home by store detectives. He denied the story.

COURT: The question is, did you believe it?

A. I didn't know whether to believe it.

At another hearing, he had testified, according to the transcript, that it was more than one book, but claimed the transcript was in error.

WIRIN: And you think that is an incorrect recording by the reporter? (Objection sustained)

COURT: However, you may answer it if you wish.

A. I don't particularly wish.

At the Bridges hearing, Judge Sears had issued a scathing denunciation of Honig's testimony and credibility and impugned his motive, but Judge Mathes would not allow our defense attorney to quote what Sears said. Since the subject matter of his testimony was the San Francisco General Strike at that hearing, substantially the same as he was to give in our trial, and it would be his word against mine, the prosecution was anxious to keep out this damming indictment of his credibility.

On direct examination. Honig testified that he had attended meetings in 1934 of the Communist International, at which he said I was present, where the policy of the American Communist Party was discussed.

SCHULLMAN: I object to this testimony and move to strike all the testimony on the ground it is introduced for the sole purpose of prejudice and bias on matters that are not relevant to any issue in the indictment and on the ground that under the law in 1934, visits by anyone to any country by any delegate for labor purpose or parliamentary purpose or any economic or social purpose was not in violation of any law.

COURT: Prejudicial is not a legal ground of objection.

PROSECUTING ATTORNEY KINNISON: I am asking only about the policy of the Communist Party U.S. with respect to overthrow of the government of this country by force and violence. . . .

An objection by the defense was denied, as was a motion for a mistrial.

KINNISON: . . . as it pertains to the allegations in the indictment in this case.

COURT: Now, Mr. Kinnison, obviously that is an improper question.

The prosecution was anxious to produce 'the smoking gun' to cinch its case, and the next opportunity came when the witness told of discussions at these meetings about the San Francisco longshore strike in June 1934.

HONIG: Lozovsky (head of the R.I.L.U.) said that perhaps the strike could be further spread into a general strike of all workers, at least in San Francisco. . . . Schneiderman said that he thought that was an excellent suggestion, he thought such a general strike could be produced. . . . Lozovsky reminded the people there that general strikes should be regarded as rehearsals for seizure of power by the Party and the working class, and the delegates become very enthusiastic about it, and they got up and endorsed what Lozovsky said, and among them was Mr. Schneiderman. He also said that was true, that he believed such a general strike would offer an excellent rehearsal for seizure of power in the United States by the American Communist Party.

Now, this movie-script version of how to "produce" a general stike and a rehearsal for revolution may sound ludicrous to anyone familiar with strikes and labor history, especially with the events which led up to the San Francisco General Strike, but is was no laughing matter for us in that courtroom. As for my own involvement, I had been away from California for four years, and the only thing I knew at the time about the strike was what I read in the brief bulletins in the English-language *Moscow Daily News* and much later in the *New York Times* when it arrived by mail. But the rebuttal would have to wait till we put on our own defense. In the meantime we would have to rely on portraying the objective circumstances surrounding the strike to show how preposterous was Honig's story.

In 1936, during another waterfront strike, the witness said another discussion of similar import took place at a meeting of waterfront leaders, at which Schneiderman and Bridges were present. (The Bridges hearing judge had dismissed Honig's account in this regard.)

KINNISON: Was the question of revolution discussed at this meeting? (Objection sustained)

LEONARD: I renew motion for mistrial on the grounds of misconduct by the prosecution in asking questions which are knowingly improper, for the purpose of prejudicing these defendants. (Denied)

HONIG: Schneiderman pointed out perhaps the same situation as had occurred in 1934 could now again be brought about, namely, he said, the bringing about of a general strike, not merely the maritime workers, but all workers of this type for the entire West Coast, and he reminded the Party members present that at the Comintern meeting in Moscow which had discussed the 1934 strike and its preparations, that such general strikes are rehearsals for seizure of power by the Party and the working class.

So I had not only "produced" a general strike in San Francisco from 5,000 miles away, but here I was a few years later getting ready to produce another one for the entire West Coast in another "rehearsal" for seizure of power. I was flying high indeed! (A standard encyclopedia notes that the general strike is "practically unknown in the U.S.," and lists only the Seattle strike in 1919 and the 1934 San Francisco strike. A child at the time of the first, I was being credited with planning the other at the still precocious age of twenty-eight.)

Recalling the period shows the absurdity of Honig's claim that a responsible Party leader would be talking about turning a strike into a revolution in San Francisco. We were supporting the Roosevelt New Deal in the thirties, and devoting ourselves to building a united front against fascism. The wave of strikes that developed at this time was the result of workers in some cases feeling free for the first time to organize into unions, and in others moving to make their old impotent unions more effective. Communists were active in these strikes around economic issues and in some cases played a leading role in the struggles.

In any case, the witness's story came apart under intense cross-examination amid a barrage of objections by the prosecution, most of which were sustained by the court.

MARGOLIS: Isn't it a fact that in this trial is the first time you ever testified, out of all your testimony in (seven) other cases, that Mr. Schneiderman had any duty to formulate policy in Moscow in the Comintern?

A. Yes, I think today is the first time I have mentioned that phrase, yes, in this trial.

Q. And the fact that you mentioned it for the first time because you invented it to help bolster the case against Mr. Schneiderman, isn't that correct?

A. No.

The defense was curious how he, a mere research worker, could be sitting in on high-level policy discussions in June, when at the Bridges hearing he had testified that in August or September (long after the strike) was the first time he had been allowed to sit in on such discussions, having been elevated to the role of "representative," according to his story.

Q. Isn't it a fact that this is the first time in which you have testified in which you said that you acted as a representative, prior to the time you became a representative three or four months after you arrived in Moscow (in May)?

A. I don't remember.

Q. Do you remember any other case in which you said that?

A. No.

Q. When did you tell any government or investigating agency or any person connected with any government or investigative agency of those two meetings?

A. I don't remember.

Q. In the Bridges case, isn't it a fact that the investigators who spoke to you about your testimony told you that they were particularly interested in anything which would show that the general strike in San Francisco in 1934 was Communist-controled.

A. I don't recall that they put it that way.

Q. Did you tell any investigators or agents of the government to whom you talked about the Bridges case about those two meetings in Moscow?

A. I am sure I did.

Q. The fact is, is it not, Mr. Honig, that in the Bridges case you gave no testimony whatsoever relating to any meetings in Moscow at which the general strike was discussed?

A. I do recall testifying about the meeting.

Q. I will ask you, Mr. Honig, to find in the Bridges transcript the reference to that testimony.

After the lunch recess, Honig stated he couldn't find any reference to such testimony in the Bridges transcript.

Q. The fact is that you did not tell these representatives of the government, with whom you spent part of days giving them what you knew, anything about these alleged incidents in Moscow where the general strike was discussed, where there was an alleged discussion about a revolution, and where there was a directive issued?

A. No, I did tell them, not about alleged, but actual discussions.

Q. And the fact is, that after you told them, they never asked you any questions about it, is that right?

A. No. I found no questions asked of me as to that in the Bridges hearing.

Q. You considered it was not a proper occasion because you knew that the story didn't exist, and you hadn't invented it yet, had you?

U.S. Attorney Binns objected to the question and it was withdrawn.

Time after time the defense brought forth Honig's statements at other proceedings which were substantially different from his allegations at this trial, to show that he tailored his testimony to fit the occasion, depending on whom he wanted to finger or what the government wanted to establish.

MARGOLIS: Isn't it a fact that you have testified about this incident on several occasions previously and have never given an answer which in substance or effect contained the part which I have read?

A. That is possible, yes.

Q. Didn't you invent that for the purpose of this case?

A. No . . . well, the testimony I gave in some proceedings may have differed in some respects with other testimony in slight degree, yes.

His explanations for giving admittedly false testimony at various hearings varied. When asked whether he had testified falsely at one proceeding, he answered that he had given the false answer "hesitantly, with accentuation . . . I was using it in the sense of sparring for time to collect my thoughts." Another time he said, "My tongue must have slipped." On several occasions he claimed the transcript of the other proceedings was wrong.

Battered and cornered, his confident air disappeared; the witness could not answer a routine question about a date, and exclaimed: "I have been on the stand all day, and I have to take a little time to think." The prosecution asked for a weekend recess, which the solicitous court granted.

But aside from puncturing Honig's credibility, the defense sought to show by the objective circumstances which led to the general strike that his story was inherently incredible. When Norman Leonard's cross-examination delved into the working conditions of the longshoremen in 1933 and 1934, the judge intervened.

COURT: How is it material?

LEONARD: We want to show the objective facts from which the jury can infer such statements were never made.

The longshoremen at the time were in the notorious "Blue Book" company union. Their jobs were dependent on the infamous "shape-up" on the docks; frequently kickbacks were required to get a job. Past strikes in San Francisco had been lost because they received no support from the seamen's union or from the longshoremen in other ports. Wages were 75 cents an hour for an eight-hour day. The average weekly wage in San Pedro was $10.45. The men might have to work 24 to 36 hours at a stretch, perhaps for a day or two, or only a few hours. (The pay of sailors started at $25 a month, or an average of $36 a month for an ordinary seaman, and about the same for a messboy in the steward's department.)

A rank-and-file movement spurred an upsurge of recruiting into the A.F. of L. International Longshoremen's Association. As the union grew rapidly, the men were blacklisted. But after a brief protest strike forced the Regional Labor Board to reinstate four longshoremen who had been fired from the Matson Navigation Company docks, the Blue Book was doomed, and the I.L.A. soon represented nearly all the longshoremen on the Pacific Coast.

When the defense tried to introduce testimony given in 1951 at a government hearing in Washington about the Blue Book and blacklisting, prosecuting attorney Neukom brought in a red herring; he rose to ask for a stipulation that Congressman Vito Marcantonio, who had elicited the testimony from a witness, was "elected on the Communist Party ticket."

MARGOLIS: I move for a mistrial on the ground it was deliberately, willfully a misleading statement intended to create bias and prejudice on the part of counsel. These are not true. (The defense later offered a stipulation that Marcantonio had been elected to Congress at various times on the Republican, Democratic, or American Labor Party ticket.)

The new militant union, 14,000 strong, voted 99 percent to strike for a six-hour day, a thirty-hour week, and $1.00 an hour, and most important of all, preferential hiring through a union hiring hall. The employers refused to bargain or recognize the union, and after months of delay and the failure of government mediation, the West Coast longshoremen struck on May 9, 1934.

From the first day the Teamsters refused to handle cargo. The seamen's unions supported the strike, and some of them struck for their own demands. The employers launched a campaign of redbaiting against the unions, charging Communist influence and control, and especially against the leading spokesman of the longshoremen, Harry Bridges.

The fact is that all of these unions were headed by old-time conservative officials, but the wave of militancy swamped them. The rank-and-file movement which brought about the rejuvenation of the International Longshoremen's Association was a reflection of the militant upsurge that was taking place in the labor movement all over the country, but on the waterfront it was inspired and led by the left, which included members of the Communist Party. The longshoremen elected a rank-and-file strike committee that took charge of the strike. Attacked from all directions by the employers, the city officials, and the press, they welcomed the support given them by the Communist Party newspaper, the *Western Worker*, which got out special strike editions carrying the official bulletins of the strike committee.

The seamen were not as well organized as the longshoremen; for one thing, the left at that time had tried to organize them into an independent union, the Marine Workers Industrial Union, which had a small membership and siphoned the most militant members out of the A.F. of L., leaving the top leadership of the International Seamen's Union an almost free hand. Nevertheless, spurred on by the fact that the Marine Workers Industrial Union had called the crews of thirteen ships on strike, the affiliates of the A.F. of L. Seamen's Union joined the strike and presented their own demands.

Negotiations broke down when the longshore strikers rejected government-proposed arbitration, at which point National Guard troops were sent in and the employers prepared to forcibly open the port of San Francisco with strikebreakers. Train crews from the State Beltline Railroad refused to work. When the employers attempted to run trucks through the picket lines, the police opened fire on the pickets with tear gas and the battle was on. On July 5th, "Bloody Thursday," hundreds of policemen, armed with tear gas, night sticks, sawed-off shotguns, and riot guns attacked and fired on the longshoremen and their supporters. The "Battle of Rincon Hill" raged all morning, and the strikers retreated from the Embarcadero to their headquarters. At noon the police attacked the pickets in front of the union headquarters with tear gas and opened fire again. Dozens were wounded, and two were dead. On the same day the National Guard took over the waterfront.

The city was outraged, and when 40,000 marched in the funeral parade, general strike sentiment swept the city, and the San Francisco Central Labor Council set up a strike-strategy committee as one union after another went out. The general strike was on.

This sequence of events was dragged out of Honig by Leonard's cross-examination, but oh, so reluctantly! But he did not recall that the waterfront employers refused an offer of arbitration proposed by the head of the Central Labor Council if the troops would be removed. He "didn't recall" that William Green, president of the American Federation of Labor, sent a telegram supporting the general strike. He couldn't explain why he said on direct examination that no troops were called and that there was no violence.

As for the policy of the Communist Party, a published resolution of the Central Committee of the Party was entered into the record, reading: "It was the capitalist class, which in panic before the rising giant of the class action of the masses, cried out that this strike, which they could have settled very quickly at any moment by the simple expedient of granting the workers' economic demands, was actually a revolutionary uprising organized by the Communist Party to overthrow the whole capitalist system. Of course this strike did not have revolution as its objective. . . . The immediate aims of this strike were not to win power, but to win the immediate economic demands of the workers as well as the withdrawal of the troops, the withdrawal of all decrees against the freedom of the strikers to picket."

On redirect examination, the prosecution tried to repair some of the damage done to their witness. Honig reversed the testimony he had given at the Bridges hearing and at this trial, that when he was in the Party he believed that socialism could be achieved by peaceful means. He also sought to dispel the implication that the reason he changed his mind about talking to the FBI was because of pressure. When he refused to talk to them, he said, he thought the FBI was antilabor. "I decided to make an independent investigation of my own. I was unable to find any antistrike or antilabor role of the FBI." (His arrest for shoplifting just at that time must have facilitated his "investigation.")

Through it all, Judge Mathes grew increasingly unhappy with the length of the cross-examination. He ruled out question after question objected to by the prosecution. He insisted the defense speed up its questioning, threatening to lengthen the hours of the court sessions and to hold court on Saturday. But even the judge got tired of Honig's "explanations" and at one point abruptly cut him short with the remark, "It does not require explanation." It was a thoroughly whipped informant who finally was excused and left the stand, his jaunty air gone, his walk reduced to a shuffle. The fireworks had fizzled, but again we wondered, how much of the poisonous fumes remained in the air for the jury to inhale?

The government rested its case. It was a shabby performance, which could only be understood by their assumption that when it came to trying Communists, anything goes. But they had not expected that the going would be so rough that it would take four months to present their case, and that the defense would so thoroughly expose their charges for the political frameup that it was. Now it was our turn.

16   Witness for the Defense

The trial had opened in February. It was now June. The tension had taken its toll among the defendants and their families, and also among the attorneys. We had to sit at the defendants' table and the counsel table, and present a calm and confident exterior to the press and the jury, even when we were seething inside. It was hard to sit still week after week and not strike back when the abominations were pouring forth from the witness stand, although there was some satisfaction when the cross-examination penetrated to the sordid means by which the prosecution had purchased its evidence, or what passed for evidence, or when the informant's tales were shot full of holes.

Oleta Yates was to be our first witness for the defense. But I was also preparing myself to go on the stand, temporarily giving up my role as counsel "pro per"; Leo Branton was to be my counsel for the questioning. What concerned us was that the prosecution, unable to produce a conspiracy on the part of any of the defendants, was relying heavily on impressing the jury with out-of-context quotations from Marxist books which left the inference that we sought to achieve our aims by force and violence.

The dogmatism of past years continued to haunt us. In earlier days, there had been some highly romanticized versions of how socialism would be achieved in the United States. There was once an obscure pamphlet in which the author let his literary imagination run loose and with a dramatic flourish described how a delegation of workers would march into the White House and tell the President he was through. There were also those who spoke of "soviets." The Party eventually repudiated these versions as individual interpretations which it had never adopted in a Party program. The educational outlines which we were presently using in our Marxist classes made clear that we sought to achieve our goals by peaceful means, and only anticipated violence from a defeated ruling class when the forces for socialism achieved a majority.

Reading from such an outline, defense attorney Wirin had quoted: "This was a line envisaging peaceful development of the revolution" and asked the witness Russell:

Q. Was that discussed in the club, substantially?

A. I believe it was.

This was to counter some lengthy quotations about "insurrection" and "the enemy" by the prosecution, given with a significant pause and emphasis on the words "in the present epoch," which caused me to rise in protest.

SCHNEIDERMAN: May we have a stipulation, Your Honor, the insurrection referred to was the 1917 Russian Revolution, and that it was quoted from a work by Lenin written about 1917, and the "enemy" referred to were the Czarists?

We had not given much thought to the question of the U.S. road to socialism. The Party had spent very little time theorizing on how it would achieve power in the United States. Being a small party, and believing that socialism was far from being an immediate issue in this country as yet, it had devoted its main attention to outlining its more immediate objective of creating the broadest democratic alliance to combat the danger of fascism and war. Beyond this, we had gone no further than visualizing a farmer-labor coalition, in alliance with oppressed minorities, becoming the basis for a popular-type government, which would make more likely a peaceful development to socialism. But we had no blueprint for revolution. There were too many complex circumstances in the world situation as well as in the United States that might determine what the future would hold in the fight for socialism.

When Oleta O'Connor Yates stepped to the witness stand, the jury saw a youngish, frail-looking, attractive woman whose appearance defied all the stereotypes of Communists they may have had in their minds. She looked and talked like a school teacher; one would not suspect that she could swear like a trooper. She carried herself with coolness and dignity, and answered questions with a sharp precision and directness that indicated a complete mastery of her subject. But the frailty of her appearance concealed a steel-like quality and valor in her inner makeup which the prosecution would soon find it could not break. The moral stature and bearing of the witness for the defense was in striking contrast to that of the miserable cast of characters dredged up by the prosecution for its case.

There were four generations of O'Connors who had lived in San Francisco, she said of her background in response to Ben Margolis's questions. Her grandfather was a charter member of the Teamsters' Union, her father one of the founders of the Union

Labor Party, the political arm of the San Francisco labor movement. She worked her way through the University of California in Berkeley during the financial hardships of the Depression by pealing vegetables, sweeping stairs, waiting on tables, washing dishes, and doing housework. She coached students in a cooperative and was paid with a box of apples. Her bachelor's and master's degrees were in her trunk when her landlady seized it for back rent. Lack of finances prevented her from continuing for her doctor's degree, and her hopes of teaching went glimmering. She translated medical pamphlets from Italian to English, but could get no steady jobs.

Among the books she had read there were More's *Utopia*, Bellamy's *Looking Backward*, and George Bernard Shaw's *The Intelligent Woman's Guide to Socialism and Capitalism*, and the works of Upton Sinclair and Jack London.

I happened to be glancing up at the jury just then, and at the mention of Shaw's *Woman's Guide* I saw my favorite juror, the writer, smile and nod her head, unconsciously indicating her familiarity with that book, too. (Had they met under other circumstances, and compared notes, they might have found they had much in common. Instead, one of them was to determine whether the other one belonged in prison for beliefs that came from the same book.)

Her reading had ranged from Beard's *Economic Interpretation of the Constitution* to Marx and Engels. From the latter she found the only reasonable explanation for the scenes of despair she saw: evictions, utilities being shut off, jobless men and women going to City Hall for grocery bags to feed their children. She rejected the current bourgeois explanations for the crisis—"the unemployed did not want to work," or that it was due to "sun spots" (yes, there was such a theory solemnly discussed).

She heard about food being destroyed, crops being plowed under, and saw fruit lying on the ground and rotting, while farm workers were starving. And this paradox was best expressed when she read in the Communist Manifesto, "Modern bourgeois society with its relations of production, of exchange, and of property, a society which has conjured up such gigantic means of production and of exchange, is like the sorcerer who is no longer able to control the powers of the nether world whom he has called up by his spells.

MARGOLIS: Explain (the quotation) "revolt of modern productive forces against modern conditions of production."

Prosecutor Neukom, who had spent days and weeks reading

into the record quotations from Marxist classics without explanation, objected.

NEUKOM: To go into all this literature and give us a person's interpretation what these words mean, unless it is contended that these are not plain English words, is invading the province of the jury.

MARGOLIS: I think they are plain English words, although sometimes from the way the government has treated them, I don't think they understand that, Your Honor. (Objection overruled)

YATES: The means of production are owned by a very small number of people to make profits; the vast majority of the people who produce do not get enough to buy all they produce, they get back only a very small amount in wages. Consequently the modern productive forces are in conflict with, are revolting against these property relations which prevent the utilization of the productive forces to their fullest capacity.

Q. Does the word "revolt" there have any connotation of force and violence in your mind?

A. No.

Oleta joined the Socialist Party in 1932. But its activities consisted of meetings and lectures about socialism, while she saw the Communist Party dealing with the day-to-day problems of the unemployed in the cities and the agricultural workers. She went to the San Joaquin Valley to see for herself, and found Communists working in the fields, while the growers were trying to prevent the organizing of unions by using the police, sheriff's deputies and vigilantes. Kern county was an armed camp, and striking cotton pickers were brutally attacked.

The report of a Special Commission investigating the situation said: "We cannot understand why scores of officers, estimated at approximately eighty, found it necessary to gas an audience of several hundred men, women, and children in a comparatively small one-story building." A report to the National Labor Board told of lettuce harvesters receiving twenty-two and a half cents an hour, and being guaranteed only five hours of work. It said: "Words cannot describe some of the conditions we saw."

In 1933 she started to attend Communist meetings, and participated in their activities—organizing relief for the agricultural workers, and sending unemployed delegations to City Hall. After failing to convince the Socialist Party of the need for unity of action with the Communists on these and other immediate issues, she led a walkout from the Socialist Party and with about 250 Socialists joined the Communist Party.

Side by side with the unemployed struggles of the period, the ferment began among industrial workers to organize into unions, and the Party was actively engaged in both. The witness quoted from "Industrial Relations in the San Francisco Building Trades," by Frederick L. Ryan: "The second major factor to influence San Francisco unionism after 1932 was the formation of radical and liberal groups. . . (who) had many adherents in the unions. The *Western Worker*, newspaper of the Communist Party on the Pacific Coast, favored industrial unionism and a labor party. During 1932 to 1933 the unemployed were organized into Unemployed Councils, led by militant workers rather than by the old trade union leaders. As fast as the government started public works, new unions arose. The Building Trades Council . . . officials were unable or unwilling to take a militant attitude for the protection of the worker. . . . These organizational activities outside of the crafts began to have an effect upon the regular labor bodies."

Oleta graphically described the violent days of the maritime strike of 1934 and said it verified her understanding of Marxist-Leninist teachings on the role of the state: "I felt that some of the concepts I had concerning the role of force utilized by the state were being demonstrated. . . . At the point that the employers determined to open the port, that all the agencies of the government, the Mayor's office, the police, the National Guard, as well as the press and the radio—all of these were put into motion to effect the employers' program to break that strike."

The *San Francisco Chronicle* helped to whip up the hysteria for the bloodbath that was to follow by reporting that a Communist army planned the destruction of railroad and highway facilities to paralyze transportation, and that the San Francisco Bay area was to be a focal point in a revolution for the control of the government. A warning from a Southern Pacific superintendent was relayed to state officials that Communist forces were nearing the Northern California border (presumably from Oregon).

MARGOLIS: Did you ever have any knowledge of any kind of Communist movement of this kind?

YATES: No. I was not planning to march on the city or the city hall or anywhere else. I was working eight hours a day on a job, and I knew of no other Communists or Communist army that was going to march to San Francisco. It would have been ridiculous if it had not been a prelude to the force and violence that followed.

Q. About the period of the general strike, did you observe any acts of force and violence with respect to the Communist Party?

A. Yes. It was July 17 or 18. I myself had just left the office of the *Western Worker*. I saw it being broken into by both police and vigilantes, who smashed the windows and threw all of the furniture out into the street, destroyed the typewriters, and scattered literature all over the place. . . . Later I saw the results of similar raids on Party headquarters in the Mission District and on Fillmore Street. I learned that the homes of private people had been invaded in a similar fashion by both police and vigilantes and havoc had been created, and people had been taken off to jail.

An ironic touch was added in Yates' description of "Bloody Thursday," when the police opened fire on pickets and spectators. A cameraman who was photographing the scene for the San Francisco *News* was slugged and pierced through the ear by a stray bullet, and was hauled off to jail. His name was Joe Rosenthal, who later won world-wide recognition in World War II for his famous photograph of the raising of the American flag on Iwo Jima. When this was mentioned, the prosecution objected.

NEUKOM: Your Honor, I move to strike that from the record. It could have only one obvious effect in this case.

COURT: The jury will understand he did not raise the flag on Iwo Jima in 1934. Motion denied.

The reign of terror spread far and wide. The following description by Mike Quin in *The Big Strike* was read into the record: "The Mission Workers Neighborhood House looked as if it had been battered by artillery fire. The cavalcade moved from building to building, and when the list of organizational headquarters was exhausted, they started in on private residences. Homes were looted, wrecked and left in shambles. By nightfall the jail was packed with some three hundred suspected Communists. Raids of this kind continued for many days and eventually spread through all of the towns and cities up and down the Pacific Coast.

"Across the Bay in Oakland the raids had begun a day earlier. Police announced they had information that the Communists were arming. Every Communist hall or headquarters was raided and wrecked. No weapons of any sort were found, but scores of men and women were crammed into the jails. Mayor McCracken announced he had sworn in 3,000 citizen vigilantes. An additional 500 were mobilized in Berkeley, and 500 more in Alameda." In San Jose, pickhandles were passed out to vigilantes with instructions to use them.

Q. Were any of these vigilantes arrested when they engaged in acts of violence?

A. Not to my knowledge.

Mayor Rossi of San Francisco issued a statement: "I pledge to you that as chief executive in San Francisco, I will to the full extent of my authority run out of San Francisco every Communist agitator, and this is going to be a continuing policy of San Francisco."

Yates continued her testimony: "Immediately following the destruction of the offices, the *Western Worker* was prepared for publication in a private home. I assisted in this. I carried typewriters and paper up and down Telegraph Hill to the private residence where work was being done to prepare the material so that the paper could be put out, despite the fact that the printing shop had been told not to publish it any more.... There was not a single break in publication, although one issue did come out in mimeographed form when it was impossible to get it printed.... It was necessary that it should not be known where the paper was being prepared or even who was working on it, because that home would have been invaded and the people arrested."

Long after the strike was over, vigilantism was still rampant. In August, 1935, an armed mob tarred and feathered two radicals in Sonoma County, and the *Oakland Tribune* carried accounts of tear gas being used against women and children. In September 1936, during a lettuce strike, 2,000 vigilantes attacked the Central Labor Council hall in Salinas with tear gas. The *San Francisco Examiner* published hysterical reports that red flags had been put up in the lettuce harvesting area with numbers on them indicating the number of Communists that would congregate at that point to start a revolution. The next day the *San Francisco Chronicle* reported that the State Division of Highways had put the red flags up as markers to have a traffic check in the lettuce fields. But by this time a stronger labor movement, inspired by the longshoremen's victory, had begun to fight back, and at least in San Francisco the terrorist acts ceased.

The witness's firsthand account of the circumstances leading up to the general strike further demolished Honig's fairy tale that it was conceived in Moscow. It also bolstered the defense's contention that the security measures taken by the Party had nothing to do with a secret plot or conspiracy, but were forced on it by the denial of democratic rights to the Communists.

She went on to show that the Party carried on political activities publicly when possible. As chairman of the Party in San Francisco, Yates was a candidate for the Board of Supervisors three times, at one time getting the endorsement of unions having 40,000 members, with 400 to 500 precinct workers volunteering in her campaign. Her last campaign was conducted the previous year, when she was in jail fighting for bail, and she received 35,000 votes. As a result of her activities in behalf of a Fair Employment Practices law, and of proposed amendments to the city charter to give more power to the people, she was appointed by the mayor to the Mayor's Committee on Civil Affairs.

When scrap-iron was being loaded for Japan during its invasion of China in 1938, Chinese and American workers marched down to picket the docks, and the longshoremen refused to cross the picket line.

Q. What did you have to do with this picket line?

A. Well, I took part in it.

Referring to the prosecution charge that the Communists opposed American foreign policy, the defense introduced a statement by the Communist Party to a hearing of the State Assembly Committee on Elections and Reapportionment, on a bill requiring candidates to take a "loyalty oath": "To fight for peace is not treason. To oppose participation in an unjust war has a long and honorable precedent in American history. Abraham Lincoln denounced the unjust annexationist war with Mexico, as did Thoreau. Carl Schurz, a minister to Spain, a Secretary of the Interior, and a senator from Missouri called for an end to the war of aggression against the Philippines; today the new Catechism of the Roman Catholic church advised its members to take up arms in defense of their country unless they are 'convinced from adequate and unquestionable evidence that the war is unjust.'"

An interruption in Yates's testimony came when the defense brought in Russell N. Anderson, a court reporter in the state of Washington. Honig had questioned the accuracy of the transcript in the Washington hearings, when our defense attorneys showed that he gave contradictory answers at different proceedings, trimming the testimony to fit the case. But Honig's protestations proved to be false when it was revealed that the transcript was not made from stenographer's notes, but from a disc; the recording was played in court, and it proved that the disputed transcript was accurate. If there was anything left of Honig's credibility, this demolished it.

Ben Margolis then turned to the question of Marxist-Leninist theory in his questioning. Oleta was eminently qualified to deal with this, as she had taught at the Marxist Institute conducted by the Party, and had herself prepared some of the class outlines which were being used. The outlines were shown to have relied heavily on American democratic traditions and history; the source material in the bibliography included not only the Marxist classics, but the writings of Jefferson, Washington, Samuel Adams, Tom Paine, Frederick Douglass, and some recent American historians.

Her exposition of Marxist-Leninist theory was clear and concise. She developed three major propositions: That revolution is a result of a historical process, and is not something that can be conceived by a group or party; that it is accompanied by violence only when there are no democratic channels left open to the people, and then the violence is initiated by the old ruling class; and that Marxist-Leninist principles have to be applied differently in each country in accordance with its own historical background and conditions. (I had outlined the same concepts in my opening address to the jury.)

The outlines she prepared for classes emphasized, the witness testified, that "there is no blueprint" for socialist revolution, and used Lenin's warning against dogmatism: "We by no means regard the theory of Marx as perfect and inviolate; on the contrary we are convinced that this theory has only laid the foundation stones of that science on which the socialists must continue to build in every direction. . . . For this theory only gives general precepts, the details of which must be applied in England other than in France, in France other than in Germany, and in Germany otherwise than in Russia. . . . No decree has yet been issued stating that all countries must live according to the Bolshevik revolutionary calendar; and even if it were issued, it would not be observed."

She showed that the prosecution's reading of isolated quotations out of context was a crude distortion of Marxist teachings. She pointed out that Marx, Engels, and Lenin had at various times believed that the revolution could take a peaceful course under certain conditions in some countries. But those dislodged from power would not allow a peaceful solution; for example, the governments established by peaceful revolutions in Hungary and Finland after World War I were overthrown by reactionary forces.

"Revolution is a process," she pointed out. "It means first of all the accession of the working class and its allies to power; but in addition, after the power has been achieved, it means the reconstruction of the social order. It means the establishment of a state machinery that will guarantee that such a social order will be constructed. . . . I believe that this can be done by peaceful means, and I have worked for that. . . . The only possible situation I could conceive of where peaceful means would not be possible would be a situation in which our present form of government was overthrown and a fascist government set up in which there were no democratic avenues of expression open for the people, and they would either have to submit to a fascist minority or find ways of effecting that social change. . . . Here it is necessary to point out that when the working class comes to power and has control of the state, that like all other states, it does rest upon force or a threat of force in order to back up its program and effect social change. It rests upon these same types of force which every state in history has rested upon."

Step by step, Oleta was taken through the testimony of the government witnesses to show that they either were ignorant of, or deliberately falsified, the interpretation of the Party's aims and teachings. At the end of the direct examination, Judge Mathes took over the questioning.

COURT: When you say that the government cannot be overthrown by the use of words, do you mean that the use of words plays no part in overthrowing government?

A. No. As I understand it, words alone will not overthrow anything; but words expressing ideas, expressing concepts to people can cause people to take certain actions . . . can cause them to build a people's movement that will become the government.

COURT: I am prepared to instruct the jury that force and violence means other forceful acts, other violent acts than speech, that speech itself, no matter how forceful or how violent it might be or appears to be, it does not constitute the force and violence we are concerned with here.

But the judge's benign attitude did not last very long when the cross-examination began.

17 Lord High Executioner: The Anatomy of an Inquisition

The prosecution had no intention of jousting with Oleta Yates on questions of Marxist-Leninist theory. It proceeded almost immediately with its game plan—to demand that the witness name names, knowing full well that she would not do so. The unsavory job was handled by Neukom. He had already demonstrated his unscrupulous tactics when he had made his disjointed, incoherent flag-waving speeches to the judge, alternately pleading with and threatening the court with dire results if the defendants were to go free. Somewhere in the course of the trial the odious nature of his job overcame him and shattered his morale. After heavy drinking he would call one of the defense attorneys in the middle of the night, and in a drunken babble assure him that he was only doing his job, and plead for understanding.

"Doing his job" consisted of turning the jury's attention away from the shakiness of the government's case.

NEUKOM: With whom of the defendants did you meet in conjunction with your duties? (Objection to the question overruled)

YATES: I am quite prepared to discuss anything that I did, anything that I said, but I am not willing to provide names and identities of people; that would be becoming a government informer and I cannot do that. (Objections by all the defense attorneys)

SCHNEIDERMAN: May I request Your Honor to instruct Mr. Neukom to cease this line of questioning. . . . I see no other purpose of this except to try to make an informer out of somebody who despises such a role; and it has only one possible purpose. It has nothing to do with the issue in this trial.

COURT: The court directs you to answer the question.

YATES: Your Honor, I cannot be an informer.

COURT: You are instructed, Madam, to answer that question.

A. I will not play the role of a witness for the government. I will not add to the prosecution's case against people who have rested (their case), who are putting on no further defense.

(This referred to the fact that ten of the defendants had rested their case, there being practically no evidence against them; only four of us intended to put on a defense.)

COURT: You understand the possible consequence of your refusal to answer, I take it?

A. I am afraid I do, but the possible consequences, grim as they may be, are not as bad as going around hanging your head in shame for the rest of your life, because you have been an informer.

NEUKOM: You know that books, articles, pamphlets have been the medium of fanning people into action, to achieve results, and could not such pamphlets or books be the medium to cause people to take steps to overthrow the government? You do not think that words could be the avenue upon which travel the thought, the incitement of force and violence?

A. People are not so stupid as to be led by words. People by their own experiences, because of certain material objective conditions are moved to a course of action. . ., words may explain and interpret their experiences and guide them toward the solution of their problems, but words in a vacuum will never accomplish anything.

Neukom then proceeded, over the objections of the defense, to read into the record the dissenting opinions of Supreme Court Justices Stone, Robert, and Frankfurter in the Schneiderman case, in which they opposed my citizenship.

MARGOLIS: I move for a mistrial. The court has permitted counsel to use the exhibit for a purpose for which it was specifically not admitted. Secondly, this was extremely prejudicial, the reading of this dissenting opinion contained the strong polemical language of those who have been overruled by the majority of the court. (Denied)

The prosecution went back to the question of names of Party members in clubs who had been mentioned by the government witnesses. Mathes warned Oleta that if she refused to answer, each refusal would be punished by a separate contempt citation consecutively.

YATES: If I were to answer, it could only lead to a situation in which a person could be caused to suffer the loss of his job, his income, and perhaps be subjected to further harassment. I am sorry, I cannot bring myself to contribute to that. . . .It means persecution for them and their families; it evens opens them up to possible illegal violence. I will not do it.

COURT: Does that mean you refuse to answer the pending question?

A. Yes, I guess it does, Your Honor.

COURT: Very well, I have no alternative to hold you again independently of all the other occasions again in contempt of court.

By that time the judge had issued four separate contempt citations. Amid a storm of objections, the jury was excused.

MARGOLIS: Your Honor does know, we all know that people even who are rumored to be Communist have a pretty difficult time these days . . . . The other day there was just a rumor of Mr. (Owen) Lattimore, although he has denied it again and again, has been called a Communist by Senator McCarthy—there was a rumor that he was going to leave the country, that he was going to apply for a passport and it became headlines all over, and there has apparently been handed down an order which makes him virtually a prisoner within the confines of this country, and he is an important man. He has a college position, has held high government positions (as an expert on China), he is powerful and has powerful and influential friends, yet that happens to him. And for a witness who sits up there on the stand in a situation such as this, where she is willing to tell everything about herself, who does not want to be responsible, when she in her heart knows that these people have not done anything wrong, that there is a real danger that by her sitting there and saving her skin she is going to destroy perhaps some figure and she is going to injure somebody else. I think Your Honor would have just as much power (as) if that lynch mob were waiting right outside the court to grab the persons named. Your Honor would have the power, and I think it would be really, if not in law, in conscience an abuse of that power to utilize it, to force a witness to destroy others, or put on no defense.

COURT: The witness does not want to be an informer. There are a great many people who do not want to be, and some people may suffer great punishment. Others will talk a great deal about it but not suffer much punishment.

SCHULLMAN: I do think the court, knowing full well that if they reveal names, there is no purpose except to prejudice the jury. I felt alarmed here because I feel that the effect is crucial.

COURT: We can all speculate what the jury thinks about it. You may admire a witness who does not inform. I do not know.

SCHNEIDERMAN: Your Honor, I will be very brief, because I subscribe to the remarks already made by other counsel. As this court has undoubtedly observed, the defendant who is on the stand is a person of strong principles. Now, it does not matter whether one agrees or disagrees with those principles. But here we have a case where a person who has searched her conscience to see whether she is abiding by the principles to which has given her life. Now, I would like to draw a parallel which indicates that the law is not always so strict as it appears on these questions. There is a law which requires all persons to be liable to military service, but there are such people as conscientious objectors who, for either moral or religious reasons, come forward and say that they believe it is against the principles by which they have based their whole life—whether it is on the basis of religion or a moral principle does not matter—and that they cannot see themselves going to battle and killing another human being. There is a law that requires that person to be liable to military service; and that law is (applied), even in times of war, so that person is not punished if it is known by his record that his moral or religious principles were the reasons why he refused to go to military service. On the contrary, the usual procedure is not one of punishment, but one which eventually allows a certain recognition or respect for that moral principle which the conscientious objector has put forward. Now I submit, Your Honor, that the issues can be tried fully by the asking of proper questions which show the intent of each defendant who goes on the stand; the government is simply trying to drag in prejudicial questions by constantly asking questions of names when they know by the evidence already given here that it is utterly abhorrent to a Communist, and certainly to these defendants, to be placed in the role of an informer. I urge upon the court to reconsider its decision.

WIRIN: Your Honor, as a lawyer and as a member of the Bar and as an officer of the court, I want to supplement the argument made by one who preceded me, who is not an officer of this court, not a member of the Bar. As a matter of fact, there are court decisions, which I have had occasion to call to Your Honor's attention when I appeared as amicus (friend of the court) or directly in behalf of persons of deeply religious conscience. The highest court of the land took the view that under certain circumstances the courts will not press their authority and their power against the exercise (of) deep inner convictions of principles of conscience. Certainly it can be said that the atmosphere is such that a court may take judicial notice that one whose name appears publicly as identified as a Communist may reasonably expect serious hardships to befall him, and to be indicted as one of the 3000 which Mr. J. Edgar Hoover has said the Department of Justice had on a list for possible or probable indictment, and the other consequences which are sometimes even more severe, the loss of job. It may be that some of the jurors may respect this defendant for exercising conscience and abiding by it. But any punishment for contempt by this court cannot help us with this jury.

COURT: Was there some other name involved?

NEUKOM: There will be others, Your Honor.

MARGOLIS: There are approximately 1000 names in this record, and it would mean for this witness to be prepared to go ahead with as many of the thousand people as the government chose, and to have that on her conscience. The government gains nothing except a contempt proceeding; nothing except having Mrs. Yates go to jail on account of this. They gain nothing but the bias and the impression that will result from that. Those are things which I think they are not entitled to gain, Your Honor.

COURT: Mr. Margolis, will you bring the defendant Yates to the bar?

The defendant stepped from the witness stand and stood before the judge. There was a stirring in the courtroom, and then a hush.

COURT: Mrs. Yates, your refusal to answer certain questions which the court directed you to answer has been adjudged contempt of court. . . . Are you prepared at this time to purge yourself of contempt?

YATES: Well, I would like to state to the court in all conscience I cannot do otherwise and I must maintain that position.

MARGOLIS: I merely want to ask Your Honor to keep in mind the matters that were presented in oral argument. . . . There is no attempt on the part of this defendant to protect herself, but arises out of the kind of deep conscience which is, as Mr. Schneiderman and Mr. Wirin have pointed out, the kind of conscience which a conscientious objector exercises. . . . In light of all this, I again, Your Honor, request reconsideration of the matter and vacating of the order.

COURT: She refused to answer the questions. That's all I can consider.

The defense then argued that pronouncement of judgment be deferred to the end of the trial, and pointed out that the jury might hear of the sentencing through the press if it was pronounced during the trial. Mathes was obdurate.

COURT: It is the judgment of the court, Oleta O'Connor Yates, as to each contempt of which you have been found guilty, that you be committed to the custody of the marshal to be imprisoned in a jail type institution until you have purged yourself of your contempt by answering the questions ordered to be answered in each instance or until further order of the court. This judgment is imposed separately and independently as to each question you refused to answer. The sentence imposed shall commence and run consecutively thereto. . . . You carry the key to your jail in your own purse. You may purge yourself at any time and be discharged from custody.

A stay of execution for twenty-four hours to allow for an appeal was denied; a stay to allow her to go home and get some personal necessities before going to jail was also denied. The judge, who was so solicitous of the government witnesses when they conveniently claimed sickness when the cross-examination was getting too much for them, now showed that he was made of sterner stuff when the next morning Margolis asked that the sentence be suspended.

MARGOLIS: She was placed on a cot out in the hall where the light shines all night, and as a result has had practically no sleep. The cells and the regular bunks are full. . . . Under these circumstances, in order that she may be able to be physically in a position to adequately face cross-examination and prepare re-direct examination, I would again like to move the court, pending the completion of her examination, that Your Honor order Mrs. Yates released, in order that she may adequately be able to present her defense and not be handicapped in this way.

COURT: The motion to suspend execution of the sentence is denied. If she is to be a martyr, if that is her desire, she should be a martyr in the best sense of the word, not one of those present-day martyrs who want all the glory and unwilling to stand the pain, but a martyr of old who is willing to take the glory and the pain with it.

MARGOLIS: I had hoped that we were living in an era where martyrdom was not required of people. . . . And I had hoped particularly, Your Honor, in an American court that would not be required of any defendant. . . . And I say not only is it a principled position, but it is a courageous position that bears the highest possible principle.

COURT: Be careful, Mr. Margolis. I would not want to catch you in contempt for advising contempt . . . . I will hear no more of it. Sit down. Call the jury, Mr. Bailiff.

So after nine and a half days on the witness stand, the victim of Mathes's vindictiveness had to continue the cross-examination. Her frail figure had lost considerable weight under prison conditions and some of her medical problems were recurring. But she bore up under it stoically, and continued to patiently answer questions hour after hour in a firm voice. It was Neukom who got so exhausted that his voice showed his fatigue and the court had to admonish him: "Keep your voice up, Mr. Neukom." But not only his voice became hazy. At one point he stopped and asked no one in particular: "Have I a question? My mind is a little hazy on it."

Book after book, quotation after quotation was put into evidence by the prosecution until there were hundreds of exhibits in the record. Neukom would fumble his way through a passage, picking out a few lines or phrases, as on abolishing the state, the meaning of which had gone completely over his head.

NEUKOM: Where is there any explanation there that a person reading that passage should interpret it as you interpreted it?

YATES: One does not use merely one line on one page. . . . One uses the whole outline. This particular reading material pertains to the position of the Marxists with respect to anarchists, and attacks the position of anarchists that the state can be abolished as soon as the working class has come to power. In the very next section it deals with the whole question of the historical meaning of revolution, and deals with the question of force and violence as weapons of the dominant class against the majority, and indicating clearly that the program of the Communist Party is one of winning the majority of the people (for) socialism, that there cannot be a blueprinting in advance the concrete method for achieving it.

Mathes was getting impatient with the cross-examination.

COURT: Let's move on to something more important and up-to-date. . . . We could be here until next fall on these matters. She has been under cross-examination, this is the third day. I expect you to be somewhere near the conclusion of it. You are wasting time now.

It soon became clear why Mathes was impatient and wanted something more up-to-date.

COURT: If you wish to ask the witness leading questions as to the names of persons previously mentioned in the testimony, you may do so.

So Neukom went back to asking for names.

YATES: This is again the same question, and if you ask it in twenty different forms, my answer is the same.

In all, nine more separate citations for contempt of court were issued by the vengeful judge. But that was not all. When the prosecution concluded its cross-examination, Mathes took over the questioning at length. He repeatedly asked the defendant to define terms like "force and violence," and made clear he was not satisfied with the answers she gave. Objections by the defense and motions for a mistrial were brushed aside.

SCHULLMAN: Your Honor, may I join in that (objection)? There are other words, "peaceful," "parliamentary," etc. Your Honor has picked out words. We are only limited to the words Your Honor used, and I submit it is prejudicial to my clients to take words out of context . . . because of prejudice created by the fact

232

that the court did not interrogate to this extent any of the prosecution's witnesses.

LEONARD: The court is selecting words to put to the witness in response to her understanding those words with respect to force and violence, illegal, and so on, and did not choose other words which are found in the same writings with respect to peace, legality, etc. . . . . The court asked the witness whether or not the words were used in a usual or dictionary sense, thereby implying to the jury that the words were used in some unusual and special sense. . . . The government had three and a half days of cross-examination, and it apparently was content with the record that developed, and it was improper for the court to engage in that examination after the government had completed.

BRANTON: The effect of the court's manner of examination was more akin to cross-examination and had the cumulative effect of conveying to the jury that His Honor was of the impression that the witness did not interpret the words in their ordinary sense, but had some peculiar interpretation of the words. . . . I believe that the manner of the court's cross-examination conveyed to the jury that His Honor had certain feelings about this witness's testimony, which I believe was highly prejudicial. . . . The witness was on the stand for many days telling about the meaning of various words within various contexts as they appeared in various writings. If the court had asked questions about them at that particular time, so that it would have been related to some specific evidence, the jury might be able to interpret that which His Honor was trying to clear up a misunderstanding about, but to save all these matters until the very end of the witness's examination, and then without relating to any particular work, but just to pick out words and say "violence" and "force" and things like that has another cumulative effect.

Mathes instructed the jury to disregard the episode, but he had accomplished his purpose. Evidently believing that the prosecution had botched the job and not put on a very convincing case, he took it upon himself to make sure the jury got the implications of his questions. Coming after his savage treatment of the defendant with thirteen contempt citations, he had delivered the *coup de grâce*. But he gave her one more chance to repent.

COURT: Mrs. Yates, there are certain questions you have not answered which the court has instructed you to answer. I shall give you another opportunity to answer them before you leave the stand.

YATES: I cannot in good conscience alter the decisions which I was compelled to make. I have as best I could attempted to speak fully, freely, honestly, without reservations, on what I did, what I thought, what my purposes were. . . . But there is an atmosphere today of a very dangerous kind, and I would contribute to that if I were to point out people that will open them up to the kind of persecutions that would ensue. I cannot do anything that would cause an injury to innocent people who have done no wrong and would only be victimized because of the political atmosphere that now exists.

Before leaving the stand, Oleta had one more ordeal to face—cross-examination by a colleague and co-defendant. This unusual situation came about because we wanted to bring the jury's attention back to the issues on trial as interpreted by the Supreme Court opinion in the Schneiderman case. We had agreed that I would question her about it, and so, remembering the saying that "Anyone who represents himself has a fool for a client," I rose to face my comrade.

SCHNEIDERMAN: Did you have any conversation with me in regard to the Schneiderman case which affected or clarified your understanding?

YATES: Yes, I did. The main point that I can recall at this time is that you stated that the majority opinion in the Supreme Court reflected fundamentally the views which you held with respect to some of the main teachings of Marxism-Leninism, particularly on such questions as the possibilities of the working class peacefully to secure state power, the character and content of the dictatorship of the proletariat, and on the question of the position of the Communist Party as expressed by you on force and violence.

Q. Was there any discussion as to whether the Supreme Court majority opinion reflected an accurate definition of the Party's position on force and violence?

A. Yes. . . . You stated you believed that the majority opinion did reflect and did state an accurate interpretation, as you understand it, on those particular questions.

Q. Do you recall any further conversations regarding my testimony?

A. Yes. It took place some time after we were arrested last year. At that time when we were preparing for this trial you suggested to me to re-examine the testimony which you gave, and you stated that you believed the main issues were essentially the same as the issues in that case, and that the books and the material that was dealt with in the Schneiderman case was the same as the books and material that were to be introduced in this case by the government.

SCHNEIDERMAN: I wish to ask for a stipulation, Your Honor, from the government regarding one of these volumes Mr. Neukom had read and questioned the witness regarding the program of the Communist International, and had specifically quoted an excerpt from that program which starts out, "The conquest of power." I now wish to ask for a stipulation from the government that this exact excerpt on the conquest of power appears in the transcript of my trial as a government exhibit introduced against me in my citizenship trial.

The prosecution made an objection and argued that it was not admissible. They were not anxious for the jury to be reminded that this volume, as well as nearly all others read to them by the prosecution ad infinitum, was before the Supreme Court when they handed down their favorable ruling in my citizenship case. But the judge, evidently content with the damage he had already done, was inclined to be generous.

COURT: The objection is overruled. The facts stipulated to are received into evidence.

We had accomplished our objective.

When Oleta Yates finally left the stand, we were confronted with a dilemma. The four of us who had not rested our case had all expected to testify for the defense. But in assessing where the trial stood, the question arose, what more could be accomplished, or would we be better off resting our case at this point?

We had done well in demolishing the prosecution witnesses. Oleta had done magnificently well on the stand. But the prosecution's strategy of inviting contempt citations and the judge's own blatant intervention in the cross-examination were clearly intended to obscure the issues and prejudice the jury. Our basic position had already been presented, through Oleta's testimony and the devastating cross-examination of government witnesses by our able staff of attorneys. The trial had now dragged on from February into July—nearly six months. There was a saturation point beyond which further rehashing of the same ground would be counterproductive. There were no acts we had to explain, no speeches we had to justify; there was the flimsiest of evidence which would point toward any illegal intent on the part of any defendant. It was a trial of books and ideas.

For the rest of us to go on the stand would mean more contempt citations, more opportunity for Mathes to tip the scales by his obvious bias, and the issues would be further obscured for the jury. We had achieved our main goals, and from now on it would be all downhill if we continued. The more we discussed it, the more we came to the conclusion that it would be best to rest our case with no further witnesses, and I so informed the court.

SCHNEIDERMAN: Your Honor, we had intended to call possibly

ten to fifteen witnesses for the defense, including the three remaining defendants who had not rested, on the position of the Communist Party and the meaning of the books and literature in evidence, as well as on the intent of the defendants. But the prosecution's seeming determination to elicit names from witnesses for the purpose of identifying them as Communists, and thus asking witnesses to be informers, places us and other prospective witnesses in a very difficult position. We have tried to make a full presentation of our defense and we are confronted with the alternative of continuing under these trying circumstances and subjecting future witnesses to the same kind of ordeal or resting our case.

COURT: Mr. Schneiderman, if the witnesses are not informers, they would not be very much witnesses. Every witness who takes the stand is called to be an informer, an informer of the truth, in every trial.

SCHNEIDERMAN: But he is not always required to be an informer against his neighbor or friend or against other people whom he believes to be innocent.

COURT: Oftentimes he is.

SCHNEIDERMAN: This, of course, is an unusual situation, but then, this is an unusual trial because it is a trial of opinion. We feel that the prosecution has put us in this position, because in place of cross-examination to meet the issue, they are trying us on the question of giving names. And therefore I wish to inform the court of my decision to rest my case without calling any more witnesses. When I have completed introducing a few remaining documents into evidence and some reading from documents to the jury and a couple of other matters, I will rest my case.

I then read to the jury portions of my testimony in the citizenship trial giving my interpretation of the Party program, and offered it into evidence on the ground that prosecution on these grounds was barred by the principle of "res judicata" (the issue has been adjudicated). The judge sustained the prosecution's objection.

An "amicus curiae" (friend of the court) brief in our behalf was filed by the American Civil Liberties Union, but no argument was permitted. We also made an offer of proof on the unconstitutionality of the Smith Act by: Dr. Eason Monroe, Southern California Director of the American Civil Liberties Union; Gifford Phillips, publisher of *Frontier* magazine; Professor Edgar Warren, director of the U.C.L.A. Institute of Industrial Relations and former chief of the U.S. Conciliation Service; and Dr. William Lindsay Young, Southern California Director of the National

Conference of Christians and Jews. Again, the court sustained the government's objections and refused to hear them. We rested our case.

* * *

"No doubt most of your relatives are still outside of the Party. Do not be intolerant of their views. Do not neglect your family, your wife or husband, your children. The whole spirit of our Party should help you being into your own home a new element of human understanding, warmth and appreciation of your family ties." This appeared in a Party pamphlet addressed to new members, written by one of the defendants, Frank Carlson, which we had introduced into evidence.

It has relevance here because United States Attorney Binns, in his summation to the jury, gave an entirely different picture of the Party: "You have heard no expression of brotherly love, kindness, charity. It is all hard and harsh. What is there about it that touches the human heart or the human sympathies?"

As he spoke, I thought of Sacco and Vanzetti, and a hundred other victims of frame-ups and lynch mobs; my mind went back to the struggles of the unemployed, and the continuing struggle of oppressed minorities. The people in power did not show much "brotherly love" in these events. The oppression which we fought surely touched the human heart and sympathies, but it was our participation in fighting the oppressors that caused them to put us on trial. And they equated this fight with "force and violence."

Binns argued to the jury: "They do not say, 'Let's get together and try to work this out.' They say, 'Let's violently struggle, let's fight, let's oppose, that is, use force and violence.'" He even discovered a new crime: "You never find one single place where they say, 'Don't read anything in the old classics.' They tell you, 'Read them.'. . . When they have meetings, they sell this literature."

Even the press did not escape Binns's list of criminal acts: "Replete throughout the literature has been the emphasis on getting subscriptions to the *People's World*, selling the *People's World*, getting people to read the *People's World*."

The summations of six months of evidence by the prosecution and defense took several days. Judge Mathes could not resist one last jab at us. It was during my summary, when I was speaking of a meeting where the witness Foard attributed to me a statement that revolution meant violence, tragedy, and bloodshed. We had brought to the witness stand the bookkeeper of the building where the meeting was supposed to have taken place, with her records of meetings in that hall. She had testified that there was no record of such a meeting within a year of the date given by Foard. The only meeting held in that hall was for an entirely different speaker from New York. In explaining this to the jury, I said: "No such meeting took place." Mathes interrupted: "Mr. Schneiderman, do you want to take the stand and testify to that?" I had evidently over-stepped the limits of what can be said in a summation, but so had the government, for that matter, without any comment by the judge. But for Mathes it was an opportunity not to be missed—to remind the jury that I had not taken the stand. I declined the invitation.

On July 30 the case went to the jury. But J. Edgar Hoover and the Justice Department had one more trick up their sleeves. As the jury filed out of the courtroom and we went outside, we were confronted on the courthouse steps with sensational headlines in the newspapers on sale. Newsboys were shouting: "Red Plot to Seize U.S. Government," "Secret FBI Report," "Stalin Calls for Forcible Destruction." Four newspapers, with a combined circulation of 1,200,000, and every radio and television station carried the story that "a long secret FBI report" revealed that "Russian Premier Stalin has decided Communists can climb to power in the United States only by 'forcible destruction' of the government—never by peaceful means."

Inured as we thought we were to the machinations of the prose-cution, we were stunned by this crass intervention of the FBI to guarantee a guilty verdict. Evidently unsure of the outcome, the Department of Justice decided to deliver one last blow. Lawrence K. Bailey, special assistant to the attorney general, who sat on the prosecution's trial staff, must have reported to Washington how shaky the government's case was.

The timing was unmistakable, as I pointed out in an affidavit which I filed for the defense with the court. The Hoover report was made to the Senate Internal Security Committee some time ago; it was held for over a month before being released for publication on July 30, the very day our case went to the jury.

The published reports gave the impression that the FBI had dis-covered a new secret "plot" or "conspiracy." What it actually consisted of was a rehash of old charges based on isolated quota-tions taken out of context from Marxist literature. The Stalin quote was completely false. It was a garbled version of a quotation from Lenin, which was already in evidence in our trial, and which we had explained in its true context.

It was impossible that the jury did not hear about the report. They had been instructed not to read about the case, but they had not been instructed not to read newspapers, or listen to the radio or television. They could not have missed seeing the headlines, or hearing the newsboys shouting them, on their way out. They could not be quarantined from the conversation of relatives and friends. In fact, if all they would learn of the story was what the headlines proclaimed, that the FBI had discovered a "secret plot" or "red conspiracy," without being able to sift the fraudulent basis, it would be worse for us than if they had read the now-familiar quotations which the defense had placed in their proper historical setting.

We went before Judge Mathes and asked for a mistrial. Schullman argued: "The very function of the jury has been usurped by reason of the widespread dissemination and circulation of the opinion and conclusion of the Department of Justice, of which the FBI is an arm. The very fact that must be found by the jury has been communicated by them to the jury through this media in such a manner that it has deprived the defendants of a fair trial. . . . None of the individuals who have collated the report in behalf of the FBI, giving their opinion of what happened in this case, have taken the witness stand, nor have they been confronted by the defendants.

"The result, Your Honor, is that the jury, under the impact of the *Herald Express*, the *Times*, the *Mirror*, the *Examiner*, all four of which were being sold immediately upon the adjournment of July 30, carried headlines and banners which, invading the province of the jury, told the jury that: 'You have been listening to a case for six months. You have heard the government contend that the entire conspiracy is based principally upon excerpts from these books. Now we tell you that . . . it is our opinion and conclusion that those books and membership in the Communist Party constitute a conspiracy to advocate and teach the overthrow of the U.S. government.' The strange part about it, Your Honor, is that it used the language of a long documented secret, and then all the newspapers, radios, and televisions carried this information, and those excerpts were as a matter of fact not made by Stalin . . . , but were made by Lenin, and were read into the record, and therefore they were taken out of context and they were taken out of this courtroom, and the impression communicated via the press, radio, and television to the jury, and to everybody else that read it, that unquestionably the Department of Justice has concluded that all Communists and these defendants are guilty . . . and as a result, no jury can possibly escape the invasion in the jury room.

"Now this is not a coincidental, accidental thing. . . . This was calculated (and) has just one purpose. To me it has another purpose, that apparently the government is convinced of the weakness of its case and it had to make sure that these defendants are found guilty. It would not take a chance that some juror or all the jurors, based upon the evidence, might believe that these defendants are not guilty. So they had to cut the chances, put on the lid, nail down the coffin, and entomb the defendants. . . . We think that there is a clear-cut, purposeful, deliberate, malicious intentional interference with the jury system, with the jury's function, with the court, with due process; therefore, we believe a mistrial should be granted so that this case may say, even to the Department of Justice, and its arm, the FBI: 'You are just a bit too zealous.'"

MARGOLIS: . . . Lawyers have come up to me and said, "I've never seen anything so rotten in my life."

COURT: I have in mind the possibility that the screaming headlines might be beyond human ability to avoid reading, or one of those agitated commentators over the radio or television.

Nevertheless, the judge refused to poll the jury, unless he could also ask them if the story changed their minds. Since no juror was likely to admit this, the defense refused the judge's condition and the jury was not polled.

The waiting began. Apprehensive as we were, there was no relaxation of tension with the daily grind over. We had to stay close to the courtroom, for there was no way of knowing when the jury's verdict might come. Our mood was not optimistic, but as day after day dragged by, a hope flickered that we might at least get a hung jury.

I put on the most cheerful front I could for Leah and Ellen (she had just recently had her eighth birthday). I reminded Leah that even if we lost, it would take a year or two for the appeals (it took five), and in any case I thought we would have our best chance there. The probability of even a temporary reprieve made the prospect of separation from my loved ones somewhat less painful to contemplate.

When five days had gone by, our hopes began to soar, but they were short-lived. On the sixth day, we were summoned mid-day to the courtroom. As the jury filed in we anxiously scanned their solemn faces. When I looked at my favorite juror, the writer of children's books, I knew the verdict. Her face was strained, and she looked as though she were holding back tears. The verdict was "guilty," and we were each given the maximum sentence of five years and $10,000 fine. Oleta Yates received an additional three years and one year for contempt of court. It was a big day for Judge Mathes, and for the blind goddess who held the scales in her hands.

18 The Supreme Court — Second Round

True to form, the judge revoked our bail, although it is only customary to do so in murder cases. When the appellate court ordered that bail be set, Mathes started the filibuster all over again. He could not assess the risk, he said, if we fled to Mexico; our extradition treaty with Mexico was such that the latter might consider us political refugees and refuse extradition. Margolis retorted that the Mexican government had no hesitation in having its agents shanghai Gus Hall, a New York Smith Act victim who had sought refuge, into the hands of the FBI and escorted him to the border. But the judge was adamant in his refusal to carry out the higher court's order. We promptly appealed again, and three weeks after we had been jailed by Mathes the federal court of appeals in San Francisco set bail of $10,000 or $20,000 for each of the various defendants, and we were released. Altogether we had spent nearly seven months in jail due to the paranoia of a judge who saluted the American flag every time he walked into the courtroom. It was a little over a year since we had been arrested, and although we did not know what the future would hold for us, it felt good to be free for the time being.

Our fight in court had positioned us well for the appeal, and my natural optimism rose to the surface again, although at the time there was little I could point my finger at to justify it. But as I sat in the plane on my way home to San Francisco, I thought to myself: "The battle isn't over; the last word has not been said yet."

I did not think of it then, but there was a curious parallel of history repeating itself between my citizenship trial and the second one. My first trial took place in 1939 in a period of anti-Communist hysteria when we were going against the stream; by the time my appeal reached the Supreme Court, the U.S. was engaged in the war against fascism as an ally of the Soviet Union, and President Roosevelt was releasing Communists from jail "in the interests of national unity." When our appeal in the Smith Act case reached the Supreme Court, the Korean war was over and the McCarthy madness had died down; there was a revulsion in the nation against the "excesses" committed during that period. Side by side with the revival of concern for the protection of democratic liberties, there was an upsurge of the civil rights movement which had its first reflection in the Supreme Court's decision outlawing segregation that was based on the notorious "separate but equal" doctrine.

Earl Warren has been credited with the change in the high court, but the role of the individual reflects the social environment in which he or she operates, and the ascension of Warren to head the Court came at the right time. Of course, we had no inkling that the court had changed enough to reverse its previous upholding of Smith Act convictions, but we felt that given the changed climate the record in our case was sufficiently different to warrant its taking another look.

When our team of attorneys appeared before the Supreme Court, we had two new faces in addition to Margolis, Wirin, and Branton. Both were friends of Earl Warren, and both had volunteered their services. Augustin Donovan was the head of the Bar Association in Oakland, where Warren came from. He represented the two editors among the defendants, Al Richmond and Phillip Connelly, and would stress the issue of freedom of the press. Robert W. Kenny, a former judge, state senator and attorney-general of California, the only Democrat in the Republican administration of Governor Warren, was a close political associate of his. He was to represent me on the issue of "res judicata." As one of the trial attorneys in my citizenship case, he was the most qualified to argue before the Court that I was being tried for the same books and ideas as in the case in which the justices, some of them the same ones who now sat, had already ruled in my favor. Black, Douglas, and Frankfurter were still there. It was Justice Frankfurter, during the bail hearing in 1951, who raised the question of "res judicata"; and although he had sided against me in the citizenship case, we thought it was not impossible that he would take the position that I should not be tried again on essentially the same evidence.

So for the second time I was an interested spectator in the august chambers of the Supreme Court, where nearly fifteen years earlier, Wendell Willkie had stood at the lectern arguing in my behalf. This time, when Warren nodded his head with the greeting "Judge Kenny," as my attorney rose to address the Court, it amused me to think that the Chief Justice might have felt that we were ganging up on him when he saw two of his old friends,

Kenny and Donovan, telling the Court that it must decide that Communists have constitutional rights, too.

Aside from these additional arguments in my behalf, our team of attorneys focused on the insufficiency of the evidence to prove either a conspiracy or the specific intent of the individual defendants, and on some technical legal points involving the judge's instructions to the jury on the meaning of the word "organize." We also hammered away at the intervention of the FBI and the Department of Justice at the end of the trial in an effort to sway the jury with headlines about a fake "Red Plot." We had doubts that the Court would accept this incident as grounds for a reversal, but we felt it was a good point to drive home both to the Court and to the public. The justices did not like to see the facade of a "fair trial" so rudely brushed aside.

Our case was not the only one that rode on our appeal. By this time, over one hundred Communists in fourteen states had been put on trial and convicted; only the New York defendants' convictions had been upheld. The fate of all the other defendants hung on our appeal. Furthermore, the Party itself would have been outlawed and the teachings of Marxism-Leninism banned; such measures had only been taken in fascist countries. The inevitable result would have been that repression would have extended far beyond the Communist Party.

The ordeal of waiting was new to the other defendants, but not to Leah and me. Just as in 1943, we went about our affairs trying to act unconcerned, but not planning too far ahead. Time dragged on. The Court was taking an inordinately long time. I wondered if they were held up and deadlocked by Frankfurter's role; I remembered how he had conducted a bitter rear-guard action to the very end, in opposing the majority opinion in my citizenship case. As time went on, he had moved more and more to the right in the Court's decisions, and I had come to realize that my fleeting hope that he had signalled a change in my case was not well founded.

It was June, 1957, five years after the trial. June was when the court adjourned for the summer, and usually some major decisions were handed down on the last Monday they met. After so much waiting, I was not sure if I wanted another delay, or whether I would rather have the suspense over with, whichever way it went. When the decision finally came down, I was walking down a downtown street, looking for a place to buy an ice-cream cone, when I saw the headlines: "Supreme Court Acquits Reds." I spent the rest of the day in a daze. That night our house was flooded with about a hundred people in a spontaneous, delerious celebration that lasted far into the night.

The six-to-two decision was not an unqualified victory, however. It acquitted four defendants outright, and the rest of us had our convictions set aside, and our cases remanded back to the Federal District Court. Back to Judge Mathes. It was up to the Justice Department and the judge whether we would be prosecuted again. Nevertheless, we rejoiced in the landmark decision which in effect wiped out all the other convictions of Communists whose appeals were pending, and to all intents and purposes nullified the Smith Act. By establishing the criterion that the specific intent of each individual must be proved, the Supreme Court made it impossible to continue prosecution under this law. While evading the issue of the constitutionality of the Smith Act, the net effect of the Court's action was a setback for the forces of McCarthyism.[1]

After a few months of playing a cat-and-mouse game, the Justice Department finally gave up and reluctantly agreed that the prosecution would be dropped and the indictments were dismissed. I got the news at the office when Leah phoned. "It's all over," she said. I wanted to jump and shout, but I had to suppress my feelings till after work. That night we had a repetition of the June celebration. One of the defendants who was originally acquitted in June good-naturedly taunted me: "What took you so long?"

Ours had not been the worst ordeal of that dreadful period. Many had suffered more than we did. Some had served long sentences. Others went into exile; a few committed suicide. The Rosenbergs were executed for a "crime" they did not commit. Careers were smashed, jobs lost, families broken up and decimated. One of our leaders, Bob Thompson, had his skull smashed in prison by a fascist and went to an early death with a metal plate in his head; another, Henry Winston, was blinded in prison through willful, criminal neglect. We were the "lucky" ones.

Well-meaning people have said to me: "Your case shows that democracy works—twice in your case an injustice was corrected." This overlooks the awful toll that McCarthyism wreaked not only on the innocent victims, but on the nation as a whole. Fear had stifled dissent. It also overlooks the fact that no victory for civil liberties is complete or permanent—the fight has to be made all over again each time reaction and racism raise their head, each time the cold war is revived, each time there is a new attack on labor.

Our experience with the FBI and the Department of Justice

pales in comparison with the revelations in later years of the crimes of J. Edgar Hoover's regime, which had the consent, to a greater or less degree, of every president during his long reign. Hoover is gone, but the instruments of repression remain in place, ready to go into action whenever the ruling circles so decree. Other laws still remain on the books, or are pending in Congress. The "dirty tricks" of McCarthy, Hoover, and Nixon were not just "excesses"; they were the most visible parts of the whole system of repression used against the people. To think that "the worst is over" is to let our guard down, for the threats to the people's rights take ever new forms. Only eternal vigilance and mass resistance can keep it from happening again.

It was the aim of those in power to destroy the Party, and with it the spirit of resistance of the American people and its potential for struggle, which threatened the proponents of nuclear confrontation and of the war against labor and its allies. But through it all the Party survived. There is something mightier than a sword, and that is an idea whose time has come. No matter what the future may bring, my belief has never faded that a new generation in the Party and the working class will find the American road to socialism.

Epilogue

Primarily the story of two political trials and their historical background, this account has covered three decades of struggle in the most eventful period of our history. The world has changed a great deal since then, and ill health has made me an observer (participating in spirit only) of most of the struggles of the intervening years. The experiences of those early years, as well as some interpretations of my own (however different the opinions of others who have lived through these times) are offered here in the hope that a new generation may find them useful—not only in judging the past, but more importantly, in gaining a perspective for the future.

My ten-year-old granddaughter asked me, "Why were you in jail?" I tried to explain that some people have gone to jail for a just cause, as when Martin Luther King, whom she had read about in school, was jailed when he fought for the freedom of Black people, even when it meant violating unjust laws. She replied, "I knew you were not a criminal."

It is not my intention to present myself and my comrades to my grandchildren or to my readers as heroes unsullied by imperfections. We had faults; we were guilty of mistakes; hindsight makes it easy to identify misjudgments. It has become fashionable nowadays to dismiss our efforts, and the role of the Party which led them. I am convinced, however, that over the years the errors and shortcomings were far outweighed by the contributions made by the Communist Party at every turning point in the modern history of our country—contributions made possible by the application of Marxism-Leninism.

We were (as we still are) engaged in a battle with a relentless adversary out to destroy us, and it has been inevitable that we should have losses from our ranks. These casualties have included some of my codefendants, who acquired illusions of an easier path to socialism. But there is no easy path.

Effective resistance to a powerful ruling class can be possible only if some of the lessons of past struggles are not forgotten. Methods and forms of struggle will not always be the same, of course, but the basic principle of the united front, based on a revitalized labor movement, which we have advocated over the years, is still the key to organizing against the corporate interests which rule the nation. One of the main weapons of these interests

246

and the media which they control absolutely is anticommunism (together with anti-Sovietism).

When other efforts to divide people uniting in resistance fail, the Red scare is used to cloud the real issues and to divert attention from genuine human problems. No distortion or outright lie is too great when it comes to depicting the role of the Communists, as was demonstrated by government witnesses in our trial, and indeed as is illustrated by propaganda poured out by the media every day. Sophisticated technology has proved more effective than in earlier days in influencing the minds of the masses, and has made more difficult the task of penetrating the smokescreen of deception.

Our experiences during the repression of the McCarthy period, exemplified in these pages by my own ordeal as a Smith Act defendant, show something of the consequences, in human and political terms, of redbaiting. Many suffered from McCarthyism, but Communists were among the chief targets, although the two laws under which they were mainly prosecuted over a period of years, the Smith Act and the McCarran Act, were many years later struck down by the U.S. Supreme Court.

Although the decisions of the Court dodged the basic constitutional issues, a lesson emerged from the McCarthy persecutions as surely as it did (far more catastrophically) in Hitler Germany: that the suppression of the Communists is the first step toward the suppression of liberties for all. Thanks to the democratic traditions and resistance of the American people, our country pulled back from the brink in time, but it is a sobering thought that it can happen again.

Communist do not have a negative attitude toward bourgeois democracy, but we have no illusions regarding its nature in the United States. The affirmation in the Declaration of Independence that "all men are created equal" did not reflect social reality, even in the earliest days of our history. It did not apply to the original inhabitants of this land. It did not apply to the Black slaves. It did not apply for some years to those without property who could not vote. It did not apply to women, who could not vote at all until the twentieth century. Capitalism did not grant equality to the poor; from its first days, the rich had the power, regardless of the facade of equality under the law. And within that basic inequality between the classes, based on the exploitation of labor, there was yet another special burden of oppression borne by the Blacks and other minorities in our own land, not to speak of that borne by the smaller nations who became victims of American imperialism.

Nevertheless, the strength of our democratic traditions is unique in that our country knew no feudalism, no monarchy, no Napoleonic era; and because of the special historical circumstances (geographic, economic, social, and cultural) of our growth as a nation. With its enormous wealth, capitalism in its earlier days could afford to make considerable concessions to the working class (primarily to its upper third) in order to keep its loyalty, and this has dimmed the memory of intermittent examples of violent suppression of labor in the last century. It was the economic disaster of the thirties, and the resulting struggles, which frightened the ruling class into a more flexible approach to dealing with economic and social issues, but its options are narrowing.

If there were illusions that the people were freer than they actually were, then these illusions made them fight all the harder for freedoms being taken away from them. This was the reaction against the Alien and Sedition laws at the end of the eighteenth century. After the suppressions of the twenties and the Hoover era came the struggles of the thirties, which brought economic and social advances during the New Deal. But in each period the fight had to be made all over again.

When I chose my lifetime commitment, I entered on a path which crossed that of the great and the lowly—politicians, judges, labor leaders, and world revolutionary figures—but more important than any of them were the pea pickers of Watsonville, the garment workers of New Haven, the iron miners of the Mesabi Range, the Finnish farmers of Minnesota, the copper miners of upper Michigan, the packinghouse workers of South St. Paul, and the maritime workers of the Pacific Coast. I had joined on hunger marches with the jobless and picket lines with men and women on strike. My journey brought me to the defense of the Scottsboro boys, Tom Mooney, Angelo Herndon, Paul Robeson, and Wesley Wells. Inevitably it led me to the prosecutors and the persecutors, the Un-American Committee hearings, Supreme Court appeals, trials and vindication, and trials again.

All this represented in the eyes of those in power a far-flung "conspiracy" of which I could not absolve myself. Nor could I renounce my advocacy of revolutionary changes to abolish economic exploitation, racism, and imperialist war. If there exists a conspiracy to advocate these goals, so be it—no inquisition can stop it. The road is long, the journey unfinished, but the struggle goes on. The greatest of the new challenges faced by the present generation are the threat of nuclear war and the robbing of gains made by the struggles of the people during the last fifty years. But at every crucial point in our history, as in the times I recount in this volume, the people have rallied to turn back the forces of reaction. And so I have high hopes for the future of our country. I believe there is socialism in that future. It will not come easily, but it will come.

Notes

Chapter 3

1   Vesselin Hadjinikolov et al., *Georgi Dimitrov* (Sofia: Sofia-Press, 1978). See also Stella D. Blagoeva, *Dimitrov: A Biography* (New York: International Pub., 1934), pp. 96-124 for Dimitrov's speech in court.

Chapter 4

1. A movie of this event, taken by an amateur photographer, is in the archives of the Southern California Library for Social Studies in Los Angeles.

Chapter 5

1. New York *Times*, June 24, 1941.

Chapter 6

1. Joseph Barnes, *Wendell Willkie* (New York: Simon & Schuster, 1952), p. 318.
2. *New Republic*, Mar. 18, 1940; cited by Barnes, p. 321.
3. Barnes, p. 322.
4. *Ibid.*
5. New York *Times*, June 24, 1941.

Chapter 7

1. Testimony is quoted from the official trial transcripts, *United States* v. *Schneiderman*, Federal District Court, San Francisco, 1939.

Chapter 8

1. Willkie brief to the Supreme Court, Schneiderman vs. U.S., U.S. Supreme Court, 1943.
2. Testimony is quoted from the official trial transcripts, *Schneiderman* v. *United States*, U.S. Supreme Court, 1943. See *The Schneiderman Case: U.S. Supreme Court Opinion*, intro. by Carol King, (New York: American Committee for the Protection of the Foreign Born, 1943), (pamphlet, 43 pages).
3. Liva Baker, *Felix Frankfurter* (New York: Coward-McCann, 1969).
4. *Ibid.*
5. Joseph Lash, ed., *From the Diaries of Felix Frankfurter* (New York: Norton, 1975), p. 249.
6. Majority Opinion, Justice Murphy, *Schneiderman* v. *United States*, U.S. Supreme Court, 1943; Dissenting Opinion, Justice Stone, *ibid.*
7. Opinion concurring with majority, Justice Rutledge, *ibid.*

Chapter 10

1. Papers in the Truman Library, Independence, Missouri. Cited by Francis L. Loewenheim in Houston *Chronicle*; Monte E. Poen, *Strictly Personal and Confidential: The Letters that Harry Truman Never Mailed* (Boston: Little, Brown, 1982), and San Francisco *Chronicle*, April 5, 1982.
2. Dean Acheson, *A Democrat Looks at his Party* (New York: Harper, 1955), p. 127.
3. The Foley Square defendants were: Benjamin J. Davis, Jr., Eugene Dennis, John Gates, Gilbert Green, Gus Hall, Irving Potash, Jacob Stachel, Robert Thompson, John Williamson, Henry Winston, and Carl Winter.
4. Green, Hall, Thompson, and Winston.

Chapter 12

1. Sharing the dock with me were: Frank Carlson, Phillip Connelly, Ben Dobbs, Bernadette Doyle, Ernest Fox, Dorothy Healey, Rose Kusnitz, Carl Lambert, Albert Lima, Al Richmond, Frank Spector, Loretta Stack, Harry Steinberg, and Oleta O'Connor Yates.

Chapter 13

1. Citations to the Smith Act trial are from the transcript, *United States* v. *Schneiderman et al.*, Federal District Court, Los Angeles, 1951.

Chapter 18

1. Supreme Court decision (on appeal), *Yates et al.* v. *United States*, U.S. Supreme Court, 1957.